Appalachia in the Classroom

D1523346

APPALACHIA in the CLASSROOM:

Teaching the Region

Edited by
Theresa L. Burriss and Patricia M. Gantt

OHIO UNIVERSITY PRESS • ATHENS

Ohio University Press, Athens, Ohio 45701
ohioswallow.com
© 2013 by Ohio University Press
All rights reserved

To obtain permission to quote, reprint, or otherwise reproduce or distribute material
from Ohio University Press publications, please contact our rights and permissions
department at (740) 593-1154 or (740) 593-4536 (fax).

Printed in the United States of America
Ohio University Press books are printed on acid-free paper. ∞

20 19 18 17 16 15 14 13   5 4 3 2 1

Library of Congress Cataloging-in-Publication Data
Appalachia in the classroom : teaching the region / edited by Theresa L. Burriss and
Patricia M. Gantt.
    pages cm. — (Series in race, ethnicity, and gender in Appalachia)
Includes bibliographical references and index.
ISBN 978-0-8214-2041-6 (hc : alk. paper) — ISBN 978-0-8214-2042-3 (pb : alk. paper)
— ISBN 978-0-8214-4456-6 (electronic)
1. Appalachian Region—Study and teaching (Higher) 2. American literature—
Appalachian Region—Study and teaching (Higher) I. Burriss, Theresa L., 1966– author,
editor of compilation. II. Gantt, Patricia M., 1943– author, editor of compilation.
F106.A575 2013
974.071′1—dc23

                                                                    2012045765

Steam

Steam rises from water
boiling knife, fork and spoon.
Floating out the screen window
it settles on the creek running
toward the French Broad River,
tumbles to the Tennessee,
merges with the Mississippi,
plunges into the Gulf of Mexico
and unites with the Gulf Stream,
making its way back to bodies
bathing in the Niger River,
rinsing sweat from picking
cassava instead of cotton,
eating *eguma bread* wrapped
in leaves instead of black eyed peas
out of spoons boiled by white women.

—Connie Aiken

CONTENTS

Contents

DEDICATION AND ACKNOWLEDGMENTS

The publication of *Appalachia in the Classroom: Teaching the Region* is bittersweet. While such a teaching aid is long overdue in Appalachian pedagogy, the release of the book was delayed due to tragic and unforeseen life events as contributors submitted their chapters. First, Appalachia lost one of its most important writers, Wilma Dykeman, in December of 2006. This "tall woman" of the mountains had served as strong inspiration for editor Patricia (Pat) Gantt; Ms. Dykeman was the focus of Pat's dissertation and many subsequent articles, including a chapter in this collection. Within a year almost to the day, Pat tragically lost her husband, Thomas Morrison Gantt, who had been her sweetheart for more than forty-five years. Yet a year later, beloved Appalachian teacher and writer Danny Miller died far too young after suffering a stroke. His name was listed on Pat's original table of contents as a possible contributor to this text. Due to the deaths of these three individuals, Pat struggled to find the energy to move forward with the collection. That's when Theresa Burriss stepped in to assist her, to add more contributors, and to prepare the manuscript for outside readers to review. As she made this push, Theresa's ninety-one-year-old grandmother, Gwendolyn K. Burriss, affectionately known as Granny Jo, died two days before Christmas of 2010. We dedicate *Appalachia in the Classroom* to these four individuals.

A special thank-you goes to Gillian Berchowitz, Senior Editor at Ohio University Press, who exhibited a sincere dedication to the completion of this project throughout the editors' trials and tribulations. Gill believed in the necessity of this project and never wavered in her support of it. Finally, thank you to all the contributors, those who were on Pat's original list and those who joined the lineup after Theresa became coeditor; we appreciate your patience.

INTRODUCTION

As we move into the second decade of the twenty-first century, the scholarly discipline of Appalachian Studies continues to evolve and change to keep pace with the living culture on which it focuses. While Appalachian Studies must remain mindful of the past to understand and inform the present, educators and scholars should maintain a contemporary focus on the region and its people in order to address current issues. Rigorous study and critique of both old and new Appalachian arts and literature legitimize this still relatively young discipline and provide students with critical thinking skills that can be applied in any context. Moreover, students acquire cultural awareness and sensitivity both particular to Appalachia and yet transcendent of it, enabling them to apply their Appalachian Studies knowledge to other cultures throughout the world.

Appalachia in the Classroom: Teaching the Region seeks to contribute to this twenty-first-century dialogue in Appalachia by offering different topics and teaching strategies that represent the diversity found within the region. And therein exists one of the challenges, yet realities, of studying Appalachia today. How do educators avoid essentialism and essentialist thinking while still acknowledging that a distinct region and culture exist? Such tension plays an integral role in postmodern Appalachian Studies as educators move beyond solely debunking reductive stereotypes and grapple with complex contemporary Appalachian subject matter in a cross-curricular context using interdisciplinary teaching methods. As some educators may struggle to come to a solid understanding of Appalachian Studies in the twenty-first century, the contributors to this collection offer several answers, although the answers are not always tightly contained or given in black and white. In fact, how do educators and students even designate Appalachia? The Appalachian Regional Commission (ARC) offers one understanding, certainly, albeit politically and geographically prescribed. Yet scholars have debated the ARC's changing boundaries since the commission was conceived in the 1960s.

Additionally, the region's image has been shaped over time by literary treatments, from frontier explorers and local color writers to more contemporary authors who hail from both inside and outside Appalachia. Even this distinction between "insider" and "outsider" proves challenging with the region's history of out-migration, as does rural versus urban Appalachia. In the spirit of deconstruction, however, must educators choose an either/or dichotomy? A "both/and" approach seems much more useful, for Appalachia comprises insiders and outsiders, rural and urban, Northern, Central, and Southern, black, white, Hispanic/Latino, and Asian. And again, it's important to emphasize that the Appalachian culture is alive and evolving, continuing to respond to and incorporate local, national, and international influences. The contributors to this work clearly believe a distinct Appalachian region exists and have focused on the cultural, historical, literary, economic, environmental, and political circumstances that bind the residents.

As a result, they offer pedagogies to reach the twenty-first-century student. While some contributors focus on their specific students and how those students have responded to the materials, others take a more general approach in offering teaching tips that could be adapted to different types of schools or students. It's important to note, however, that with both types of chapters, the editors did not want to present lesson plans that were too prescriptive or canned. Appalachian Studies, and really education in general, should not promote a one-pedagogy-fits-all approach because it cannot. We value academic freedom and promote individual teaching strategies and choices. In fact, not all contributors to this collection even teach Appalachian Studies in Appalachia. The educators hail from as far as Texas and Utah. They range from the seasoned and retired to the new and nascent. Additionally, students attending a large public Research I institution can be quite different from students at a small private liberal arts college.

Nevertheless, the editors did want to offer practical strategies that educators could acquire by simply reading these chapters and then trying them in their own classrooms. The most obvious educators the collection will appeal to are those already teaching Appalachian Studies or who have a desire to start. Even those who may have been incorporating regional materials for several years will find unique pedagogical approaches that can energize and freshen their teaching. Education professors will find the collection useful as they share with student teachers the value of place-based education and how certain faculty members go about implementing it in their classrooms. Because *Appalachia in the Classroom* is a pedagogy book, education majors can analyze and critique the methods put forth by the contributors and at the same time expand their own teaching repertoire. All of the chapters will be useful to instructors in two-year and four-year postsecondary institutions, and even some graduate faculty will benefit from the teaching ideas contained in the collection. Some chapters, however, may not be appropriate for high school students due to the adult content of the arts and literature. Outside the traditional classroom, the text would be a great resource for Appalachian cultural competency trainers as they educate health-care providers, business professionals, human resource specialists, and community organizers. Such professionals would benefit from the contributors' discussion and analysis of the region, its inhabitants, and the environmental, political, and social factors affecting day-to-day living. When I conduct these trainings, I always incorporate poetry into my presentation, and as a result, many participants ask me to provide an Appalachian reading list of poetry, short stories, and novels. Whatever the level of teaching or intended audience, *Appalachia in the Classroom* seeks to inspire educators to try new strategies with their students.

This collection is timely in that many of the chapters intentionally problematize neat categorization of Appalachia and Appalachian Studies, a distinct postmodern move, while drawing from fresh research and teaching methodologies. Moreover, the contributors offer teaching strategies on topics and literature that range in dates from several decades old to newly published or discovered. *Appalachia in the Classroom* is different from other recent and useful edited collections, such as *An American Vein: Critical Readings in Appalachian Literature* (Miller, Hatfield, and Norman 2005) and *A Handbook to Appalachia: An Introduction to the Region* (Edwards, Asbury, and Cox 2006), yet it complements these texts and others. While the first of these is devoted to the use of literary theory and criticism in the service of Appalachian poetry and prose, the second is focused on providing students with a broad overview of topics that help explain the region. Attempting to fill a need with practical how-to teaching strategies, *Appalachia in the Classroom* contributors draw primarily from literature, along with history, film, folktales, and photographs and diaries, to educate students and demonstrate several ways those materials can be used to do so. We believe instructors from various disciplines not only will find ready-to-implement delivery strategies but also will use these pedagogical approaches as catalysts to create their own, which could very well make their way into a second volume. After all, one collection cannot even come close to incorporating the vast body of work on Appalachia that exists now.

Readers will find that the book is divided into sections, with chapters grouped according to themes. "Creative Teaching of Appalachian History" serves as the beginning section and lays a foundation for the entire collection.

In Emily Satterwhite's contribution, "Intro to Appalachian Studies: Navigating Myths of Appalachian Exceptionalism," she discusses the necessity of not only dispelling certain students' pervasive negative stereotypes of the region but also problematizing other students' overly romanticized views, which can be just as limiting and downright erroneous. As with any culture and place, complexities and contradictions, strengths and weaknesses abound in Appalachia. Satterwhite stresses the importance of teaching the truth of the region and challenging students to think critically about the power of myth creation and persistence, whether in Appalachia or in any other culture.

Elizabeth Engelhardt offers a most unique subject matter and provocative approach to teaching it as she exhumes stories of black Appalachian laundrywomen through photographs, letters, and diaries. At the start of her chapter, she situates her research within the tradition of African American scholars who have documented the resistance of black women to reveal too much of their stories for reasons of privacy and self-protection. Engelhardt goes on to deconstruct photographs of Appalachian African American laundrywomen, and the accompanying text provided by the white women photographers who were their employers. Through an evaluation of black female, and racially charged, archetypes, such as the mammy, Engelhardt highlights the intersection of race, class, and gender issues in a real, material way.

John Inscoe takes on Hollywood in his chapter as he offers various approaches to teaching Appalachian history through film. Dealing with nine films, ranging in date from the early 1940s to 2003, Inscoe summarizes each and then provides specific pedagogical methods he has found useful when teaching the films. Whether grappling with universal moral dilemmas and gender conflicts or focusing on issues unique to Appalachia, he furnishes educators with ideas that enable them to compare and contrast the films, as well as evaluate the films' merits and shortcomings. All in all, Inscoe demonstrates how film brings a rich dimension to teaching and depicts yet another interpretation of the Appalachian region.

Erica Abrams Locklear launches the second section of the collection, "Appalachian Literature and Folktales In and Out of the Classroom." In her chapter she provides an intriguing example of collaboration between college and high school students focused on one novel, Ron Rash's *The World Made Straight* (2006). Of particular relevance is the novel's setting in Western North Carolina, where both groups of students attend school. Not only does such a partnership naturally generate mentor/mentee relations, thereby stimulating thoughts of college attainment in first-generation students, but it also empowers the high school students as they serve as local tour guides for the college class. Despite some of the challenges Abrams Locklear and her cooperating high school teacher, Angela Sanderson, encountered, the experiential learning opportunities and partnered learning that resulted from their collaboration serve as a solid model to emulate.

Part autobiography, part teaching strategy, Jeff Mann's chapter begins with the metaphor of feasting, or plain and simple eating, to describe the immense satisfaction that occurs when students ingest great Appalachian literature. As Mann discovered the poetry and prose of his home, a region he had so desperately tried to escape, he experienced a literary awakening that he in turn shares with his own students, especially those at risk and marginalized. His experiences as a gay Appalachian man have fostered empathy for students who are oppressed for various reasons, and his purposeful selection of Appalachian texts, such as Harriette Arnow's *The Dollmaker* ([1954] 2009), prompt class discussion on topics such as assimilation and the social pressure to conform.

Linda Tate extols the value of integrating Appalachian literature into a general education American literature class and uses author Lee Smith as role model and guide as she encourages students to consider the stories that have shaped the students' lives. Despite Tate's primary use of canonical, widely anthologized American writers, she saves the Appalachian writers for the end of the semester; in that way, students can situate these authors into the larger American literary tradition and recognize the consistent desire of all the authors to tell stories, to share their perspective of the human condition. Tate utilizes video clips, along with written passages, of Lee Smith telling her own story of finding her Appalachian voice, thereby inspiring students to take pride in their Appalachian heritage.

In her chapter, Tina Hanlon rejects the notion that folktales appeal only to children, and in the process validates the worthiness of this great, rich, and long oral tradition for serious scholarly study. Methodically spelling out both the strengths and the challenges of using this literary genre in the classroom, Hanlon provides historical, world contexts for many well-known folktales, while specifically celebrating those that have made their way to Appalachia or even originated in the region, such as Cherokee tales shared by Marilou Awiakta. Hanlon is quick to point out the tremendous experiential learning opportunities associated with teaching folktales due to the many storytelling festivals in the area, while also presenting contemporary assignments for modern-day students.

The third section of the collection, "The Novel in Appalachia," offers three contributors who focus on vastly different works and authors from different time periods. Selecting one of Wilma Dykeman's lesser-known and -taught novels, Patricia Gantt enumerates multiple themes and lessons *The Far Family* (1966) offers students. While she distinguishes this work from Dykeman's other fiction and nonfiction, Gantt demonstrates how the novel is united with the others through its great attention to detail and its authenticity of Appalachian culture. Of particular importance is Dykeman's treatment of the "insidious racism" found in the region, a reality that has existed since the first people of color entered the mountains more than a hundred years ago. *The Far Family* can well serve as catalyst for class discussions of racism, civil rights, and social justice.

Ricky Cox tackles the difficult-to-categorize work *I Am One of You Forever* (1985), by Fred Chappell. Despite the author's claim that the book is indeed a novel, Cox points out that students will find much to debate about this assertion, along with seemingly random insertions of magical realism or tall-tale qualities. Such issues lead students to question the reliability not only of the narrator but also of the author himself. Moreover, Cox notes that Chappell's "novel" offers a different, though just as valid, picture of Appalachia in the mid-twentieth century when compared to Arnow's *The Dollmaker* ([1954] 2009) and James Still's *River of Earth* ([1940] 1978). Gender roles and expectations, as well as class privilege, provide even more fodder for literary analysis and critique, thereby providing students with much to consider in their formal papers and in-class discussions.

Felicia Mitchell extols the value of using literature to study the environment and ecology as she examines Barbara Kingsolver's novel *Prodigal Summer* (2000). Identifying Kingsolver as an established "literary activist," Mitchell places the author within the environmental literary tradition of Rachel Carson. She classifies the issues raised in Kingsolver's novels as a branch of deep ecology and proceeds to provide question prompts useful for thinking critically and ethically about the environment. In the rest of the chapter, Mitchell examines the various characters in *Prodigal Summer*, as well as their sometimes conflicting eco-philosophies. And finally, Mitchell highlights some challenges teachers of ecofiction may encounter, such as the resistant, contrary student. Yet opportunities for civil debate, centered on humans' role in protecting the environment, or even their place within it, abound when ecofiction is incorporated into curricula.

In the final section, "Appalachian Poetry and Prose," the contributors present a sampling of the vast writing talents in the region. Parks Lanier provides readers a broad and sweeping introduction to Appalachian poetry, including a catalog of writers that extends from such historical staples as Louise McNeill, James Still, and Jesse Stuart to contemporary favorites like Darnell Arnoult, Ron Rash, and Frank X Walker. Lanier's chapter is useful to literature teachers as he illuminates various and distinct characteristics of Appalachian poetry, as well as discusses basic literary concepts in the poetry, whether tone or dialect. Importantly, he highlights the role of nature and religion in many Appalachian poets' work, citing Jim Wayne Miller's (1980) "Brier Sermon" as one oft-used example.

In contrast to Lanier's vast poetry sampler, Theresa Burriss homes in on a specific group of relatively new writers on the Appalachian literary landscape as she focuses on three of the Affrilachian writers, Frank X Walker, Nikky Finney, and Crystal Wilkinson. She points out the cultural, political, and literary links between writers of the Harlem Renaissance and the Black Arts Movement, tying them to the emergence of the Affrilachian writers in the early 1990s, and demonstrates how their writing specifically draws inspiration from those earlier African American literary periods. In the process, Burriss also situates the writers within a larger Appalachian tradition as the Affrilachians strive to dispel reductive caricatures and stereotypes of the region and make a place for Appalachians of color not only in the literary canon but also in the general history books.

In her chapter on Cherokee Appalachian Marilou Awiakta, Grace Toney Edwards provides key biographical information on this multigenre author before delving into her poetry and prose. Edwards sprinkles "Teaching Tips" at various points throughout the essay, which prove most helpful to new educators yet also prompt veterans to reevaluate old, staid delivery of material. Utilizing both *Abiding Appalachia* ([1978] 2006) and *Selu: Seeking the Corn-Mother's Wisdom* (1993), Edwards addresses topics such as Native American philosophy, history, and custom, along with specific literary issues, including identifying themes and genres. She clearly articulates the richness of Awiakta's work and the wealth of creative and critical thought available to be mined therein.

In the final chapter of the collection, Robert West discusses the poetic evolution of Robert Morgan, one of the most highly celebrated Appalachian authors, who began writing poetry in the late 1960s with an intense attention to "compression and brevity." In the process, West provides educators lacking confidence in teaching poetry recommendations for supplemental texts to make sense of Morgan's formal poetic styles and to situate Morgan's work within a larger historical global context. West goes on to discuss how Morgan became more conversational in his poems, which led to a natural exploration of prose writing, first through short stories and then with novels and nonfiction. In the spirit of coming full circle, however, West documents how Morgan now dedicates himself to meter in all of his most recently published poems. West's analysis of Robert Morgan's stylistic changes, primarily in his poetic oeuvre, can easily be applied to many Appalachian authors as students come to understand their creative development and growth.

Given the abundance of books on Appalachia produced over the past couple of centuries, and in particular the latter twentieth century and the beginning of the twenty-first century, one book-length project can respond to only a limited amount of material. But it is a start and offers a variety of authors, approaches, and considerations for teaching Appalachia. Selecting Connie Aiken's poem "Steam" to serve as the epigraph to the collection, editor Pat Gantt was drawn to the poet's intentional linking of the individual to the universal. A natural element, steam/water, bonds women across the globe, from Appalachia to Africa, despite the women's superficial differences. Indeed, their common humanity is celebrated. And all of this is a key aspect of great literature and teaching, no matter the subject or region. As Pat explained to me recently, employing the words of Wilma Dykeman, who was describing her own mother, "Connie Aiken is 'of the leaf and flower of Appalachia.'" Clearly, such a poet establishes the right tone and timbre for a collection on teaching Appalachia.

Theresa L. Burriss, Radford, VA
August 2012

References

Arnow, Harriette. 1954 (2009). *The Dollmaker*. Reprint, New York: Simon and Schuster.

Awiakta, Marilou. (1978) 2006. *Abiding Appalachia: Where Mountain and Atom Meet*. Blacksburg, VA: Pocahontas Press.

———. 1993. *Selu: Seeking the Corn Mother's Wisdom*. Golden, CO: Fulcrum.

Chappell, Fred. 1985. *I Am One of You Forever*. Baton Rouge: Louisiana State University Press.

Dykeman, Wilma. 1966. *The Far Family*. New York: Holt, Rinehart and Winston.

Edwards, Grace Toney, JoAnn Aust Asbury, and Ricky L. Cox, eds. 2006. *A Handbook to Appalachia: An Introduction to the Region*. Knoxville: University of Tennessee Press.

Kingsolver, Barbara. 2000. *Prodigal Summer.* New York: HarperCollins.

Miller, Danny L., Sharon Hatfield, and Gurney Norman, eds. 2005. *An American Vein: Critical Readings in Appalachian Literature.* Athens: Ohio University Press.

Miller, Jim Wayne. 1980. "Brier Sermon—'You Must Be Born Again.'" In *Appalachia Inside Out: A Sequel to "Voices from the Hills."* Vol. 2, *Culture and Custom,* edited by Robert J. Higgs, Ambrose N. Manning, and Jim Wayne Miller, 423–26. Knoxville: University of Tennessee Press.

Rash, Ron. 2006. *The World Made Straight.* New York: Holt.

Still, James. (1940) 1978. *River of Earth.* Lexington: University Press of Kentucky.

PART ONE

Creative Teaching of Appalachian History

ONE

Intro to Appalachian Studies:
Navigating Myths of Appalachian Exceptionalism

EMILY SATTERWHITE

> When I walked into the room for the first day of Intro to
> Appalachian Studies, . . . I was half expecting to see a man
> dressed in plaid with few teeth going on about what it was
> like living in Appalachia.
>
> > —First-year student, College of Engineering,
> > Williamsburg, Virginia (Virginia Beach–
> > Norfolk–Newport News consolidated
> > metropolitan statistical area)

> I love country music and southern food so I was excited
> for the class to begin. I was surprised when you began by
> disproving everything I thought to be true of the region
> on the first day of class. I believe that this surprising turn
> of events allowed me to learn much more about the region
> than I had initially expected.
>
> > —Senior, College of Liberal Arts and
> > Human Sciences, Chesapeake, Virginia
> > (Virginia Beach–Norfolk–Newport News
> > consolidated metropolitan statistical area)

> In the beginning of the course I was frustrated with
> Wilma Dunaway's quest to take away everything about
> Appalachia that I like. Her argument would probably be
> that I romanticize the region . . . based off of memories of
> visits and relatives. Throughout the course of the semester

I realized the importance of Dunaway and busting other Appalachia myths.

> —Sophomore, College of Liberal Arts
> and Human Sciences, Chester, Virginia
> (Richmond metropolitan statistical area)

This class made me realize that I grew up in Appalachia. . . . As embarrassing as it is to admit, I was one of those . . . people that thought of Appalachia as poor white people that lived in ramshackle houses in the mountains. This class helped me . . . to establish my identity.

> —First-year student, College of Natural
> Resources, Augusta County, Virginia (in
> Appalachia, outside Staunton)

THESE EPIGRAPHS[1] REPRESENT FOUR STANCES toward the idea of Appalachia that I see at the beginning of each semester when I teach Introduction to Appalachian Studies. About a third or more of my students come to Blacksburg and Virginia Tech from the metropolitan areas of Hampton Roads, Richmond, and Northern Virginia (oriented to Washington, DC), plus a small sprinkling from metropolitan places outside Virginia. Like the first three students quoted above, metropolitan students often arrive with unexamined assumptions about the region—predominantly negative stereotypes, but also romantic views of Appalachia as a simpler, more wholesome place that is homogeneous in landscape and culture. About another third grew up in rural or urban parts of Appalachia.[2] Many if not most of these students are well aware of negative stereotypes and have worked to distance themselves from poor whites who live in ramshackle houses (to paraphrase the fourth student above). But some of these students from the region eagerly seek support for their regional pride; they have generally learned, by way of self-defense, to talk about the region in glowingly positive terms not unlike the romantic stereotypes held by the metropolitan "outsiders." The remainder of the students (fewer than a third) are mostly from farming areas, often in central or southern Virginia but also in Pennsylvania and elsewhere. Their views are usually a complicated mix of the rural pride and rural shame that help feed both negative and positive visions of Appalachia.

When I walk into a classroom, my foremost challenge as a teacher and a scholar is to stimulate critical thinking. In the Intro to Appalachian Studies classroom, this entails confronting both the negative *and* the positive assumptions that students bring with them. I have found that the positive assumptions are far more difficult to unseat. There are fewer materials available that complicate romanticizations of Appalachia, and students' faith in them is more intransigent, more defensive and self-justified, and in some cases more psychologically necessary than students' unexamined beliefs in negative stereotypes. My students' "final reflection" papers (from which I take the majority of student quotations for this essay) have repeatedly offered testimonials about conversion experiences from bigotry to understanding, as well as declarations that students have learned to "refrain from stereotyping, not to judge people, and to think beyond superficial concepts."[3] Yet for several years I found that students initially holding romantic views often ended the semester clutching them with an unshakable ferocity. And some students who began with essentialist negative views moved by the end of the course to an equally essentialist celebratory approach.

The problem with a purely celebratory stance is that a romantic view often relies on superficial understandings that can be just as reductive as negative stereotypes. Overly celebratory approaches therefore rob students of a full understanding of the complexities of the region's history and their own experiences of the region. Essentialist approaches furthermore tend to reinforce judgments about "insiders" versus "outsiders" that make little sense; farming students from outside the region frequently find common cause with farming students from inside the region, whereas students from locales that pride themselves upon cosmopolitanism—whether Abingdon (in Appalachia) or Fairfax (in the DC area)—find themselves reconsidering hierarchical assumptions about the relative worth of urban versus rural places. When we unpack essentialist assertions about who counts as an Appalachian "insider," we enable more students to identify with the region. Some, like the Augusta County student quoted above, realize that they, too, can claim Appalachian identity. Others become allies ready to join forces in solidarity with the region rather than feeling relegated, irrevocably, to the outside looking in.

After having taught this course ten times in the past six years (2005–2011), I'd like to do some of my own end-of-term reflecting about the way I conceptualize the course. As I hope to show, students' end-of-semester assessments suggest that when confronted with challenges to positive as well as negative generalizations, they can be trusted to sift through them and learn to recognize nuance in historical and contemporary realities. The nuances empower, rather than confound, their abilities to craft sense of self and build relationship to place.

Framing the Course

Like many other instructors, I have found it useful to frame the opening weeks of Intro to Appalachian Studies in terms of addressing stereotypes. *Yawn.* Stereotypes are old news. I find debunking them a rather clunky and simplistic approach. I feel dissatisfied when students describe their learning in my course primarily in terms of flagellating themselves for having ever believed in stereotypes and vowing never again to be taken in by unfair labeling of any sort. On the other hand, debunking stereotypes is for students a readily recognized and relatively easy way into highly complex materials. As one student put it, "I . . . like how the class is structured in a way that we aim to disprove the myths of Appalachia as opposed to simply explaining conditions on the ground. I think it helps me generate a better understanding of the course material when I am able to contrast it with preconceived notions that are popularly held, [by] myself included."[4] Addressing stereotypes can also be a necessary first step. Most conventional "learning" really consists only of adding content to already-existing frameworks for seeing the world rather than forcing the frameworks themselves to change.[5] If I don't address students' preconceptions head-on, I have found, then students undergo all sorts of contortions in order to force the new materials to conform to their prior expectations about the region.

I'd like to give a quick sketch of the first three days of class before filling in some details about the ideas I employ in my attempts to deconstruct overly simple views of the region. On the first day of class, an interactive "Where is Appalachia?" small-group mapping activity and a lecture help students begin to think about the region—not only where it is and what it is as a place, but also why it exists as an idea. On the second day of class, I use a PowerPoint slide presentation to make a case for my own pet peeves, "Five Myths of Appalachian Exceptionalism," that exist in the twenty-first century. I adapt this title from "Taking Exception with Exceptionalism," by Dwight Billings, Mary Beth

Pudup, and Altina Waller, the introduction to the anthology *Appalachia in the Making*, edited by the same three scholars. Billings, Pudup, and Waller note that the essays in their collection diverge from "a long tradition of Appalachian regional studies" in that they do not claim the phenomena they examine "were necessarily *unique* to the highland South" nor "general to the *whole* mountain region" (1995, 3, emphasis mine). Similarly, I show how the generalizations of rurality, poverty, whiteness, and mountainous topography are neither unique to Appalachia nor true of the whole region.

On the third day of class, we move backward from the twenty-first century to the origins of ideas about Appalachia in the 1700s. I assign one of the shortest readings of the semester: the first three pages of Wilma Dunaway's *The First American Frontier* (1996), in which she describes the Jeffersonian "Agrarian Myth" and its relevance for what she calls a national "long-running love affair" and "romance" with Appalachia grounded in eighteenth-century ideals (1–3). This excerpt sets the stage for the first unit of the course.

For the sake of this article, I will wait to discuss the second class period's "Five Myths of Appalachian Exceptionalism" until the second part of this essay, partly because the Five Myths fast-forward to contemporary beliefs about the region. In other words, I will explain my two "undoing myths" projects in chronological order rather than pedagogical order. I'll first describe how I teach and address the Agrarian Myth and then discuss the ways I delineate and address my "Five Myths of Appalachian Exceptionalism."

The Agrarian Myth

The reading for the third day, from "Appalachia and the Agrarian Myth" (the opening portion of the first chapter in Wilma Dunaway's *First American Frontier* [1996]), describes the ways in which European settlers associated Appalachia, as "the first western frontier," with the "American dream of freedom and equality" (1).[6] Dunaway claims that "Americans have kept alive their romance with Appalachia" both through tourism and through the "myth of the happy yeoman" (2, 3). Dunaway argues that since the 1700s, Americans have linked the Jeffersonian "folk hero" of the "idealized" "yeoman farmer" with the Appalachian region (2). The yeoman was praised for his honesty, independence, egalitarianism, and his "ability to produce and enjoy a simple abundance" (3)—in other words, for his self-sufficiency, lack of materialism, and love of the simple life. Jeffersonians believed that the uniqueness and greatness of America resided in the continent's vast (supposedly) unsettled open land, which "would guarantee the preponderance of the yeoman"[7]—whose presence would in turn guarantee equality and democracy in the nation.

The "myth of the happy yeoman" is based on the wishful belief that frontier America "was characterized by fiercely egalitarian subsistence economies that offered ... upward economic mobility" (Dunaway 1996, 3). In 1890, Frederick Jackson Turner announced that the frontier had been closed because European settlers had advanced to the western edge of the continent. The ideal of the yeoman farmer's easy access to self-owned, self-farmed land was threatened: Without a frontier on which yeomen could be yeomen, whither America? Dunaway observed that anxious Americans turned to Appalachia for reassurance that an internal frontier had been spared the "forward march of progress" (3). From the late 1800s through the 1970s, commentators falsely "contended that isolation froze Appalachians into 'a folk world of small, isolated, homogeneous societies' shaped by the traditions of early settlers" (3). (These idealized homogeneous folk societies, it must be noted, were white.) Even into the twenty-first century, "the southern mountains have been idealized ... as one of the strongest bastions of such self-sufficient farmers" (3). Thanks to its association with the happy yeoman farmer, the Appalachian region "has been romantically envisioned as the living representation of the nation's egalitarian goals" (3).

(There is a peculiar contradiction here, Dunaway notes. On the one hand, Appalachia is imagined as "the quintessence of rural America, described by many as the avatar of what is best about country life and family farms" [1996, 3]. Appalachia is seen as America at its finest, as the most American place of all. On the other hand, Appalachia is at the same time imagined as a deviation from the norm, "one of the most distinct subregions left in the United States" [3]. This distinctiveness has been perceived alternately as a problem and a welcome relief.)

Dunaway confronts the myth of the happy yeoman in two ways. First, she points out that much of what people claim about the rural parts of Appalachia is equally true of other rural parts of the country. Second, she critiques what she argues is a false premise that the "preindustrial Appalachian economy" was "characterized by five central features: a wide and equitable distribution of land ownership; subsistence agriculture; reliance on local barter networks rather than upon commercial markets; utilization of family labor; and autonomy from external trade" (1996, 4). Over the course of the first unit of the class, I assign readings that support Dunaway's challenges to the idea that

Appalachia was and is the home (solely or primarily) of happy subsistence farmers who don't care about making money. More on this soon.

These few pages of Dunaway's text comprise some of the most difficult reading of the semester. We spend an entire class period parsing and discussing them. First, students get into small groups and jointly complete a worksheet with the following prompts:

1. What beliefs does Dunaway say people hold about Appalachia?
2. Find places in the text where you can tell that Dunaway wants to criticize the beliefs Americans have about Appalachia. Write down the words that give you clues about her position regarding the beliefs she describes.
3. What is the "Agrarian Myth," and what does it have to do with Appalachia?

As you may surmise from the second prompt, students' reading comprehension skills are often not sophisticated enough to gather, from three pages read out of context, that Dunaway is describing and vehemently *criticizing* rather than *advocating* a romantic view of the region. Often, students' preclass discussion board posts demonstrate that those with romantic proclivities eagerly seize upon the idea of Appalachia as a wholesome and unique preserve. They quote Dunaway to fortify and promote their sense of the region as embattled and virtuous. The second prompt allows the careful readers to help the less-accomplished or less-attentive readers see that Dunaway's use of words such as "infatuated," "glorified," "idealized," "nostalgically," "fascinated," "romantically envisioned," "generalizations," and "love affair" should tip us off that she is not pleased with these interpretations of the region. ("Dunaway is a scholar," I remind these students from majors such as civil and industrial engineering and animal and poultry sciences. "How many of your professors, do you think, look with favor upon romanticization, generalization, and nostalgia?") Astute students point out that in a "love affair," one doesn't necessarily really know the object of one's infatuation but views him or her with rose-colored glasses that gloss over flaws.

After we review the worksheet together, I ask the students if the idea of a romance with Appalachia seems familiar. Do they recognize the tendency to idealize the region—either in themselves or in others? Occasionally a student will insist that the romantic view is accurate, that the region is populated by families like his or her own who are hardworking, virtuous, self-sufficient farmers isolated from the rest of the world. Students from outside the region sometimes pipe up to readily acknowledge that they were drawn to attend Virginia Tech in part because of their idealistic image of Appalachia. Often a student raised in the region will report a time when she or he traveled outside the region and encountered a romanticized view of the mountains that s/he found insultingly simplistic.

I share with the class some of the things that I heard while interviewing visitors to the Smithsonian Folklife Festival's 2003 "Appalachia: Heritage and Harmony" program on the National Mall in Washington, DC. One visitor comment in particular highlights the desire to believe in Appalachia as continuing to harbor a subsistence economy. When asked to describe the region, this visitor told me that it was reassuring to know there was "a place to go" if something like the events of September 11, 2001, were to happen again—a place where one could live off the grid, so to speak, without reliance on electricity, computers, grocery stores, or technology of any sort. Sitting in the heart of the mountains in a well-equipped classroom in a sprawling research university with "Tech" in its name, the proposition that the entire region could be described in this way strikes the students as particularly far-fetched.

Before I describe the texts that I assign to help deconstruct the Agrarian Myth, I should mention that, in addition to the "Taking Exception" essay, a number of scholarly works have helped me navigate the complex ways in which "myths" of Appalachia are exaggerations that have grown from kernels of truth. These include especially Dwight Billings's introduction to *Confronting Appalachian Stereotypes: Back Talk from an American Region* (1999); and Ron Lewis's contribution to that volume, "Beyond Isolation and Homogeneity: Diversity and the History of Appalachia" (1999).[8]

CHALLENGE #1 TO THE AGRARIAN MYTH: H. TYLER BLETHEN, "PIONEER SETTLEMENT"

On the fourth day of class, we begin to discuss readings that dismantle the Agrarian Myth of the happy yeoman farmer. H. Tyler Blethen's "Pioneer Settlement" (2004) is the second chapter of the anthology coedited by Blethen and Richard Straw, *High Mountains Rising: Appalachia in Time and Place*. "Pioneer Settlement" draws partly on Wilma Dunaway's *The First American Frontier* (1996) but also on a vast body of scholarship regarding the region from European contact in the 1500s until 1865. Blethen emphasizes the period from the American Revolution up to the Civil War—a period more appropriately identified as the "displacement and repopulation" of Appalachia, as historian John Alexander Williams points out (Williams 2002, 30).

More thoroughly and clearly than any other text I've found, Blethen's chapter addresses the five assumptions about the pre–Civil War Appalachian economy that Dunaway wants to complicate: (1) widespread and equitable land ownership, (2) subsistence agriculture, (3) reliance on family labor alone, (4) use of bartering to the exclusion of commercial markets, and (5) insulation from external trade. Blethen acknowledges that "the goal of Appalachian settlers in the antebellum period was to own their own land, thereby achieving economic independence (and fulfilling Thomas Jefferson's dream of a country of yeoman farmers)." "But," he points out, "not all succeeded" (2004, 21). In contrast to the myth of widespread and equitable land ownership, Blethen provides Dunaway's argument that many of the region's residents were tenant farmers who did not own the land that they worked. "Contrary to stereotype" about subsistence agriculture, Blethen observes, few farming households were "completely self-sufficient" (22). Some sold their labor to wealthier residents, which, in conjunction with slavery (which we discuss a few days later), confounds the picture of family labor only.

When we meet to discuss Blethen, students get into groups of four to complete a worksheet (see fig. 1). I have asked them to come to class with certain information extracted from Blethen's chapter during their reading of it so that they will be prepared to complete the first half of the worksheet. First, "From what parts of the world did the eighteenth-century residents of Appalachia originate? (Hint: Remember that Blethen refers to Appalachia in this era as a 'triracial society.')" The worksheet directs students to reference their notes on this question and then, on a map of the world that I provide them, circle those three parts of the world: Europe, Africa, and North America. Second, students should have noted as they read "from what three areas of Europe did the largest number of settlers in Appalachia emigrate?" The worksheet directs them to draw arrows from these three European places: England, Germany, and Northern Ireland. (Having off-loaded the seek-and-find portion of the exercise into their reading time helps us move through Blethen's highly detailed chapter more quickly during class.) These questions and mappings remind the students about Blethen's description of the "triracial society" (2004, 19) and contact zone that existed in early Appalachia. These two concepts confront the common misapprehension that the region can be understood with reference solely to isolated white or Scots-Irish people and practices.

FIGURE 1. Instructions for Group Work on Tyler Blethen's "Pioneer Settlement (2004)."

Pioneer Settlement of Appalachia, 1540–1865
(More aptly described as the "displacement and repopulation" of Appalachia,
according to John Alexander Williams.)

Tyler Blethen's chapter on "Pioneer Settlement" concentrates on the period between
the American Revolution in 1776 and the beginning of the Civil War in 1861.

The following questions are designed to help you draw on Blethen's overview of
the settlement of Appalachia in order to *complicate long-standing assumptions about
Appalachia.*

I. All groups complete the following activity. Carefully review the first two pages
   of "Pioneer Settlement" (pp. 17–18).
   A. From what parts of the world did eighteenth-century residents of
      Appalachia originate? Outline them on the map. (Hint: Remember that
      Blethen refers to Appalachia in this era as a "triracial society.")
   B. From what three areas of Europe did the largest number of settlers in
      Appalachia emigrate? Circle them. Then represent the movements of
      migrants on your map with arrows, including the intermediary moves they
      made as they journeyed to the Appalachian region.
II. Your group should complete just one of the following (marked with *).
   1. Blethen describes the region as a "*frontier*" that required people to "rely upon
      and borrow from others who came from alien cultures" (p. 20). A better
      term for this (because less romanticized and more descriptive than the idea
      of "the frontier") is *contact zone.*
      A. What kind of economy was forged by this *contact zone* for multiple
         cultures?
      B. What contributions did Europeans make?
      C. What contributions did African Americans make?
      D. What contributions did Native Americans make?
   2. Although Appalachia is imagined as an isolated land of subsistence
      farmers, Blethen describes the region's inhabitants as active in a *global
      market economy.* He argues that, "contrary to stereotype, few [farming
      households] were completely self-sufficient" (p. 22).
      A. What *cash crops* or other surplus products did Appalachian households
         cultivate?
      B. What goods and services did they *export* to local, national, and world
         markets?
      C. What *imported* goods did Appalachian households purchase?
      D. What *industries* flourished in Appalachia before the Civil War?
      E. What was the region's most extensive extractive industry in this period?

There is so much material in this chapter that for the second part of the worksheet I use a "jigsaw" system to invite students to identify additional evidence they will need in order to challenge the Agrarian Myth of a homogeneous and isolated society of yeoman farmers. Half of the small groups hammer out what Blethen means by a "triracial society" through considering what traditions and values Native Americans, Africans, and white Europeans (most prominently English, German, and Scots-Irish) each contributed to the region's contact zone. For example, Europeans contributed crops such as grains and various peas, and introduced cattle, sheep, and hogs. Africans contributed medicinal plants as well as edible crops like watermelon, okra, peanuts, and yams. Native Americans contributed crops such as corn, beans, squashes, and tobacco, as well as agricultural practices such as planting beans and squashes among irregular rows of corn. The English contributed legal and governmental institutions and language, while Native Americans taught Africans and Europeans how to dress, track, decoy game, and live off the land while hunting (Blethen 2004, 19–21).

When these groups share their answers, I make some additional clarifications. Students sometimes mistake this "synthesis on which Appalachians of all ethnicities came to rely to sustain themselves" as a result solely of cooperation and mutual regard rather than also of the conflict endemic to a contact zone (Blethen 2004, 20). I address confusion about the Scots-Irish (emigrants from Northern Ireland who were descended mostly from Lowland, *not* Highland, Scots) with an additional information sheet about this group. Finally, I highlight Blethen's point that white settlers in Appalachia weren't "pure" carriers of their home countries' traditions, having often arrived there after first interacting with immigrants from other cultural groups (for example, while living in Pennsylvania before migrating down the Great Wagon Road). Conflict, diversity, and hybrid traditions of the triracial contact zone complicate the story of the isolated pioneer yeoman.

The remaining small groups tackle perhaps the most essential materials for confronting the Agrarian Myth in terms of antebellum Appalachian inhabitants' participation in a global market economy. I ask students to pick out evidence of Appalachian households' involvement in a market economy through (1) cash crops (or other surplus products), (2) exports, (3) imports, and (4) industries. A small minority of households specialized in cash crops (such as tobacco or cotton) and "purchased most of their household goods" (Blethen 2004, 22). Most households, however, cultivated at least some surplus grain or livestock for trade and purchased some household goods. As farming began to take predominance over hunting, the "primary cash crop" was livestock, especially hogs (23).

Never autonomous from external trade, early settlers exported forest products such as deerskins, furs, feathers, beeswax, and snakeroot. Other settlers exported "corn and livestock, . . . butter, tanned hides, and ginseng to markets in Savannah, Charleston, Washington, Baltimore, Philadelphia, and New York" (Blethen 2004, 23), with ginseng ultimately traveling to China via London. Appalachian "cotton, oats, wheat, corn, tobacco, hemp, and ginseng" went to New Orleans and later Nashville (23).

As opposed to maintaining purely subsistence households, early settlers imported goods, including weapons, clothing and clothing components (cloth, buckles, buttons), and kitchen items. In time, residents bought import goods from Europe that included hardware, yarn, shoes, liquor, drugs, bonnets, silk goods, and books. Most Appalachian households "regularly purchased salt, coffee, refined cane sugar, tea, spices, chocolate, and rum" (23).

Regional industries complicate a picture of families working their own subsistence farms without interactions with commercial markets. Early industries included gold, salt, iron, small amounts of coal, and, especially, "extensive" amounts of timber, which then supplied "fuel for saltmaking, charcoal for ironmaking, bark for tanning leather, support beams for constructing mine shafts, barrels for transporting salt and meat," and building products (24).

Finally, students are often surprised by Blethen's observation that the region was not only well-integrated into a market economy but also a "comparatively wealthy region" of the nation until after the Civil War, when Midwestern products gained a competitive advantage in reaching eastern markets and Appalachia's resources became strained by rapid population expansion at a time when it struggled to recover from the devastation of the war (23–24). I supplement Blethen with maps of early long-distance routes that crisscrossed the region and of railroads and towns in 1860 to point out that trade required methods of ingress and egress that complicate notions of regional isolation (Williams 2002, 36, 150).

CHALLENGE #2 TO THE AGRARIAN MYTH: APPALACHIAN MUSIC AND DANCE

The first time I taught Intro to Appalachian Studies, I ended the course with a lecture on Appalachian music and dance as a soft landing to a long semester—a day that I thought the students would enjoy and that required of them zero preparation.[9] At the suggestion of one of my students, who thought early exposure to "music day" would whet students' appetites for more, I moved this lecture to the beginning of the semester rather than the end. Not only does the topic have the virtue of engaging students, but I discovered that it allows me to reinforce Blethen's messages about Appalachia in the 1800s as a multicultural contact zone influenced by, rather than sequestered from, worldwide currents in isolated and homogeneous white societies. After all, in order to learn about music and dance in the American backcountry, one must learn about English, Scots-Irish, and African immigrants (the latter largely forced immigrants) to the region.

In an hour and fifteen minutes, we can barely scratch the surface. The lecture emphasizes secular traditions to the exclusion of sacred ones. I now have the students complete a short listening and reading assignment before coming to class since we don't have time to sample everything during class. Using a PowerPoint presentation as our guide, we listen to and talk about the old-time music traditions based on voice (British a cappella ballads), fiddle (British), and banjo (African). We talk about the unique fiddle and banjo duet that was likely forged in the region thanks to the precise demographic mix found there. Video excerpts of *River Dance*, buck dancing, and solo and group clogging reinforce the notion that Anglo traditions and African traditions influenced one another in ways that are visible in the clogging dance traditions historically common in parts of Appalachia. Our discussion of the introduction of instruments such as the guitar (from the mid-1800s) and the mandolin (from 1900) via mail-order catalogs brings home the notion that the region wasn't totally self-sufficient, divorced from national markets, or culturally isolated. Finally, students are quick to notice that the commercialization of country music that began in the 1920s doesn't entirely fit with the myth of the happy yeoman farmer.

CHALLENGE #3 TO THE AGRARIAN MYTH: WILMA DUNAWAY, "SLAVERY'S GRIP ON THE MOUNTAIN SOUTH," AND A FIELD TRIP TO SMITHFIELD PLANTATION

Clearly not all of the region's inhabitants relied on the use of family labor associated with the Agrarian Myth. I've experimented with a number of different texts on slavery in this course and finally settled on using excerpts from the first chapter, titled "Slavery's Grip on the Mountain South," of Wilma Dunaway's *Slavery in the American Mountain South* (2003, 15–47).[10] Paired with a field trip to an Appalachian plantation, this reading helps students recognize that not all the region's inhabitants were yeoman farmers without a care in the world for financial gain or worldly status.

Dunaway notes that the traditional claim has been that plantations did not exist in the Mountain South because this type of economics was alien to Appalachian yeomen farmers. But, Dunaway maintains, the reality is that slavery existed in every mountain county, as did slave supporters. Where slavery was practical and profitable, she argues, it was used. In 1800, Appalachian slave ownership ranged from nearly 50 percent of households in Appalachian Virginia to nearly 20 percent of households in West Virginia (Dunaway 2003, 25). The extent of slaveholding varied by terrain, from 8 percent of residents in mountain counties to about 16 percent of hill-plateau households and 18 percent of ridge-valley families (26). Rather than being headed by yeomen farmers, most Appalachian households between 1800 and 1860 were either landless (nearly half) or slave-owning (nearly 20 percent) (26).

According to Dunaway, statistics suggest that slavery had very little presence in about half the land area of Southern Appalachia, had a weak hold on about one-quarter of the counties, and reached intensive Deep South proportions in only about one-quarter of the land area. Nonetheless, she asserts, despite relatively low numbers of slaveholders compared to the lowland South, slave owners had a huge influence on Appalachian economy and society. According to Dunaway (2003):

- Slaveholders monopolized land and created a self-perpetuating inequitable class society that led to class antagonism.

- Slaveholders' over-investment in agriculture and slaves stunted manufacturing and prevented the growth of a diverse, sustainable economy.

- Slaveholders ensured that they would not be taxed for public education, but they supported higher education like the University of Virginia, "accessible only to the sons of the wealthy planters of the eastern part of the state and to the southern states" (47).

- Slaveholders' values were dominant, including their lack of respect for manual labor.

As Dunaway puts it, elites in Southern Appalachia were tied to slaveholding elites in other parts of the South and remained loyal to their political and economic agendas.

In addition to reading about slavery, the class takes a field trip to observe firsthand the Smithfield plantation house (see fig. 2). Because Smithfield is

FIGURE 2. Historic Smithfield Plantation, Blacksburg, Virginia. (Photo courtesy of Historic Smithfield.)

located on Virginia Tech's campus, it is possible for us to visit during our regular class time; the students pay the $3.50 admission cost themselves. Built in 1774, Smithfield was owned by Col. William Preston, a politically prominent surveyor with connections to George Washington and Thomas Jefferson. Preston's vast holdings included parcels from Southwest Virginia to Louisville, Kentucky. Under Preston's wife's management after her husband's death in 1783, the plantation's fifty to eighty slaves raised hemp, corn, and flax.

Though Smithfield may appear modest as mansions go, tour guides emphasize the ways in which the house was designed to flaunt its owners' wealth and status. Its architecture is similar to the Tidewater plantation style. The house boasts glazed windows, Chinese Chippendale staircase railings, transom windows in the entryway, expensive Prussian blue paint in the master chamber, and an impressive drawing room mantel similar to one in the Raleigh Tavern in Williamsburg (Virginia Wind 2006; Virginia Is for Lovers 2006). One student, reflecting upon what she had learned from the Smithfield field trip, noted the "'elitist' lifestyle" of the Preston family, whose "slaves ran the house." She wrote: "I had imagined the Appalachian frontier people to be living in little log cabins, wearing clothing made of animal skins—almost like Davy Crockett or *Little House on the Prairie*. While this may have been the case for some, there definitely was a variety of lifestyles and incomes present in this area."[11] Whereas the Agrarian Myth imagines Appalachia as a land of freedom-loving, equality-loving, hardworking, landowning, and profit-eschewing yeomen, the realities of slavery and tenant farming in the region suggest a much more complicated picture.

Following these three challenges to the Agrarian Myth, we shift our focus to post–Civil War local color fiction that simultaneously raced mountain people as pure white and not-quite-white and sensationalized mountain violence and feuding in order to rationalize industrial exploitation. Though we continue to be alert to romanticizations of the region, we have plenty of opportunities to explore the motivations for and consequences of negative stereotypes about the region in this second unit.

Five Myths of Appalachian Exceptionalism

I have alternately presented the Five Myths of Appalachian Exceptionalism prior to or following class discussion of the Agrarian Myth. Although I place my discussion of the Five Myths second in this essay, I have learned that it works better to introduce them on the first or second day of class, prior to introducing the Agrarian Myth. I then emphasize that the course is jumping backward from there to start with the colonial era and move forward in time, eventually coming full circle back around to the Five Myths. Otherwise, students experience confusion over chronology and begin to mix evidence challenging the Five Myths with evidence challenging the Agrarian Myth, and vice versa.

You might call the Five Myths my personal pet peeves in contemporary representations of Appalachia, though some of them are rooted in the Agrarian Myth dating to the 1700s. In a PowerPoint presentation, I present the following as common overgeneralizations about the region:

1. Appalachia is *all* poor and the poorest place in the United States.
2. Appalachia is *all* rural and also the most rural part of the country.
3. Appalachia is *all* white and the whitest place in the United States.
4. Appalachia is *all* mountains.
5. Appalachia is premodern.

In order to complicate these overgeneralizations, we look at maps, charts, and images.

Persistent rural poverty exists dramatically in Appalachia. Maps demonstrate that poverty rates of more than 20 percent also exist in the Deep South's Black Belt and Delta, on Native American reservations, and along the Mexican border (see fig. 3). I suggest to students that it's not so much that Appalachia is the only poor or the poorest place in the United States as that it is the

Nonmetro high poverty counties by race, 2000

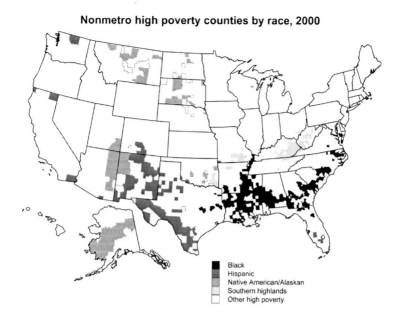

Black
Hispanic
Native American/Alaskan
Southern highlands
Other high poverty

Data source: U.S. Census Bureau, 2000. High poverty is 20 percent or higher.
Map prepared by Economic Research Service.

FIGURE 3. Nonmetro counties with high poverty (20 percent or more), 2000. Shaded areas reference the following populations: Black along the Mississippi River Delta and in a crescent across the Black Belt in the Southeast; Hispanic in the far western states, Colorado, New Mexico, Texas, southwestern Oklahoma, and southern Florida; American Indian/Alaskan native in the Midwest, the borders of New Mexico/Arizona/Utah, Oklahoma, and Alaska; Southern Highlands in eastern Oklahoma, south-central Arkansas, Kentucky, West Virginia, Tennessee, and Ohio. (Image courtesy of United States Department of Agriculture Economic Research Service)

whitest poor place in the United States—which may be why it has received more attention than other areas and become a poster child for American poverty. We then look at a more detailed map of economic conditions in Appalachia. A large number of counties, particularly in areas where the coal industry has dominated, show great economic distress, but economic conditions vary across the region (see fig. 4).

When we discuss the myth that Appalachia is uniformly rural and the most rural place in the country, we first look at images of Asheville, North Carolina; Charleston, West Virginia; Knoxville, Tennessee; and other cities in the region. But we also look at images of strip development and coal camps. Although these locales don't fit our ideas of "cities" or "urban" places, they

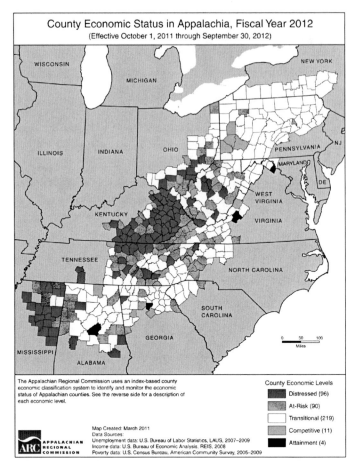

FIGURE 4. Economic Conditions by County, fiscal year 2012. Distressed and at-risk counties fall largely in Mississippi, Kentucky, Ohio, West Virginia, and Tennessee. "Transitional" areas are shown in white. "Competitive" counties fall largely in Georgia, North Carolina, and Pennsylvania. The few "attainment" counties are outside Birmingham, Alabama; Atlanta, Georgia; and Roanoke, Virginia. This map shows the federal definition of Appalachia, by far the most expansive definition. (Image courtesy of the Appalachian Regional Commission)

complicate the idea of Appalachia as purely "rural." Population density maps of the United States strikingly demonstrate that, for the most part, Appalachia is almost as well-settled as the rest of the eastern half of the country; the West, by contrast, looks rural (see fig. 5).

In order to tackle the myth of Appalachia as white, we first look at maps of the region from the 1800s. A map of slaves as a percentage of the population in

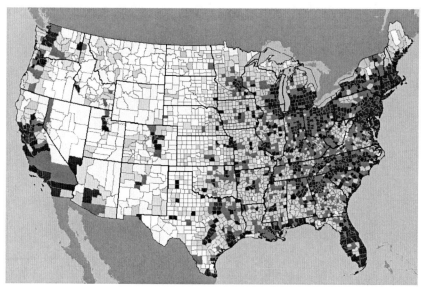

FIGURE 5. Population density in persons per square mile (contiguous U.S. only), 2000. Averaged on a per-county basis. Legend, from light (0–1) to dark (250–66,995). (Image courtesy of *National Atlas of the United States,* accessed 16 October 2011, http://en.wikipedia .org/wiki/File:USA-2000-population-density.gif)

1860 shows some counties, especially in West Virginia and Eastern Kentucky, with under 5 percent slaves. In Montgomery, the county that is home to Virginia Tech, however, one in five residents were enslaved African Americans. In neighboring Roanoke County, one in three residents were enslaved African Americans (see fig. 6). Present-day maps, on the other hand, demonstrate that most of the region is more than 90 percent white (though the Hispanic population is surging in some areas).[12] We talk about both the push and the pull factors that sent freed slaves out of mountain counties following the Civil War as part of the whitening of the region begun earlier with the forced removal of Native Americans. I also mention the surge of African Americans working in the region's coal-mining and railroad industries in the early twentieth century. Finally, we look at a map that demonstrates that many places in the United States in addition to Appalachia are disproportionately white compared to the national average.[13]

The most common definition of Appalachia offered by introductory students is that it is mountainous, but the region's topography is far from homogeneous. Plateau, ridge and valley, Blue Ridge, and Piedmont landscapes shaped the ecosystem, history, and traditions in various parts of the region (see fig. 7).

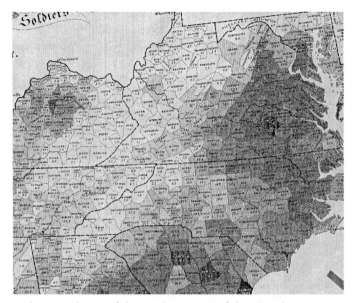

FIGURE 6. Slave population of the southern states of the United States, 1860. African American slaves made up forty to eight per cent of the population in the darkest areas. Counties where slaves represented thirty to forty percent of the population include Lincoln, Garrard, Madison, Montgomery, and Bath in Kentucky and Roanoke and Franklin in Virginia. A light gray band, which follows the present-day I-81 corridor in Southwest Virginia and East Tennessee, indicates those counties where slaves represented ten to thirty percent of the population. Slaves comprised up to ten percent of the population in the lightest counties. (Image courtesy of the US Coast Guard)

Finally, I remind students that the region today is not premodern, as myth and legend would have it. People in Appalachia do not live as people did two hundred years ago. Time did not stand still. A lot of different evidence might be marshaled to make this point. I like to show a map of Wal-Marts to suggest how far the region is from being uniformly populated by yeoman subsistence farmers with no need to buy anything at the store.[14]

Conclusion: Evidence of Student Learning (and Mislearning)

> I had originally thought "it's such a simple and plain place, what is there to learn about it?" The answer was a lot.
>> —Senior, College of Science, Virginia Beach, Virginia
>> (Virginia Beach–Norfolk–Newport News
>> consolidated metropolitan statistical area)

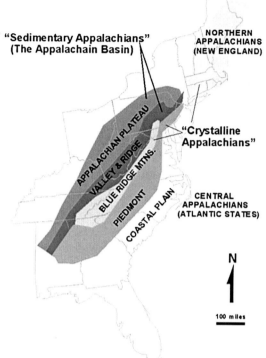

FIGURE 7. Major relief regions of Appalachia. Courtesy of USGS, Phillip Stoffer.

Appalachia is a real place to me now, rather than a nostalgic ideal. . . . Real people live there, and are not too different from me or [people from] other parts of the US.
> —Sophomore, College of Business, Charlottesville, Virginia (one county east of Appalachia)

I thought [this class] would be learning about the mountains, bluegrass music, flat-footing, and other "norms" of Appalachia. Instead, I got Dr. Satterwhite, who took what I thought to be "norms" and turned it upside down. . . . All the myths I thought were true were turned against me. Then I was expected to be able to explain how and why all this was occurring. A major brain workout.
> —Sophomore, College of Liberal Arts and Human Sciences, Pittsylvania County, Virginia (outside Danville, two counties east of Appalachia)

I have had plenty of opportunities to feel discouraged about the extent to which my pedagogical strategies can succeed in shaking the assumptions that students bring with them to the class. On one recent exam, a student wrote with misplaced confidence, "As the world becomes more urban . . . we know we will always have the Appalachian wilderness."[15] Despite my attempts to show students that the yeoman farmer was always more of an ideal than he was ever a uniform reality throughout the region, another student was proud to have learned that Appalachians "no longer live as s[e]lf sufficient yeomen farmers."[16] Nonetheless, I have also seen plenty of evidence that students from all geographical backgrounds—Appalachian and not, metropolitan and not—come to see the region in a more complicated light. And somehow the antiexceptionalist "warts-and-all" approach nurtures rather than undermines students' appreciation for Appalachia.

For the most part, students who entered the class with negative assumptions about the region found those assumptions shaken. Frequently, they claimed in their final reflection papers to have learned the error of their ways. As one student from Northern Virginia put it, "I have gone from just accepting the Appalachian stereotypes out of laziness and ignorance to being able to tell you . . . what mountain top removal does to the environment and the people, all three races of the tri-racial society . . . racial violence in the region, what local color writing is, industrialization['s] effects on the region and economy, and much more!"[17] A junior from the Virginia Beach–Norfolk–Newport News consolidated metropolitan statistical area wrote that the course "made me realize the depth and complexity of Appalachian culture and society. . . . Now I realize that Appalachia is as much an idea as a place." He tracked "exaggerated and romanticized views of Appalachia" to nineteenth-century local color writers and investors "looking to exploit the people and land/resources."[18] A student in the College of Engineering was amazed that "one place can have such contradictory stereotypes." She recognized that an idealized Appalachia "consists of these yeoman farmers who are all patriotic, simple, hard-working, living off the land, supporting their family type of men." At the same time, she recognized that "the Local Color Movement helped to spread the idea that Appalachia's people were hillbillies, ignorant, less civilized, frozen in time, and lived in a backwards sort of way."[19]

Again and again, students described advances in the complexity of their thinking not only about Appalachia but about stereotyping more generally. A first-year student wrote that "looking at how and why those false or exaggerated ideas are created has caused me to look at ideas I have of people and places throughout the world that may heavily lean on stereotypes, overgeneralizations, and ignorantly assigned characteristics. . . . In a nut shell, by focusing on Appalachia, my perception of people worldwide has changed."[20] A student from Ohio learned to "not stereotype anyone, not from Appalachia and not from other parts of the country and world. We all come from somewhere that is special to us, and no one wants other people judging them because they come from a certain region."[21] "I got to hear the firsthand experiences of many of my Appalachian classmates during discussions," wrote a sophomore from Maryland, and learned "that they are very similar to people who I know back home."[22]

Some students were more successful than others in being able to go beyond the idea that stereotypes are unfair to articulate the motivating forces behind the social construction of reality—or, in the above words of the student from Pittsylvania County, Virginia, "to be able to explain how and why all this was occurring." A sophomore from Appalachian Page County in northwestern Virginia admitted that initially, "I was so excited to finally be able to take a class about Appalachian traditions like wild plant uses and quilting, just like my beloved *Foxfire* Books talk about" and that "I was surprised to find out that this class did not focus on those." This student not only broadened her notions of Appalachian traditions, she also found that "this class challenged me to ask . . . Why did the author write this piece? Who is the intended audience? Who does it benefit?"[23] A junior from Winston-Salem, North Carolina, felt the "class provided me with complex and logical explanations for why I had heard what I had about the region." "While I still have a romanticized opinion of Appalachia," he admitted, "I now consider the why, the how and the what in terms what Appalachia is."[24]

It was not always immediately clear to students that demystifying the region was compatible with loving and nurturing it. One student from outside Roanoke ended the semester feeling incredibly torn. A sophomore, she visited the family of a new Virginia Tech friend at their home in the region. She wrote that the family recognizes "that not all Appalachians follow every one of the stereotypes," but "they believe that most do." They were very agitated by her description of the course because they felt that "squishing the stereotypes, both good and bad, squishes their entire culture." She worried, "Are we then destroying something important to [the region] by disproving the common beliefs about these people? . . . Sitting in the [family's] kitchen, I feel that I am trying to take their identity and replace it with a blank, empty slate." In the end, she hoped to be "able to articulate the importance of the Appalachian Studies class to people" because she believed "that it is important to work through the falsehoods."[25]

Sometimes at the opening of a semester I will have a student very much in agreement with this family and visibly angered that I would challenge the notion that all Appalachians are simple, white, honest, isolated, even "backward" farming people living on land that's been in their families for generations. I attempt to give them the space to cherish what they hold dear about the region but also the opportunity to expand their notions of Appalachianness. Rather than "replace" traditions with a "blank slate," I offer explanations for which cultural traditions are historically grounded in the region, and show students the ways that those cultural traditions are inheritances of a triracial contact zone.

Given that positive generalizations about the region have been critical in regional identity construction, it is fair to worry that a course that objects to romantic views of Appalachia risks joining forces with those who would seek to denigrate the region and its people. Sometimes the opposite seems to be the case. As one student from New Jersey put it, "I'm not sure Dunaway would be happy to hear this, but I think I've fallen in love with Appalachia."[26]

For most students hungering to hold on to or boost regional pride, the course appears to do more good than harm. A young woman whose family moved to Ohio when she was a child wrote that bullies called her brother "hillbilly," and "We always had to work extra hard to prove to locals that we were capable of doing anything that they could do. . . . This class gave me the background of how all the labeling began and helped me understand how to prove them inaccurate."[27] A student from the coal fields conceded, "I came into this class thinking that it would be a breeze because 'that's where I grew up,' [but] you definitely proved me wrong" and "open[ed] my view of my hometown community." She learned that Americans "wanted to make up the best fairy tale they could" when it came to describing the region. Nevertheless, she reported that she would "walk away with an appreciation that is greater for the Appalachian Region."[28] Another student from a rural part of the region wrote, "When I began this class, I did not really think that I was from Appalachia. . . . I am embarrassed about that now, that I was not more educated about the place I have spent my entire life."[29] A coalfields Virginian wrote, "Being a native Appalachian from the 'stereotypical' white, poor, and rural town, it was refreshing to understand more about the history and culture of the region."[30] One student, from a suburb technically outside of Appalachia, wrote, "This class was important to me because it helped me to better understand my region and my heritage. I may have grown up in Appalachia but I never quite understood its history. This class gave me that knowledge and respect for the area."[31]

Research has shown that residents of the region believe that a hillbilly is always someone who lives farther up the holler than oneself (Campbell 1994). This course invites students with such beliefs to identify as Appalachian. A student from Charleston, West Virginia, wrote that he had always been "conscious of the stereotypes that plague my home state" and "often felt ashamed." "For better or for worse," he explained, "I never felt that I fit the stereotypes of a typical West Virginian growing up," in part because "my father was a bankruptcy judge, we lived in a brick house with paved roads . . . I had never hunted anything, I attended a reputable public high school, and I was not interested in marrying anyone in my family." Learning about "prejudice based on stereotypes that I never felt I fit somehow caused me to embrace my heritage rather than attempt to distance myself from it. . . . Overall I feel as though taking this course has served only to deepen my passion for my home."[32] A student from Abingdon, Virginia, mentioned in particular a field trip the class took that semester to the declining coal-mining town of Pocahontas, Virginia, and the historically wealthy town of Bramwell, West Virginia. He wrote, "The trip to Bramwell helped me realize the error in my ways in regards to stereotypically categorizing Appalachians." Before the trip, he viewed "the people" of the region as "backwards," but "meeting and talking to the mayor [of Bramwell, Louise Stoker] and others really changed my view. I realized my town is not a rarity in the Appalachian region as much as I assumed it was. The same kinds of people exist in the parts of Appalachia I assumed to be part of what has been coined 'the Retarded Frontier.'"[33]

By the end of this antimythologizing course in Intro to Appalachian Studies, students with ties to Appalachia express greater assurance in their identification with the region. They approach the region's various historical legacies equipped for both knowledgeable critique and confident affirmation. "When I began the class," wrote a student from Russell County, Virginia, "I was on the defense about the area because I am from Appalachia. Knowing that Dr. Satterwhite loves the area and carries a much bigger torch for Appalachia than I do, makes me realize that you don't have to come from Appalachia to truly love the area (something I think people in my class are beginning to do—hopefully!)."[34] She was correct about her classmates, some of whom came to feel a deep sense of obligation and respect for their university's home region.

At its most successful, the course prepares students to exercise suspicion regarding all generalizations, inquisitiveness about the motivations driving any given representation, and a willingness to approach questions of identity with greater nuance and flexibility. Rather than viewing identity from an essentialist, all-or-nothing position, students learn to embrace Appalachia and Appalachianness on their own terms. A student from Virginia Tech's host town, Blacksburg, wrote: "It has also been interesting for me to re-evaluate the definition of an Appalachian. I certainly have not lived in an area dominated by mining or poverty, but I am indeed an Appalachian."[35] As one of the Russell County student's classmates from the Washington, DC, area explained, "Maybe you were born here, maybe you were not, but I do know that you can develop a love and an appreciation of Appalachia's culture, music, and way of life. I know I have. Through this class, I have learned to have a sense of pride in my adoptive home" even though "I am cognizant that Appalachia is not a fairy tale land of rural simplicity."[36]

On one of the final days of the semester, I share with students some excerpts from Jim Wayne Miller's "Brier Sermon—'You Must Be Born Again'" (1980). My favorite lines suggest that we have to know and value the past, but we don't have to relive it:

> You don't have to live the way your foreparents lived.
> But if you don't know about them
> if you don't love them
> if you don't respect them
> you're not going anywhere.
> You don't have to think ridge-to-ridge,
> the way they did.
> You can think ocean-to-ocean. (426)

We can know and appreciate ridge-to-ridge, and at the same time we can practice our understanding and our activism through the lens of ocean-to-ocean. After examining negative, romantic, and historical perspectives on the region, students learn that one doesn't have to embody or endorse all the values or behaviors found in a place over time in order to respect it, love it, defend it, and commit oneself to it.

Notes

1. Most of the student quotes in this essay are taken from their final reflections (an assignment I borrowed from Prof. Catherine Nickerson at Emory University). Students write a one-page, single-spaced paper in which they discuss what they learned in the course. Completion of the reflection virtually guarantees the student an A or B on

the assignment, with higher grades reserved for those who convince me of the extent and nuance of their learning and their ability to apply course concepts beyond the classroom.

For the sake of student privacy, when students' hometowns have populations below two thousand, I have identified only their home counties. I have labeled counties or localities "Appalachian" according to John Alexander Williams's "consensus" definition of the region, because his definition of "core" Appalachia omits the northwestern tier of Virginia's mountainous counties. For an explanation of "consensus" versus "core" Appalachia, see Williams (1996).

2. See note 1 above regarding the way in which I define "Appalachia" for the sake of this essay.

3. Sophomore, College of Agriculture and Life Sciences, from the more rural western portion of Loudon County, Virginia (Washington-Baltimore–Northern Virginia consolidated metropolitan statistical area), final reflection. See note 1 above regarding the final reflection assignment.

4. Senior, College of Liberal Arts and Human Sciences, Fairfax, Virginia (Washington-Baltimore–Northern Virginia consolidated metropolitan statistical area), teaching assessment. The teaching assessment assignment, due once or twice during the term, is a one-page response to the following prompt: "Please tell me what about this course helps you learn, what about this course frustrates your learning, and just generally how things are going for you in the course."

5. For a simplified account of Jean Piaget's theories of learning, see Atherton (2011).

6. I assign only pages 1–3, though the top paragraph of page 4 is useful in summing up five misconceptions about the early Appalachian economy.

7. Richard Hofstadter, quoted in Dunaway (1996, 2–3).

8. See also Inscoe (1995); and Shapiro (2002). I once assigned Shapiro's article outright, but nibbling away at the myths with the readings I discuss here has proved a more accessible and successful strategy.

9. I gleaned the materials for this lecture from Cecelia Conway's *African Banjo Echoes in Appalachia* (1995); and from Prof. Allen Tullos's (2001) undergraduate course American Routes, for which I was a teaching assistant while a graduate student at Emory University.

10. The excerpt I adapted for classroom use emphasizes a few key statistics but omits a multitude of other statistics in an attempt to help those students who otherwise might not see the forest for the trees.

11. Sophomore, College of Business, Blacksburg, Virginia (in Appalachia), final reflection.

12. For a map of racial demographics, see "Figure 3.1: Percent of Population in the Appalachian Region That Is Minority, 2010," in Appalachian Regional Commission, "The Appalachian Region in 2010: A Census Data Overview," 15, accessed 16 July 2012, http://www.arc.gov/assets/research_reports/AppalachianRegion2010CensusReport1.pdf.

13. For a map of counties according to which races in each county have a population greater than the national average, see "Geographic Variations," CensusScope, accessed 16 July 2012, http://www.censusscope.org/us/map_common_race.html.

14. See, for example, Wal-Marts mapped in Kentucky, http://www.allstays.com/c/walmart-kentucky-locations-map.htm; Virginia, http://www.allstays.com/c/

walmart-virginia-locations-map.htm; and West Virginia, http://www.allstays.com/c/
walmart-west-virginia-locations-map.htm (accessed 16 July 2012).

15. Junior, College of Science, Brick, New Jersey (in the southernmost county of the New York metropolitan statistical area), exam response.

16. Sophomore, College of Engineering, New City, New York (New York metropolitan statistical area), exam response.

17. Junior, College of Agriculture and Life Sciences, Burke, Virginia (Washington-Baltimore–Northern Virginia consolidated metropolitan statistical area), final reflection.

18. Junior, College of Liberal Arts and Human Sciences, Norfolk, Virginia (Virginia Beach–Norfolk–Newport News consolidated metropolitan statistical area), final reflection.

19. Sophomore, College of Engineering, Lakeland, Florida (east of Tampa–St. Petersburg–Clearwater consolidated metropolitan statistical area), final reflection.

20. First-year student, College of Liberal Arts and Human Sciences, Floyd County, Virginia (in Appalachia), final reflection.

21. Sophomore, College of Agriculture and Life Sciences, Salem, Ohio (in federally defined Appalachia but not in consensus Appalachia), final reflection.

22. Sophomore, College of Business, Burtonsville, Maryland, final reflection.

23. Sophomore, College of Agriculture and Life Sciences, Page County, Virginia (in Appalachia, near Harrisonburg), final reflection.

24. Junior, College of Natural Resources and the Environment, Winston-Salem, North Carolina (one county east of Appalachia), final reflection.

25. Sophomore, College of Agriculture and Life Sciences and College of Liberal Arts and Human Sciences, Bedford County, Virginia (outside the Roanoke metropolitan statistical area, one county east of Appalachia), final reflection.

26. Sophomore, College of Agriculture and Life Sciences, Monmouth County, New Jersey, final reflection.

27. Sophomore, College of Agriculture and Life Sciences, Wytheville, Virginia (in Appalachia), final reflection.

28. Junior, College of Business, Buchanan County, Virginia (in Appalachia), final reflection.

29. Senior, College of Science, Covington, Virginia (in Appalachia), final reflection.

30. Senior, College of Business, Dickenson County (in Appalachia), final reflection.

31. Senior, College of Science, Bedford County (rural suburb of Lynchburg, one county east of Appalachia), final reflection.

32. Senior, College of Engineering, Charleston, West Virginia (in Appalachia), final reflection.

33. Junior, College of Engineering, Abingdon, Virginia (in Appalachia), final reflection.

34. Junior, College of Science, Lebanon, Virginia (in Appalachia), teaching assessment.

35. He proceeded to explain, "Living in a college town like Blacksburg, the local education system is pretty strong. Despite the fact that I have not struggled to get by or been held back in my education, I have experienced good wholesome family values, an appreciation for the land, and a love for my neck of the woods in the Appalachian mountains." His insistence on associating Appalachia with family values and appreciation for the land

is a testament to the unevenness of student learning in a class that argues Appalachia isn't the only place where one can find those virtues. Sophomore, College of Liberal Arts and Human Sciences, Blacksburg, Virginia (in Appalachia), final reflection.

36. Sophomore, College of Science, Herndon, Virginia (Washington-Baltimore–Northern Virginia consolidated metropolitan statistical area), final reflection.

References

AllStays. 2012. "Wal-Marts Locations by State." Accessed 28 September. http://www.all-stays.com/c/wal-mart-locations.htm.

Appalachian Regional Commission. 2012. "The Appalachian Region in 2010: A Census Data Overview." Accessed 16 July. http://www.arc.gov/assets/research_reports/AppalachianRegion2010CensusReport1.pdf.

Atherton, J. S. 2011. "Assimilation and Accommodation." Accessed 16 October. http://www.learningandteaching.info/learning/assimacc.htm.

Billings, Dwight B. 1999. Introduction to Billings, Norman, and Ledford 1999, 3–20.

Billings, Dwight B., Gurney Norman, and Katherine Ledford, eds. 1999. *Confronting Appalachian Stereotypes: Back Talk from an American Region.* Lexington: University Press of Kentucky.

Billings, Dwight B., Mary Beth Pudup, and Altina L. Waller. 1995. "Taking Exception with Exceptionalism: The Emergence and Transformation of Historical Studies of Appalachia." In Pudup, Billings, and Waller 1995, 1–24.

Blethen, H. Tyler. 2004. "Pioneer Settlement." In *High Mountains Rising: Appalachia in Time and Place*, edited by Richard A. Straw and H. Tyler Blethen, 17–29. Urbana: University of Illinois Press.

Campbell, Roberta. 1994. *Appalachian Experience and Appalachian Self-Concept: Toward a Critical Theory of Regional Identity.* PhD diss., University of Kentucky.

Conway, Cecelia. 1995. *African Banjo Echoes in Appalachia: A Study of Folk Traditions.* Knoxville: University of Tennessee Press.

Dunaway, Wilma A. 1996. *The First American Frontier: Transition to Capitalism in Southern Appalachia, 1700–1860.* Chapel Hill: University of North Carolina Press.

———. 2003. *Slavery in the American Mountain South.* Cambridge: Cambridge University Press.

Inscoe, John C. 1995. "Race and Racism in Nineteenth-Century Southern Appalachia: Myths, Realities, and Ambiguities." In Pudup, Billings, and Waller 1995, 85–97.

Lewis, Ronald L. 1999. "Beyond Isolation and Homogeneity: Diversity and the History of Appalachia." In Billings, Norman, and Ledford 1999, 21–43.

Miller, Jim Wayne. 1980. "Brier Sermon—'You Must Be Born Again.'" In *Appalachia Inside Out: A Sequel to "Voices from the Hills."* Vol. 2, *Culture and Custom*, edited by Robert J. Higgs, Ambrose N. Manning, and Jim Wayne Miller, 423–26. Knoxville: University of Tennessee Press.

Pudup, Mary Beth, Dwight B. Billings, and Altina L. Waller, eds. 1995. *Appalachia in the Making: The Mountain South in the Nineteenth Century.* Chapel Hill: University of North Carolina Press.

Shapiro, Henry D. 2002. "Appalachia and the Idea of America: The Problem of the Persisting Frontier." In *Appalachia: Social Context Past and Present*, edited by Phillip J. Obermiller and Michael Maloney, 36–42. Dubuque, IA: Kendall Hunt.

Social Science Data Analysis Network. 2012. "Geographic Variations." Census Scope. University of Michigan. Accessed 28 September. http://www.censusscope.org/us/map_common_race.html.

Tullos, Allen. 2001. American Routes class lectures, Emory University, Atlanta, Georgia.

Virginia Is for Lovers. 2006. Accessed 13 February. http://www.virginia.org/site/description.asp?AttrID=10247&CharID=12388.

Virginia Wind. 2006. Accessed 13 February. http://www.virginiawind.com/virginia_travel/smithfield.asp.

Williams, John Alexander. 1996. "Counting Yesterday's People: Using Aggregate Data to Address the Problem of Appalachia's Boundaries." *Journal of Appalachian Studies* 2 (1): 3–27.

———. 2002. *Appalachia: A History.* Chapel Hill: University of North Carolina Press.

TWO

Listening to Black Appalachian Laundrywomen:
Teaching with Photographs, Letters, Diaries,
and Lost Voices

ELIZABETH S. D. ENGELHARDT

IN 1989, SCHOLAR DARLENE CLARK HINE proposed the
concept "culture of dissemblance" to discuss the challenges and ethical issues
of recovering black US women's lives. In her influential "Rape and the Inner
Lives of Black Women in the Middle West," Hine focused primarily on the
legacy of rape and domestic violence African American women might try to
hide when interviewed by scholars. Believing it might be better to say nothing than risk being exploited again, and believing it better to agree there was
no story to tell than to lose the right to control what was told to whom, black
women often deliberately kept their voices out of the public record. After
lifetimes of alternatively misinterpreted and explicitly stolen knowledge, and
the reality of exploitative US race, gender, and employment discrimination,
women of color felt protective of their own stories. According to Hine, the
combination of a culture of dissemblance by subjects and racism or ignorance
among researchers severely hindered historians' picture of US social history.

Hine built on the work of fellow historian Deborah Gray White. Both
scholars agreed that African American women themselves may have hesi-
tated, resisted, and outright rebelled—for very logical reasons—at having
family papers and memories put in archives. In a 1987 article titled "Mining the Forgotten: Manuscript Sources for Black Women's History," White

argued that black women's hesitation to donate papers stemmed from a "perennial concern with image, a justifiable concern born of centuries of vilification" (238). She also identified the "adversarial nature" of relations between many black women and public institutions, as well as the perception of "being undervalued and invisible" that led many women to believe their materials were not inherently collectible (238). In addition, though, White turned the focus more fully onto researchers and the archives upon which they base their work. White suggested that archives overlooked the lives and social histories of African American women by at best negligent and at worst racist collecting practices. Even when black women's lives were located in archives, they rarely were cataloged under their own names, joining women of all races in being listed under a husband's or father's papers. The scrapbooks, cookbooks, and oral histories that women may have favored as autobiographical writing were frequently dismissed as ephemera by archives accustomed to formal definitions of genre or writing. Black women who were enslaved joined black men in antebellum collections, by often being listed only in tax or property lists of their owners.

Neither Hine nor White mentioned African American women in Appalachia specifically; in addition, the articles are both twenty years old. One might ask whether they are relevant today in teaching about Appalachia. Certainly national collecting practices, often from the hard work of feminist and African Americanist archivists, have improved. As disciplines open up to scholars with more diverse interests, the politics of subject and researcher shift as well, helping to erode the culture of dissemblance. But I deliberately evoke Hine and White as touchstones for teaching about Appalachia. In the following paragraphs, I consider briefly details about the mountains, the canon of Appalachian Studies, and our classrooms. I do so to propose that Hine's and White's concerns were writ so large in Appalachia that we still have important work to do to answer them. One piece of the answer, though, involves going with our students to those archives and manuscripts, finding the obscured voices, and building such work into our syllabi. The body of this chapter is an example of such an assignment. Coming from my own research, I offer it more as a work in progress than as a finished model; the more such efforts we make, the more our classrooms expand, and the more our students expect our syllabi to incorporate all of the voices of Appalachia.

Today I teach in Texas, at the University of Texas in Austin. My home location is the Department of American Studies, and I have a joint appointment in the Center for Women's and Gender Studies. Most of my courses are cross-listed between the two. While I do not often have the opportunity to teach undergraduate courses entirely in Appalachian Studies, I do regularly teach an upper-division undergraduate seminar titled "Southern Cultures." In that course, I incorporate a unit on Appalachia and its diversity.

Other sections of the syllabus include a close study of urban Houston rap and hip-hop cultures; the traditions of tamales in Delta Mississippi foodways; the imagined and exported South in American and transnational media cultures; and a study of Asian-owned companies' entry into NASCAR business models. Certainly, that is a lot of ground to cover in a semester; of all the topics, though, the section on Appalachia serves as a linchpin for the course. The Appalachian unit challenges students not to accept stories at face value, to question their sources, and to be aware of how methodology shapes outcomes. Those lessons then inform our discussions for the rest of the semester.

While I certainly would argue that a deeper understanding of Appalachia is necessary to any course titled "Southern Cultures," I also encourage the comparative insights about Texas and other Southern communities that emerge from studying Appalachia. Such comparisons initially surprise the students who begin the unit foggy on who Appalachians are and where the mountains are located. In one class, exasperated, I finally said, "If you keep confusing North and South Carolina, I'm going to start saying you're all Oklahoma Sooners." A strong football image, certainly, but not my best teaching moment. Nonetheless, the exchange illustrates a common classroom starting point.

Students who do know the word "Appalachia" often follow with one of two unsurprising but persistent statements. Either they start listing Appalachian stereotypes (including "Appalachians are all white people"), or they talk about the region as a place that needs help ("I went on a mission trip with my church to Appalachia when I was in high school"). The teaching example I discuss in the pages that follow traces the roots and consequences of both assumptions. Research papers at the end of the course similarly question assumptions, even when they take topics far from the mountains: one student traced the street-level geography of a Houston ward and analyzed the space between mainstream media coverage of street hustlers and the success people dismissed as such have had in the Houston music scene. Another began with a family history of narrow food choices from Jewish kosher eating in the small-town South and found a genealogy of concern for local and ethical foodways across religious and secular groups in those same communities today. Both projects had to set aside stereotypes and then develop innovative interdisciplinary methodologies. Studying diversity, photographs, and Appalachia helps students practice those very skills.

Readers may find some of what follows frustrating. I am not outlining a four-point how-to for studying diversity in Appalachian archives that can be lifted to any location and any teacher. I do not list six other photographs to plug into similar lesson plans. I am describing an upper-division seminar; for such seminars, I do not prepare lectures ahead of time, nor do I ask the same discussion questions each time I teach the courses. As a result, I describe here the broad discussion topics in which my students and I engage. I am offering what comes before daily lesson planning: a concrete and deeply personal example of how my research, teaching, and archival collecting inform my upper-division university classroom.

Thus, this narrative traces how I created a line of communication between Appalachia's nineteenth-century laundrywomen along creeks and streams in the mountains and my twenty-first-century, urban Austin, college classrooms. I describe here a series of lessons and questions that emerged from an unexpected discovery during the course of my own research and that I subsequently developed into examples, discussion questions, and theoretical and methodological challenges I pose in the class. I rely on the interplay between students, with me, and through the sources to lead us to insights similar to the ones I describe.

The Hidden Background

The mountains themselves have long had diverse populations. Appalachian literature and history carry around with them a century of mass-produced portraits emphasizing the whiteness of the population, but Appalachia in 1900 was not purely white. The lingering and tenacious assumption that it and the larger South was "an inscrutably 'Old, Weird America' where folks divided their electricity-free evenings between playing murder ballads on homemade banjos and sitting around waiting for the end times," according to American Studies scholar J. M. Mancini, "tends to obscure a larger trend that marked the period: the integration of disparate rural areas, including isolated regions, into a nationally consolidated consumer economy" (2004, 209, 215). The national economy in which Appalachia participated was also bringing diverse immigrants to the mountains, and was allowing long-residing nonwhite mountain residents to cohere into distinct communities. Mountaineers were African American, Native American, and, increasingly in the 1890s, Jewish, eastern European, and Hispanic.

One finds, however, very little evidence of these changing demographics in the sociological and literary texts written by activists to Appalachia at the turn of the century, texts likely to be elsewhere on one's syllabus. For years, even dictionary definitions erased the possibility of a racially diverse region, asserting that Appalachians were white residents of the East Coast mountain range. Popular and scholarly opinion until quite recently was that slavery either did not exist or was somehow nicer in the mountains. Literary fashions and publishing industries either confined black characters to bit players whose sole role was to establish the mountains as inevitably Southern or caused black writers to choose between their racial and regional identities.

As a result, we have set up a scholarly solipsism. If an underfunded archive (and most of ours for Appalachia are) has as its mission to collect Appalachian materials, and if the dictionary and popular definitions say Appalachians are white, how can that archive collect or catalog black Appalachian families' stories? Then, when scholars turn to those archives, how do they find evidence of Appalachia's diversity? Such a self-selected body of materials could discourage black families from telling alternative stories of slavery, racial discrimination, and prejudice in such a climate. It is rare to find cross-disciplinary conversations between African American Studies and Appalachian Studies, even when scholars in each take as their subjects the same historical locations and people. Certainly, we have lost many of our important nineteenth-century black figures to these definitional problems; Booker T. Washington, Martin Delaney, and others simply chose or had chosen for them black identities over Appalachian ones. Only today are black Appalachians such as the Affrilachian poets revisiting this last practice—previously, authors such as Effie Waller Smith, who claimed both identities, seem to have negotiated such wrenching decisions in isolation.

Fortunately—although still, I would argue, too slowly and eccentrically—a recovery and revisioning project is at work in Appalachian Studies. Memoirs, such as that of Memphis Tennessee Garrison, a black West Virginian activist (Bickley and Ewen 2001), are being reconstructed from oral history tapes. Literary republications, such as the Schomburg edition of black Kentuckian Effie Waller Smith's poems ([1909] 1991), are being supported. Contemporary writers, such as Henry Louis Gates Jr., in his memoir *Colored People* (1995); or William Drennen Jr. and Kojo Jones Jr., in their shared meditation *Red, White, Black, and Blue: A Dual Memoir of Race and Class in Appalachia* (2005), are beginning to give us resources for learning about the experiences of being black in the mountains today. We can and should incorporate such materials into our syllabi about Appalachia.

Simply using the few works back in print, though, runs the risk of emphasizing, even tokenizing, extraordinary nonwhite Appalachians. What of the women about whom Hine spoke, women with everyday lives, who did not or could not write their own stories? What of the process by which a culture of dissemblance was built? What specific historical and cultural pressures existed in the mountains to which a culture of dissemblance responded? What would happen if we entered a dialogue with historical black Appalachian women whose stories were misrepresented and outright stolen or fictionalized? Why should we not explore with our students the historical, archival, and political legacies of particular black Appalachian women? By crafting portions of our syllabi to examine larger print culture, incorporate material objects such as photographs, and deliberately seek and listen to previously erased voices, we just might, if we proceed carefully and thoughtfully, emphasizing listening and criticism, prevent such practices from being revised in the future.

Research Finds

In the course of my own research on late nineteenth- and early twentieth-century Appalachia, I stumbled across the same three photographs in three different archival collections. One shows a woman leaning over an outdoor washtub next to a creek; piles of laundry surround her. The other two are close and long-distance shots of a group laundering on the rocks of a shallow river; the laundry tubs steam as two adult women and four children take a break from washing to pose for the camera. The photographs are notable for being the only early-century images of African American Appalachians in the papers of Russell Sage Foundation researcher Olive Campbell (1882–1954), the letters of Berea college student Bertha Nickum (ca. 1870–1903), and the joint collection of settlement school educators Katherine Pettit (1868–1936) and May Stone (1867–1946).[1] While Campbell, Pettit, and Stone knew one another, their bases of operations were more than one hundred miles and two states apart, and none of the women suggest the photographs were connected to one another. It is highly unlikely that Nickum was known by any of the other women, as she was an additional hundred miles away and a much younger college student living in a dormitory; yet, Nickum is the only person who admits purchasing the photographs in a studio. While it is possible (if we stretch to a series of unlikely coincidences) that Pettit, Stone, Campbell, and the photographer were standing together beside the stream, just out of the camera's view, and that the photographer gave copies to the three women before taking the negatives to sell in studios around Appalachia, it is not possible that all four women knew these laundrywomen well. All four speak as if they do, however. From these three photographs, I built a unit on the daily experiences and scholarly construction of African American Appalachians. A detective chase through research methods runs parallel, giving students chances to practice valuable research skills as well.

First, students need context. In the early 1890s, activists who were primarily college-educated, middle-class white women came by the droves to the mountains of Appalachia. Their goal was metaphorically to clean up the needy mountaineers with education, health care, and moral lessons in citizenship. What they called "the mountain work" was often a literal cleaning up, with lessons in hygiene, domestic science, and laundry in mountainous West Virginia, Eastern Kentucky and Tennessee, and western Virginia and North Carolina.

To understand laundry in the mountains, we need to break traditional disciplinary and intellectual boundaries. For instance, the philosophical and cultural role of cleaning in late nineteenth-century imperialist cultures is illuminating. Philosopher Aritha van Herk argues in her article "Invisibled Laundry" (borrowing from Anne McClintock) that "cleansing with soap was an important aspect of imperialism's 'civilizing' agenda, but the hands that did the scrubbing were still peripheral" (2002, 894), and students may find this to be an especially intriguing perspective for Appalachia. I am generally suspicious of the often-heard formulation "Appalachia is the third world of the United States" with which students frequently enter the room, because it dismisses the privileges, however slight, citizenship and whiteness conferred to many Appalachians. However, the turn of the century *did* mark a concerted effort by mainstream and capitalist America to conquer and civilize certain Appalachian populations. Activists such as Campbell, Pettit, and Stone were at the forefront of this effort. Through laundry we can achieve a more complicated discussion of power in the mountains, one that considers how white activists' strategy was first to construct Appalachians as what we might call a "not quite white" race, and then to civilize them into being "just white enough." The ability to be successful at this cleaning up was predicated on keeping people of color firmly out of the so-called Appalachian race—done, as the photographs show, by putting their hands to work scrubbing out beside the mountain stream, keeping them in what van Herk called the periphery. In other words, looking at laundry in activists' texts allows us to address the frequently asserted but rarely analyzed fiction of Appalachia's pure whiteness because they put the laboring black Appalachian female body to work, even as they go to great lengths to minimize her existence in the region. Black Appalachian laundrywomen were hired to meet what van Herk describes as the "fetish for clean clothes (white, white, white) [which] accompanied a colonial imperative" (2002, 894). That fetish bleaches the multihued realities of Appalachia, just as black laundrywomen had to battle the color out of the activists' proper Victorian petticoats.

Students can prove for themselves the actual diversity that existed in Appalachia at any given time with census and courthouse records, as well as secondary scholarship such as William H. Turner and Edward J. Cabbell's (1985) classic *Blacks in Appalachia* or John C. Inscoe's more recent (2005) *Appalachia and Race*. The detective work for students continues as they ask: Who lived where? How many black characters appear in novels? What sleights of hand are performed in works like John Campbell's (1921) *The Southern Highlander and His Homeland* to erase black Appalachia? In other words, does van Herk's periphery model fit for turn-of-the-century mountain cultures?

The Stakes Involved

Once students investigate the whitewashing of Appalachia, I push them to ask why the whiteness of the activists' clothes is so closely tied not only to the whiteness of their own bodies, but also to their ideological investment in the whiteness of Appalachians. Because activist work elsewhere in the post-Reconstruction South was going badly, funding and charitable organizations were looking for worthy projects that might avoid the land mines of Southern racial politics and violence. "Mountain work" seemed to be just the answer, especially when activists presented "evidence" of pure white, Anglo-Saxon mountaineers who were needy and deserving recipients of aid—noble Americans who were, in the parlance of the day, "contemporary ancestors" in a "land out of time." As a land out of time, Appalachia also could be and was constructed as untouched by national patterns of immigration that were transforming the nation. Despite the realities of industrial development and racial diversity, Appalachia in the late nineteenth and early twentieth centuries carried the ideological weight of being a (so-called) pure and unsullied region of the United States. Constructed as the whitest part of America, Appalachia was therefore—at least imaginatively—free of both immigration and post–Civil War racial politics.

In order to justify to their families, funders, and mainstream society why the activists—as young, single women—should undertake the founding of schools, settlement homes, and clinics to usher Appalachians into the nation, the activists got to work writing. Not only did they need to convince others to support the work, they also needed to make the case for why they were the very best people to lead the effort. And they needed to be persuasive in the face of powerful rhetoric of domesticity, frailty, and purity for women such as themselves, all of which were potentially threatened by the wild, harsh, and uncivilized mountains. Their writings, then, are fascinating documents in the history of American womanhood and whiteness.

With this context of constructed pure mountain whiteness, I provide students texts to read closely for how white activists wrote about dirt and laundry. The activists' concerns with dirt and cleanliness carry weight beyond the mere dust of travel, and it is a topic to which they frequently return—but it comes in bits and pieces. For instance, Stone and Pettit are inflexible about the proper degree of whiteness clean clothes should achieve—even if those clothes are washed in a creek. This is met with puzzlement (and occasional outright resistance) by the mountain residents and inspires one woman to comment after watching their elaborate preparations for bed, "Ye all must be a lot of trouble to yerselves" (Stone and Pettit 1997, 139). Stone, Pettit, and the Hindman teachers insist on wearing white, full-length, properly petticoated dresses, even though the rivers are swollen, the paths are muddy, and the days are exhausting. They make their explicit goals "to live among the people, in as near a model home as we can get, to show them by example the advantages of cleanliness, neatness, order, study along both literary and industrial lines" (94). Identifying women's domestic practices as the key to improving society's health, morality, and intellect sets up the argument for why these activists are the best choice to live and work in the mountains, and it expands the scope of the mountain work.

The irony, of course, of the activists' reactions to dirt is that just as women such as Pettit and Stone were escaping the confines of domesticity in their home communities by coming to the mountains to work, they were teaching mountain women to embrace those confinements. As Adele Perry reminds us in an article about activists' encounters with First Nations people in Canada, "'Although the metaphor is one of hygiene, the objective condition of 'cleanliness' is in fact order and discipline.' Discourses of dirt were powerful and flexible ones throughout the nineteenth-century . . . world, but they were rarely unto themselves" (Perry 2003, 593).[2] Like the indigenous women Perry studies, some mountain women might have had more personal freedom and mobility before they learned new, upper-class standards of cleanliness or propriety that were often predicated on household help. Students notice at this point, however, that the lessons for mountain women did not include every mountain woman present.

Beyond Assumptions

Around the turn of the previous century, black women were the South's washerwomen, and activists to Appalachia seem to have assumed that the household help in their new Appalachian communities would be no exception. There is some evidence that suggests the truth of their assumption was dependent on which part of Appalachia and at which time. For instance, in the coal region, many women, black, white, and Jewish, "earned cash by taking in boarders and laundry," according to oral history interviews conducted by Janet Greene. She concludes, "More black women in the . . . coal communities described themselves as domestic wage workers than white women, but both black and white women said they did domestic work for pay" (Greene 1990). Thus, while Pettit, Stone, Campbell, and Nickum are in Kentucky and North Carolina, not West Virginia, we might tentatively conclude that laundry was always a job option for African American women, but they were not the only women who turned to it when needs required paid work. Yet upon arriving in Appalachia, activists such as Pettit and Campbell focused on interior ideologies of domesticity for local white women even as they hired black women to clean their clothes outside in the creeks and streams of the mountains, as the pictures show in vivid testimony.

The descriptions Nickum, Campbell, and Stone and Pettit wrote of the pictures highlight not only their concern with cleanliness, but also their inherent racial anxieties. Campbell, for instance, speaks as if she knows particular details of the washerwomen's lives. In her photograph album, all three pictures are grouped on a single page. The accompanying caption is one of the longest and most detailed in the album: "There are some Negroes in the mountains— this is wash day near Manchester, Kentucky, which because of its salt works was settled by bluegrass families who brought their slaves with them."[3] By reading the caption closely and in its context, students can have productive discussion about why Campbell anxiously explains away African American mountain residents as anomalies; the lengthy and detailed caption suggests her nervousness that the images might trouble funding agencies' confidence in the pure whiteness of mountain work. By making sure readers know that the black people were transplanted from elsewhere (i.e., Kentucky's Bluegrass region), outsiders' beliefs in the mountains' whiteness are never challenged.

Nickum, however, treats the images as generic—as a representation that can stand in for any African Americans around Berea. She neither names the women pictured, nor does she name anyone whom she or the college might have hired to help with her own clothes. Of the picture with a single figure, Nickum says: "A king might envy her content." The contentment that Nickum romantically assigns to the woman is challenged by the traditional low wages and hard work of laundering and by internal evidence of the picture—it portrays the difficulty of the work (with, for example, the washboard and long drop to the creek), the age of the woman, and the pile of work remaining to be done. Although the woman may have felt content with her life and labor, such a conclusion could be justified only from talking with her—something Nickum has not done. In a letter about both photographs, Nickum explains: "I took the negro views especially for Mother. There are any number of old Mammies like the one[s] washing here."[4] Speaking more to social expectations than evidence in the pictures, Nickum describes the women as "old Mammies" despite the fact that only one of the adult women seems older; the other two look quite young, especially as they are posing with their children, the eldest of whom looks only eight or nine. The hint in Nickum's letters that the pictures are, in fact, generic—in other words, available for purchase— further disenfranchises these particular women as owners of their own images. In other words, by having their images so commodified, the women become not some African Americans in Appalachia, but *the* African Americans in Appalachia. Reading the letters, diaries, photographs, and captions together, students see a classic example of African Americans' stories being misused and a culture of dissemblance likely being birthed. What if the women had said what they really felt about the laundry? Would they still have a job? Did they want their picture taken? How would they have posed given the opportunity?

Finally, Stone and Pettit mention at length the various African American washerwomen they employ and whose pictures they collect. Here, I challenge students to reread to uncover the narrative; it is divided into phrases and throwaway comments, but it is present in the archives. In their earliest diaries, they say, for instance, "A colored woman came early to do the washing under Miss McCartney's directions and it was a picturesque scene by the creek between the house and Comfort Nook. There was a great fire under the kettle heating the water and the merry sound of the battling of the clothes echoed from mountain to mountain" (1997, 177). The next day's entry continues: "I spent part of the morning out on the loom house step writing and showing the colored woman how to do the ironing" (179). On another day, they write, "Miss McCartney made bread this morning and showed the washwoman how to make it. She gave her first lesson in reading" (180). And later, Stone and Pettit claim, "Sarah Lizabeth, a sixteen year old negro girl, came to wash for us. Miss Pettit stayed by her all day teaching her to wash by kitchen garden rules" (217–18). The teaching involved in hiring each woman makes it unclear whether they had never taken in washing before or whether they had never encountered the activists' "kitchen garden rules"—although one suspects the latter. Here, we can see enacted how cleanliness becomes a process of order and discipline. Washing is managed as a lesson with specific steps, rules, and goals even beyond its purported end product of clean clothes. Further, laundry quickly bleeds into other process-oriented lessons such as baking and reading; as such the activists can reward themselves for teaching as many different washerwomen as possible. And this is fortunate, because, as their early diaries reveal, they are teaching the laundry lesson anew practically every other week.[5] With a sleight of hand that denies laundrywomen even their own knowledge of their profession, teaching many becomes the goal. Framing laundry as a lesson thus relieves Pettit and Stone from wrestling with why no laundrywoman seems to be able to stand them for more than one week at a time.

Alternate Methods and Sources

The investigation takes one step further for the classroom. Challenging the idea that history is simply a list of absolutely objective "facts," I offer students three versions of the history of Pettit and Stone's school. Students read the archival diaries (now collected in Stone and Pettit's *Quare Women's Journals* [1997]); Lucy Furman's [1913; 1923; 1925] autobiographical novels about Hindman; and Jess Stoddart's recent history of the school, *Challenge and Change in Appalachia: The Story of Hindman Settlement School* [2002]. Women around Pettit and Stone had a practice of cleaning up (pun intended) the diaries when later they fictionalized the work in order to raise money for the school. The early diaries of 1899–1901 were reworked into the novels of the 1920s; these in turn were revised for the remembrances of the school produced in later decades. For instance, the description of African American women washing clothes was completely erased from the Hindman story: in the 1920s novels, Lucy Furman describes a white woman washing by "lifting clothes out of a steaming kettle by the water's edge and battling them on a smooth stump" (1923, 164; 1925, 60), essentially a verbatim account from Pettit and Stone's 1900s diaries with a crucial change of race. By the time of school memoirs, students had taken over the job formerly done by black laundrywomen, as "girls did general housecleaning. . . . The most disliked job was working in the laundry. . . . The major washing took place on Saturday mornings in giant iron pots of scalding water, with wooden sticks to move the linens and clothing around" (Stoddart 2002, 121). By this point in their collective narrative, we cannot know what has happened to women like Sarah Lizabeth and the women in the photographs, who have borne the brunt of the historical forgetting.

Philosopher Anna Julia Cooper would find this unsurprising, and she makes a final example of pulling from beyond the borders of traditional Appalachian Studies to understand the context and connections between Appalachia and the nation. Writing in 1892 about the national context of activism, she especially targets how little thought white middle-class women activists were giving to African American laundrywomen:

> One often hears in the North an earnest plea from some lecturer for "our working girls" (of course this means white working girls). . . . I am always glad to hear of the establishment of reading rooms and social entertainments to brighten the lot of any women who are toiling for bread—whether they are white women or black women. But how many have ever given a thought to the pinched and down-trodden colored women bending over wash-tubs and ironing boards—with children to feed and house rent to pay, wood to buy, soap and starch to furnish—lugging home weekly great baskets of clothes for families who pay them for a month's laundrying barely enough to purchase a substantial pair of shoes! ([1892] 1988, 254–55)

Cooper reminds us to ask questions such as: Who was buying the soap and starch with which to wash Pettit's and Stone's clothes? Where did Sarah Lizabeth live, and how did she make her rent or buy her food once Hindman students took over the laundry? Did she think of applying to be a student? Was she thinking of shoes and soap while Miss Pettit was explaining the kitchen-garden rules? Students are highly skilled at these kinds of questions. Each one could be the basis of a research project or reflection paper.

As Cooper argues, and as Darlene Clark Hine and Deborah Gray White reminded us, it is not enough to stop with the erasure. The final step is to ask: Can we find not just silent images but lost voices also? Sarah Lizabeth's voice is most likely silenced. But the memoirist Memphis Tennessee Garrison (1890–1988) gives voice to another black Appalachian laundrywoman, Cassie Harston Carter (ca. 1849–1941), her mother. Working in southern West Virginia, Carter lived within a hundred-mile radius of Sarah Lizabeth. Garrison says, "My mother was a worker. She had a hand laundry; she would wash all day for fifty cents, and she worked for the rich people who had the fine things. There were no laundries; there was no dry cleaning then, and she always had a good job with the rich people" (Bickley and Ewen 2001, 22). Garrison describes the range of jobs her mother held. She speaks to how often laundry had to be combined with other work to support a family: "When she wasn't housekeeping with them, she was the nurse with the children in the yard, or she was doing laundry. After her time there, she would work in the small hotels of boarding houses. When she'd leave there, she'd meet this laundry at home; she'd wash and iron half the night" (22–23). Garrison explains that the "rich people" in West Virginia were similar to activists like Pettit and Stone, in that "they brought the reforms, and they had the nice houses—and they wanted a good laundress" (23). Finally, Garrison establishes the physical labor involved that women like Nickum were inclined to gloss over in calling such women "contented." Garrison, in fact, links the physical demand for strength in laundering to her ancestors' experiences of slavery, saying, "Oh, when I look at the washing machines now, I wonder how she did it. It was the survival of the fittest. She had to be strong. No wonder Great Gran survived the Middle Passage; she was unusual; she had to be. And my mother got some of that strength" (23).

The rest of Carter's story provides two provocative details. First, Garrison implies, Carter would occasionally put on the clothes she was hired to wash, and she introduces the story by telling us just how intentional the gesture was: "My mother was unlettered but highly intelligent. Sometimes when we were at home, she would dress up and she would say, 'I put my head up and strut like Miss Grace.' Miss Grace was the lady of the house. And bless my mother, she would have been a black Miss Grace if she had had the training and the money to have been so; she was that kind" (23). Imagine Pettit and Stone, with their kitchen-garden rules and their trouble to themselves, finding their laundrywoman-of-the-week trying on their clothes! Second, Carter uses her position to give her own daughter options other than the job she held. Garrison says, "Sometimes the people for whom she worked would say, 'Aunt Cassie, would you like to have this book? If you take this washing home, take Mr. So and So's shirts home and do them, you may have the book.' That was it. Those shirts—no sooner said than done. The book was for me" (26). Garrison explicitly states that she would not have been able to have the career that she had, had her mother not taken care of her home for her. That career was firmly based in education—all the way back to those books her mother bargained for over the laundry tub—and included fund-raising for the NAACP in West Virginia and nationally, pioneering education for special-needs children in the state, bringing cultural and arts events to black communities in the coalfields (including opera), and performing wide-ranging, complicated work for labor issues in the southern counties. In using her job to build her daughter's literacy and her own dignity, Carter helped the women in her family move from laundry workers to race workers, even as the surrounding mountain work and our historical memory are trying very hard to pretend women like them did not exist.

Conclusion

Yet they look back at us from photographs. They stand as silent presences unable to be completely erased from the diaries and novels of American women writers. They put on the clothes, inspire their daughters, and tell their own stories through family memories. Black Appalachian laundrywomen, white Appalachian employers and competitors, and white activist teachers highlight the intersection of race, class, gender, and region that stains the cleaned-up story nineteenth-century writers and even the contemporary canon of Appalachian Studies want to tell. Deborah Gray White provided us with a strikingly appropriate metaphor for Appalachia in her title from twenty years ago. Rather than accepting stories at face value, we do indeed need to pick up our shovels and realize the forgotten can be mined. We need to encourage ourselves and our students to go and look for whatever stories seem to be absent. We can find a way to teach the hidden veins, find the seams, and thereby build a more complete picture and narrative of life in the mountains.

Notes

I am grateful to the Southern Historical Collection at the University of North Carolina at Chapel Hill and the Hutchins Library at Berea College for permission to quote from their collections.

1. John C. Campbell and Olive Dame Campbell Papers, 3800, Southern Historical Collection, Wilson Library, University of North Carolina at Chapel Hill (hereafter cited as Campbell Papers). Bertha Daisy Nickum Letters and Photographs, Record Group 8:

Students, Berea College Archives, Hutchins Library, Berea, Kentucky (hereafter cited as Nickum Papers). I first viewed the photographs connected to Katherine Pettit and May Stone's papers at Berea College as well; two of the photographs have been reprinted in my own *The Tangled Roots of Feminism, Environmentalism, and Appalachian Literature* (Engelhardt 2004). They also appear in May Stone and Katherine Pettit's *The Quare Women's Journals* (1997). Note that Stoddart tentatively identifies one of the figures as Mary Stacy, a white Appalachian woman. I follow Nickum's and Campbell's handwritten captions to suggest all of the women are African American or were perceived to be at the time. As the recent controversy over Emma Dunham Kelley-Hawkins shows, making racial identifications on the basis of photographs (which can reprint skin color too dark or too light) is haphazard at best; nevertheless, what is important here is the way Nickum, Campbell, Stone, and Pettit use and discuss these pictures of laundrywomen.

2. Again, articles such as Perry's must be used cautiously since there are profound differences between Canada's indigenous peoples and Appalachian residents, especially if we are not discussing Appalachia's indigenous Native Americans; yet there are similarities also, enough to open the discussion.

3. Campbell photograph album, PA-3800/9, Campbell Papers.

4. Nickum to family, 12 March 1902, and photographs, Nickum Papers.

5. Laundry lessons were given on 9–11 July (Stone and Pettit, 177–80), 9 August (217–18), 20 August (230), 26 August (236–37), 2 September (250), 10 September (260), and 23 September (273).

References

Bickley, Ancella R., and Lynda Ann Ewen, eds. 2001. *Memphis Tennessee Garrison: The Remarkable Story of a Black Appalachian Woman*. Athens: Ohio University Press.

Campbell, John C. 1921. *The Southern Highlander and His Homeland*. New York: Russell Sage Foundation.

Campbell, John C., and Olive Dame Campbell. Papers. 3800, Southern Historical Collection. Wilson Library. University of North Carolina at Chapel Hill.

Cooper, Anna Julia. (1892) 1988. *A Voice From the South*. Schomburg Library of Nineteenth-Century Black Women Writers. New York: Oxford University Press.

Drennen, William M., Jr., and Kojo (William T.) Jones Jr. 2005. *Red, White, Black, and Blue: A Dual Memoir of Race and Class in Appalachia*. Athens: Ohio University Press.

Engelhardt, Elizabeth S. D. 2004. *The Tangled Roots of Feminism, Environmentalism, and Appalachian Literature*. Athens: Ohio University Press.

Furman, Lucy S. 1913. *Mothering on Perilous*. New York: Macmillan.

———. 1923. *The Quare Women: A Story of the Kentucky Mountains*. Boston: Atlantic Monthly Press.

———. 1925. *The Glass Window: A Story of the Quare Women*. Boston: Little, Brown.

Gates, Henry Louis, Jr. 1995. *Colored People: A Memoir*. New York: Knopf.

Greene, Janet W. 1990. "Strategies for Survival: Women's Work in the Southern West Virginia Coal Camps." *West Virginia History* 49:37–54. www.wvculture.org/HISTORY/journal_wvh/wvh49-4.html.

Hine, Darlene Clark. 1989. "Rape and the Inner Lives of Black Women in the Middle West: Preliminary Thoughts on the Culture of Dissemblance." *Signs: Journal of Women in Culture and Society* 14 (4): 912–20.

Inscoe, John C., ed. 2005. *Appalachians and Race: The Mountain South from Slavery to Segregation.* Lexington: University Press of Kentucky.

Mancini, J. M. 2004. "'Messin' with the Furniture Man': Early Country Music, Regional Culture, and the Search for an Anthological Modernism." *American Literary History* 16 (2): 208–37.

Nickum, Bertha Daisy. Letters and Photographs. Record Group 8: Students. Berea College Archives. Hutchins Library, Berea, Kentucky.

Perry, Adele. 2003. "From 'the Hot-Bed of Vice' to the 'Good and Well-Ordered Christian Home': First Nations Housing and Reform in Nineteenth-Century British Columbia." *Ethnohistory* 50 (4): 587–610.

Smith, Effie Waller. (ca. 1909) 1991. *The Collected Works of Effie Waller Smith.* Schomburg Library of Nineteenth-Century Black Women Writers. New York: Oxford University Press.

Stoddart, Jess. 2002. *Challenge and Change in Appalachia: The Story of Hindman Settlement School.* Lexington: University Press of Kentucky.

Stone, May, and Katherine Pettit. 1997. *The Quare Women's Journals: May Stone and Katherine Pettit's Summers in the Kentucky Mountains and the Founding of the Hindman Settlement School.* Edited by Jess Stoddart. Ashland, KY: Jesse Stuart Foundation.

Turner, William H., and Edward J. Cabbell, eds. 1985. *Blacks in Appalachia.* Lexington: University Press of Kentucky.

Van Herk, Aritha. 2002. "Invisibled Laundry." *Signs: Journal of Women in Culture and Society* 27 (3): 893–900.

White, Deborah Gray. 1987. "Mining the Forgotten: Manuscript Sources for Black Women's History." *Journal of American History* 74, no. 1 (June): 237–42.

THREE

The Southern Highlands according to Hollywood:
Teaching Appalachian History through Film

JOHN C. INSCOE

ONE OF THE COURSES THAT I MOST ENJOY TEACHING
is a freshman seminar called "Appalachia on Film." At the University of
Georgia, I'm an academic exile from the region (though I take comfort on
occasion that Athens is only one county away from official Appalachia, according to the ARC's skewed reasoning). I rarely get the chance to teach
Appalachian history at the undergraduate level, so I jumped at the chance
to develop this course when freshman seminars were added as a curricular
option at UGA several years ago. It is an opportunity many faculty members use to bring to the classroom interests sometimes far afield from their
home disciplines; it has been fun to see a microbiologist offer a course on
Wagnerian opera, a physicist take on Tolstoy and his philosophy of war,
and a mathematician enlighten students on baseball statistics and saber-
metrics. Many of us in the History Department seem to be film buffs;
although we don't seem to stray very far from our areas of historical exper-
tise, my colleagues have designed seminars focused on screen depictions
of scientists, the French Revolution, the civil rights movement, and the
Middle East.

Perhaps too predictably, I focus on the region I know best, Southern Appalachia. I have built my course around nine films:

- *The Journey of August King* (1995): A well-received production of a yeoman farmer in frontier North Carolina who aids a fugitive slave girl at great sacrifice to himself, based on a John Ehle novel.

- *Cold Mountain* (2003): The big-budget version of Charles Frazier's best-selling saga of the Civil War among Carolina highlanders and its protagonist's odyssey in returning home to the woman he loves.

- *Songcatcher* (2000): An independent film based loosely on Olive Dame Campbell and her discovery and documentation of English ballads and folk music in the turn-of-the-century Blue Ridge Mountains.

- *Sergeant York* (1941): Gary Cooper's Oscar-winning portrayal of Alvin York, the homespun Tennessee pacifist who became the most celebrated hero of World War I.

- *Matewan* (1987): John Sayles's meticulous re-creation of a West Virginia coal-mining community and the strike that led to an infamous "massacre" in 1920.

- *Wild River* (1960): Director Elia Kazan's story of a TVA agent's struggle to remove a determined old woman from her island home on the Tennessee River just before it's to be flooded.

- *The Dollmaker* (1984): Jane Fonda plays Gertie Nevels in a faithful, if much compressed, adaptation of Harriette Arnow's classic novel of Appalachian displacement during World War II.

- *Deliverance* (1972): A wilderness horror story of Atlanta canoers who find themselves in "hillbilly hell," based on James Dickey's best-selling 1970 novel.

- *Foxfire* (1987): A television adaptation of a Broadway play based on the clash between real-estate dealers and an elderly widow clinging to her right to live out her life on her north Georgia farm.

These cover a broad spectrum of film types: three are major studio productions and box-office hits (*Sergeant York*, *Deliverance*, and *Cold Mountain*; the first two were Hollywood's biggest moneymakers of 1941 and 1972); two are more modest studio productions (*Wild River* and *The Journey of August King*); two are independent films (*Matewan* and *Songcatcher*); and two are television productions, both part of CBS's Hallmark Hall of Fame (*The Dollmaker* and *Foxfire*).[1] Four were adapted from novels (*August King, Dollmaker, Cold Mountain,* and *Deliverance*); two were original screenplays that adhered reasonably close to historical events (*Sergeant York* and *Matewan*); and the other two (*Songcatcher* and *Foxfire*) are heavily fictionalized stories based loosely on real characters or situations.[2]

I cannot claim any overarching rationale for these selections, other than that they are all films I very much like and thus enjoy teaching; in different ways, each engages students at some level, and often multiple levels, and as such, they easily evoke discussion or debate; finally, and perhaps most importantly, each offers some element of "truth" regarding the historical realities of the Mountain South and its past.

We spend the first week discussing major themes in Appalachian history and the reasons behind the many misconceptions and stereotypes to which the region has long been subjected.[3] I have found particularly useful as a working theme for the course a statement by David Whisnant explaining Olive Campbell's mission in the 1920s in his book *All That Is Native and Fine.* "Popular understanding of the Appalachian South at the time [early twentieth century]," Whisnant wrote, "reflected virtually every shade of opinion. While for some, mountain people were 'backward,' unhealthy, unchurched, ignorant, violent, and morally degenerate social misfits who were a national liability, for others they were pure, uncorrupted 100 percent American, picturesque, and photogenic pre-moderns who were a great untapped national treasure" (1983, 110). This vast range of perceptions applies to far more than the early twentieth century; it encapsulates to varying degrees nearly all of the depictions to which the students will be exposed on-screen.

Hollywood has never been known for its historical accuracy, and yet historians have found it far too easy to throw out the baby with the bathwater, and dismiss any value in cinematic treatments of historical subjects. In his book, *Reel History: In Defense of Hollywood,* Robert Brent Toplin urges his fellow historians to take a more open-minded view of cinema and argues that movies can communicate to students of history important ideas about the past. The very nature of the medium prevents it from presenting factual realities in the same way one would expect of a written work of history, or even a documentary film. Nevertheless, Toplin insists, "in many important respects, the two-hour movie can arouse emotions, stir curiosity, and prompt viewers to consider significant questions" (2002, 1).

I admit that I originally conceived this course as one that would examine these films in terms of how they perpetuate misconceptions, stereotypes, or clichés. Yet, early on, I came around to Toplin's perspective. Although there is plenty to talk about in terms of stereotypes and distortions in most of the films, more importantly, I think, each of these stories encompasses human struggles that are brought to life through skilled writing and often great acting that grow out of actual historical situations. As such, I see these films as appealing and accessible means of drawing students into discussions of the realities conveyed—or at least suggested—on-screen. Students are certainly astute enough not to accept what they see on-screen as literal truth or documentary filmmaking, and thus not as much of our class discussion has focused on separating fact from fiction as I had anticipated in designing the course.

I show and discuss the films in chronological order by content, rather than by their dates of production. For all but the latter two, we have specific dates in which each is set: 1815, 1864–1865, 1907, 1917–1918, 1920, 1935, and 1944–1945. The last two are contemporary depictions of the times in which they were made—the 1970s and 1980s. There are merits to both chronological approaches. (I also teach a freshman seminar on Southern race relations in film, and there, the order in which the films were produced is far more integral in that we use those films to explore the changing racial attitudes of Hollywood itself and how it reflected—or failed to reflect—such attitudes in the rest of the country and in the South.) For this course, when the films were made is less integral to my purposes than is their historical subject matter. Six of these nine films were made after 1984 (only *Sergeant York*, *Wild River*, and *Deliverance* were not), so they do not lend themselves to an assessment of changing views of Appalachia over the course of the twentieth century.

The class meets twice a week. On Tuesdays, we view a film after I offer fairly brief and basic introductory remarks. Based on notes made during the screening, students write a three- to four-page analysis that they turn in on Thursday. I ask them to respond in some way to a set of questions I pose centered on the tone taken by each film toward Appalachian life (contemptuous? respectful? romanticized? satiric?, etc.); the virtues and vices of the characters, major and minor; the narrative techniques used to shape viewers' attitudes toward the region; what aspects of the film—music, speech patterns, location shooting—contribute to or detract from its regional authenticity; and what impact the movie likely had on how American filmgoers view Appalachia.

On Thursdays, when we convene again, I provide far more historical context on the film, and then we spend most of the class period discussing the issues the students have written about, discussions that grow richer and more rewarding over the course of the semester in that each film builds on those seen earlier and students are able to assess them in increasingly comparative terms. It was only as I taught the course for the first time that I came to fully appreciate this cumulative effect: that the juxtaposition of these particular films offered far more insight into both realities and perceptions of Appalachia than one would have any right to expect from Southern California's "dream factory" or than any one or two of these films alone could offer. And I took great satisfaction in that, more often than not, the students themselves picked up on these parallels and comparisons, and in so doing, often shaped their own conclusions about the region and its depiction in film.

The most obvious commonality shared by all but one of these films is the interaction of Southern highlanders with outsiders—either through the incursion of the latter into the region, or the movement elsewhere by Appalachian natives. (Only *August King* is regionally self-contained, with all of the characters and conflict limited to Appalachian residents, though even its plot is centered on the efforts of one native—a slave—to move beyond the region.) The intentions of the strangers coming into the region vary greatly in these films, as has indeed been the case historically, particularly over the course of the twentieth century. Academic fieldworkers, union organizers and company agents, government officials, tourists, and the developers who cater to those tourists all serve as catalysts that drive the plots of *Matewan*, *Songcatcher*, *Wild River*, *Deliverance*, and *Foxfire*. In each, it is the reactions of local highlanders to these individuals or groups and their various agendas that provide the tension, conflict, and emotional weight that in turn propel the plot and provide the dramatic tension.

For those highlanders who move beyond the bounds of home and region, it is usually larger historical forces that push them away; none leave willingly. It is war that takes Inman, Alvin York, and Gertie Nevels far from home and into alien environments. They carry with them skills honed in the mountains— whether shooting prowess or wood carving—that have much to do with their survival in hostile circumstances far from home, and yet all are profoundly troubled by their displacement and seek desperately to return to the comfort and security of their highland households and communities—or merely the natural world. (Inman, in particular, seems drawn back home by the aesthetics of the mountains themselves—oh, and by his sweetheart, Ada Monroe.)

A related theme that students readily detect is Appalachians' strong attachment to land. August King, Alvin York, and Gertie Nevels seek to own it ("I know a piece of bottomland to be had and I'm a gonna' git it," states York; Nevels declares to her youngest son, "You ain't goin' work your life away plowing another man's land"). The plots of both *Wild River* and *Foxfire* are driven by desperate struggles to hold on to land already owned. In both cases, it is an elderly widow who is forced to defend her property against forces far more powerful than she is, respectively, TVA officials and real-estate developers. A somewhat more vague, but equally pervasive sense of loss is evident in *Deliverance*. As in *Wild River*, the damming of a river is the impetus for the threats felt by its central characters, though the losses they fear couldn't be more different. While Ella Garth has far more at stake in defying the TVA, which is about to flood her island home and destroy her way of life, the suburban adventurers on the Cahulawassee are merely interested in "doing the river" one last time before it is turned into a lake. Yet *Deliverance* director John Boorman suggests that there's more than a wild river that's about to be destroyed. Perhaps borrowing from Kazan's film, the final scene of *Deliverance* depicts graves being dug up prior to the cemetery's flooding, a ritual no doubt reenacted many times under TVA's incursion throughout the region, and a major point of concern to Ella Garth.

The moral dilemmas that stem from these conflicts are often obvious in these films, with right and wrong, good and evil, characterized in fairly simplistic form, and yet closer examinations often reveal more subtle and complex factors that defy such easy judgments. August King (Jason Patric) is obviously on the side of angels as he facilitates a slave's escape and makes ever-growing sacrifices to protect a seventeen-year-old girl, Annalees, as she eludes her brutish master. No question of good guys or bad guys here, and yet, students enjoy discussing the fact that sexual attraction might well have served as part of King's willingness to give up so much to protect this alluring young woman (played by Thandie Newton). Would he have risked as much for a male fugitive, or for an elderly or unattractive woman?[4] And while students recognize the strong antiwar message of *Cold Mountain*, the internal strife that plagued Carolina highlanders is stripped of any moral ambivalence as home guardsmen are consigned the roles of villains in far too simplistic a take on the realities of guerrilla warfare that so racked much of that society from 1861 to 1865.

Much of the effectiveness of Kazan's *Wild River* lies in the moral ambivalence of TVA agent Chuck Glover (Montgomery Clift), his protagonist. Glover fully recognizes the benefits of TVA and the New Deal in improving the lives of the East Tennesseans, and yet he also comes to exhibit increasing sensitivity to and admiration for Ella Garth (Jo Van Fleet), the elderly woman who refuses to abandon her island farm. In an interview, Kazan once said of these characters: "I think Miss Ella's right to want to stay on her land. I think Glover is right, too. There's a need to do things for the good of the majority, which in this case is to establish inexpensive electric power and to control the erratic, devastating flooding of the Tennessee River. . . . But when you do that, some individuals are just ruled out, and I think that's a real loss and should not be ignored" (Young 1999, 258–59). This is an issue that resonates strongly in southern Appalachian history, as thousands of residents were forced off land claimed by the federal government for its creation of the Great Smoky Mountains National Park, the Blue Ridge Parkway, and the Shenandoah's Skyline Drive.

Students recognize the similar dilemma facing Annie Nations in *Foxfire* (portrayed by British actress Jessica Tandy, who spent much of her latter career playing Georgia women).[5] This elderly widow faces pressures from land-hungry developers to give up her north Georgia farmstead so that they can make big profits from the scenic vistas of that mountaintop property. The more ambiguous, and perhaps universal, issue in her story is simply her age, and the concern of her son (John Denver) as to how much longer she can live independently given the physical demands required of her in that remote environment.

Some of my students at UGA are familiar with the scenario behind Annie Nation's story—the incursion of tourism and second-home development in the north Georgia mountains. The families of some have vacation homes there or they have visited friends or relatives who do. But they admit that their contacts with natives of the area have been minimal, and they've never thought in terms of the human and cultural costs of that development. Given how many of our students come from suburban Atlanta, they react even more strongly to *Deliverance*. (Some female students are repulsed by the film and find it very difficult to sit through the rape scene at its core, a reaction I don't recall when it first appeared in 1972 and became the biggest box-office hit of that year.) But as Jerry Williamson has so astutely observed, "*Deliverance* is not about mountain people; it is rather a critique of city people" (1995, 157–58). By shifting discussion from the harassment by grotesque hillbillies and viewing the four Atlantans as something other than simply the victims of mountain violence, we open a new frame of reference that informs several of the other films as well.

These films also provide a very effective venue through which to explore gender issues. Strong women play such key roles in so many of these films that students could easily conclude, based on Hollywood's version of Southern mountain life, that Appalachia was a matriarchal society. In a chapter of *Hillbillyland* devoted to "Hillbilly Gals," Jerry Williamson notes, "If a hillbilly is a democrat, then hillbillyland grants extraordinary equality to women ... at times" (1995, 232). It certainly does so in the films under consideration here; one cannot help but be struck by the nearly reverential treatment with which mountain women are depicted in nearly all of these movies. Only *Deliverance* lacks a memorable female character.

Jane Fonda, Jessica Tandy, Nicole Kidman, and Renée Zellwegger made the most of formidable yet vulnerable heroines in *The Dollmaker*, *Foxfire*, and *Cold Mountain*, respectively. They all face seemingly overwhelming odds that force them to fight for their families, their homes, or their own survivals, usually with little or no support from men. Fonda's performance, in particular, is an extraordinary blend of fortitude and vulnerability that embodies much of both the stereotypes and the reality of Appalachian women. (She has said that Gertie Nevels is the role of which she is most proud; she won an Emmy for it [Osborne 2007].) Jessica Tandy plays an equally poignant character in *Foxfire*, whose fragility—due only to age—and stubborn attachment to her way of life, her land, and her memories suggest what Gertie Nevels might have been thirty years later in life.

Equally memorable and worthy of analysis are the rich array of secondary female characters in nearly all of these films. They are even stronger mountain women, played by able character actresses: the previously acknowledged Jo Van Fleet as the island matriarch of *Wild River*; Pat Carroll as Viney Butler, the curmudgeonly midwife who becomes the champion of *Songcatcher's* title character Lily Penleric (Janet McTeer) and the most authentic source of the music Penleric is collecting; Mary McDonnell as Elma, the boardinghouse operator and widow in *Matewan*, who stands her ground in supporting the strike and factors prominently—and triumphantly—in the film's climactic shoot-out; Eileen Atkins as the "goat woman" who rescues Inman and nurses him back to health in *Cold Mountain*; and perhaps the ultimate of mountain matriarchs, Ma York, played by British stage actress Margaret Wycherly, whose stalwart dignity commands the respect and submission of her wayward son Alvin (Gary Cooper) and makes their relationship as much the emotional center of *Sergeant York* as his courtship of his young sweetheart Gracie (Joan Leslie).[6]

Not all such women are admirable: Geraldine Page plays Gertie Nevels's overbearing and needy mother, who insists that Gertie join her husband in Detroit, which in effect forces Gertie to give up the farm she had scraped and saved so hard to acquire. In *Matewan*, Bridey Mae, a rather empty-headed and man-hungry young widow (played by Nancy Mette) is easily manipulated into betraying the coal miners and their community, of which she herself had been a part.

None of these women bow to the authority or power of men (though Gertie's mother forces her daughter to do so); on the other hand, only Ma York is defined by her influence on a male. Her quiet authority and moral suasion over not only Alvin, but her entire household of children, render her a pivotal character despite what is a surprisingly small speaking part. Although her role was based heavily on the real Mary York and her relationship with her son, one cannot help but wonder if another influence on screenwriters was the character of Ma Joad in *The Grapes of Wrath* (1940), produced a year earlier, and earning an Academy Award for actress Jane Darwell. Her influence of her grown son Tom (Henry Fonda) and management of a large family much resemble Ma York's role; both films served as tribute to American motherhood as the backbone of the nation's pioneering spirit in an era of strong patriotic and historic sentiment. (There are perhaps even stronger parallels between *The Grapes of Wrath* and *The Dollmaker*, and of the stalwart women, Ma Joad and Gertie Nevels, who attempt to hold their families together during the traumatic displacement forced upon each by the Great Depression.)[7]

These films provide plenty of opportunity for students to scrutinize masculinity as well. It is the very essence of *Deliverance*, and one in which students by this point in the course recognize as most striking in the fact that it—alone among the films we view—depicts a mountain society devoid of women, and thus a far bleaker and more threatening one because of that. (Is it mere coincidence that Drew [Ronny Cox], the most sensitive of the four Atlantans, and the only one to connect with a local resident—through their banjo duet— is the only one killed by those locals?) There is no shortage of violence in these films, but only occasionally is it portrayed as endemic to mountain society—the decadent brutality in *Deliverance*; good-ol'-boy rowdiness and barroom brawls in several films, from *Sergeant York* to *Songcatcher*; a gut-wrenching execution of a slave in *The Journey of August King*; and vigilante retribution rendered by local hoodlums upon Montgomery Clift's TVA agent in *Wild River*. Just as often, if not more so, the violence is instigated by outsiders, as in

Matewan, or results from larger outside forces, such as the guerrilla warfare in *Cold Mountain*.

If one were to keep score, it quickly becomes apparent that mountain men are not nearly as appreciated by filmmakers as are mountain women. Of male protagonists, only August King, Inman, and Sergeant York qualify as heroes in terms of standing up for principles (and in each case, much of their motivation in doing so is shaped by a woman); in *Matewan* and *Wild River*, it is outsiders, pacifist union organizer Joe Kenehan (Chris Cooper) and TVA agent Chuck Glover (Clift), who embody the moral compasses of their films when confronted with wrongs that need to be righted. More often than not, the native men in these movies are seen as weak, irresponsible, rowdy, even emasculated, malevolent, or intolerant. Women emerge as the guardians, even the repositories of values, of culture, of tradition. This is particularly evident in *Songcatcher*, which features no fewer than six major female characters; it is probably no coincidence that it is also the only film under consideration here that was both written and directed by a woman, Maggie Greenwald. For the most part, these films affirm the final speech delivered by that archetypal screen matriarch Ma Joad in *The Grapes of Wrath*. Just before her upbeat declaration that "We're the people," she muses as to how her family has responded to the challenges and crises they've faced in seeking work as California migrants: "A woman can change better than a man. Man, he lives in fits and jerks. Woman, it's all one flow, like a stream." And so it seems with Hollywood's Appalachian men and women as well.

These films can trigger fruitful discussion of other key topics in Appalachian history, such as race, religion, and community. Slavery is central to *August King*, of course, although Annalees is the only black character with a speaking part in the film, and despite her tough, determined exterior, she remains a rather passive character whose fate remains fully in the hands of white men. Racial divisions among labor forces are evident in the strikebreakers (led by James Earl Jones, no less) who so alter the dynamics of organizing efforts in *Matewan*, and in local white resentments over the New Deal policy of equal wages to black workers in *Wild River*. The sheer absence of racial issues can generate good class discussion as well, the most conspicuous example being the lack of African American characters in the highland scenes in *Cold Mountain*, despite the fact that Ada Monroe is a slaveholder.[8]

Preachers appear as influential members of Appalachian communities in *Sergeant York*, *Matewan*, *Cold Mountain*, and *Songcatcher*, sometimes as social activists, sometimes as their moral consciences. Each of these films features at least one church scene that serves to reveal vital truths about local values and/or prejudices. It's a fourteen-year-old preacher, Danny (Will Oldham), whose perspective provides the crucial narrative thread through which the Matewan massacre is told in hindsight. A church meeting makes up the climax of *Songcatcher*, as the local community is forced to deal with its persecution of the mission workers in its midst (and ends, rather improbably, with a woman shooting her abusive husband in front of the congregation).

Sergeant York opens with a church service, the primary point of which is the rowdy Alvin's absence from it. His conversion experience, along with his quest for bottomland (and a marriage that's contingent on that land), forms the dramatic crux of the movie's first half. "Folks say you're no good 'cept for fightin' and hell-raisin'," states his sweetheart (Joan Leslie), "and I'm thinkin' they're plumb right." Prodded by Pastor Pile (Walter Brennan) and the two women in his life, York quickly matures into a responsible adult, and his new-found faith spurs the pacifist convictions and the moral struggle he faces in becoming a soldier.

The sense of community is more sharply defined in some of these films than others. *Matewan* is certainly the epitome of community studies; in fact, I would argue that no other film has portrayed as complete and complex a portrait of a single community as that re-created by John Sayles in this film. Others, such as *The Journey of August King*, *Sergeant York*, and *Cold Mountain*, make the collective values and agendas of particular communities central to the protagonists' own dilemmas and actions, though *Cold Mountain* does so far more superficially, as students notice, particularly through comparison with the other two. All three, like *Matewan*, thus provide useful reference points for discussions of class differences, of shifts in power and powerlessness, of mob (or mere group) mentalities, and of how outside forces serve to either unite or divide local residents.

Revealing too are those characters, such as August King, Inman, Gertie Nevels, and Annie Nations, who for various reasons either forced upon them or self-imposed, are alienated or removed from the communities of which they once were a part or could have been a part. The resulting tensions between these characters and those in whose midst they live can tell us much about the shifting dynamics within Appalachian society at various eras in its history.

Students become sensitized to the use of music and settings as barometers of how authentic an Appalachian experience filmmakers seek to capture on celluloid. With only two exceptions (*Sergeant York*, filmed entirely in Hollywood; and more famously, *Cold Mountain*, filmed in Romania), these films were produced on location in or near the regions in which they are set, and are generally effective in making not only the mountain scenery, but mountain life—buildings, agriculture, flora, fauna and other natural resources, and physical isolation or remoteness—integral elements of the highland experience.[9]

Nearly all of these filmmakers use authentic music to add credibility to their productions and to enhance the sense of mountain life and culture—English ballads and folk tunes, gospel music and labor songs, and, of course, "Dueling Banjos." Most drew on established musicians from the region as either consultants or performers or both. It is interesting to explore correlations between the authenticity of how Appalachia is depicted and the choices of music used and the locales at which a movie is shot. It is obvious that Georgia's Chattooga River is integral to *Deliverance*'s impact, but what effect does its banjo score have on the film's tone and mood? How much does the blending of multiple musical traditions in *Matewan* reflect the multicultural components—Baptist, Italian, African American, for instance—that so characterized the workers' struggle there?[10] Are the relatively minor though egregious stereotypes and inaccuracies in *Songcatcher* ultimately redeemed by the filmmakers' close attention to what most matters in the film—its music—so meticulously re-created under the supervision of Sheila Kay Adams? And what of the irony that *Sergeant York*, the most romanticized and stereotyped depiction of the region among these films, and the only one in which no attempt was made at either location shooting or mountain-based music, may have been the most authentic film of all, given that it was made in consultation with Alvin York himself, who had not only full script approval, but also specified that Gary Cooper should portray him on screen?[11]

Unlike the hillbilly images stressed by Jerry Williamson through mostly different films than those discussed here, there is a pervasive sense in these films of Appalachians fighting back. They are constantly under siege and regularly exploited, and yet, there is no instance in which they become merely victims. These characters don't take their oppression lying down. Whether they're fighting for property, for family, for community, or for tradition, culture, a way of life, or for their very lives, they all take on heroic qualities that make us admire their willpower, their courage, and their determination, sometimes in the face of unbeatable odds. That this spirit is captured so effectively and through so many different stories and such a range of multifaceted characters brought to life in powerful performances is a point not often appreciated by those who have focused on the misrepresentations of Appalachia by outsiders—journalists, fiction writers, and playwrights as well as filmmakers. (Given the dominance of this view, it is no wonder that *Deliverance* has received far more attention from Appalachian scholars—and almost always in defensive mode—than nearly all the rest of these films combined.)

These are of course partial truths, often oversimplified, romanticized, or much embellished. Again, no one expects historical authenticity from Hollywood. And yet each of these films provides entrée into very real issues and aspects of the Appalachian experience, which allows students to recognize and examine them through these stories' very concrete and tangible terms.[12] In his book *The Invention of Appalachia* (1990), Allen Batteau stresses the extent to which the region has often served far more national than regional agendas, and that in the American imagination Appalachia has long represented far more than deprived and depraved hillbillies. As pervasive as those images are, Batteau argues that they have been offset by more positive images, which, he notes, "have become less symbols of Appalachian particularity than of shared American values—the dignity of labor, self-sufficiency, pioneering spirit, patriotism, and independence" (17–18). In essence, much of what he labels "Holy Appalachia" has been Hollywood's Appalachia. That's certainly the case in most of the films considered here.

Alvin York and the filmmakers reproducing his story on-screen certainly bought into this notion that "Appalachia is somehow a special repository of 'fundamental Americanism,'" the one region in the country that has "preserved traditional American values in their purest form" (Lee 1985, 104).[13] York, his family, and his neighbors represented for filmgoers as well the spirit of what made this nation great, and no doubt much of the film's success lay in the timing of these patriotic sentiments on the eve of the United States' entry into another world war.

But Hollywood's sense of "Holy Appalachia" was neither unique to 1941 nor limited to periods of national crisis. In some sense, nearly all of these films share to one degree or another ennobling depictions of the values of home, of family, of land, and of tradition; and it is as important to recognize and discuss these themes as "inventions" as it is to debunk more denigrating stereotypes and distortions. Yet, even if those positive images of the region may be no more historically accurate than the negatives are, the mere fact that these films take on as their subject matter real issues and events should allow us to approach them as glasses half full rather than dismiss them as glasses half empty.

This is certainly the approach Robert Brent Toplin has taken in his defense of Hollywood history. To grant him the last word, he claims in *Reel History* that such screen depictions of the past are successful when "audiences receive a modicum of information about broad historical events but are, nevertheless, emotionally and conceptually rewarded. Memorable films address important questions about the past and attach viewers' emotions to the debates about them. Hollywood gives life and personality to individuals and groups that often appear rather sterilely in the pages of history books. Cinema helps transform stale, one-dimensional stories into lively, two-dimensional experiences to which audiences can readily relate" (2002, 204).

So it is, I would argue, for all of the films discussed here. Their redeeming value as teaching resources lies not in any literal truths that they convey, but in the mere fact that they embrace real issues and present them in a dramatic context that provides students—as they have provided American moviegoers for much of the past century—accessible, appealing, and multifaceted introductions to the region, its people, and the struggles they have undergone.

Notes

This essay, while commissioned for this collection, first appeared as chapter 17 in Inscoe (2008).

1. For brief descriptions of each of these films except *Foxfire*, see individual entries in Abramson and Haskell (2006). The fullest scholarly assessment of Appalachia on film is *Hillbillyland* (Williamson 1995). Three of the films I teach were released after the publication of *Hillbillyland*; of the others I use, Williamson offers extensive commentary on only two: *Sergeant York* (207–24); and *Deliverance* (155–67).

2. *Foxfire* was produced first as a Broadway play in 1982—by actor Hume Cronyn and his daughter Susan Cooper—which in turn was adapted as the CBS movie five years later.

3. The literature on Appalachian stereotypes and imagery is an increasingly vast one. The best of these works include Williams (1961); Shapiro (1978); Cunningham (1987); Batteau (1990); and Billings, Norman, and Ledford (1999).

4. For a debate on the merits of *The Journey of August King*, see Wright and Inscoe (1997).

5. Tandy followed *Foxfire*, for which she won an Emmy, with starring roles in *Driving Miss Daisy* (1989); *Fried Green Tomatoes* (1991); and the TV film *To Dance with the White Dog* (1993).

6. For a full discussion of Ma York's pivotal role in *Sergeant York*, see the chapter on "The Mama's Boys" in Williamson (1995, esp. 215–22).

7. Coincidentally, Henry Fonda played Ma's son, Tom Joad, in *The Grapes of Wrath*; while his daughter Jane played Gertie Nevels, leading one critic to declare her role in *The Dollmaker* to be "Jane Fonda's Tom Joad, for sure."

8. For a discussion of the role of race in *Cold Mountain*, both book and film, see Inscoe (1998); Crawford (2003); and "*APPALJ* Roundtable Discussion" (Arnold et al. 2004; especially comments by Tyler Blethen, John Crutchfield, and Gordon McKinney); and film review by Inscoe (2004).

9. *Matewan* was filmed in Thurmond, West Virginia; *Deliverance* and *Foxfire* in Rabun County, Georgia; *Wild River* in and around Cleveland and the Hiwassee River in Tennessee. *Songcatcher* was filmed primarily in Madison County, North Carolina; and *The Journey of August King* was filmed in several other Western North Carolina counties. The Kentucky-based scenes in the first third of *The Dollmaker* were filmed in Sevier County, Tennessee, while Chicago doubled for Detroit. Excellent book-length accounts exist of the filming of two of these: *Matewan* (Sayles 1987); and *Deliverance* (C. Dickey 1998). Christopher Dickey is the son of James Dickey, and was with his father during the making of the film.

10. See pp. 109–13 on the scoring of *Matewan* in Sayles (1987). For another good discussion of the film, see Foner (2004).

11. The details of *Sergeant York*'s production are recounted in Williamson (1995, 207–24); Toplin (1996, chap. 3); and Lee (1985, chap. 6). For a discussion of the film within the context of other frontier films of the era, see Smyth (2006, chap. 8).

12. There are other films one could use that would perhaps reveal different patterns and different "truths" about the Southern highlands. *Thunder Road* (1958), *The Trail of the Lonesome Pine* (1936), *I'd Climb the Highest Mountain* (1951), *Coal Miner's Daughter* (1980), *The Molly Maguires* (1970), and *October Sky* (1999) are all mainstream films that I would consider adding to an expanded version of my course, either because they address other significant aspects of the Appalachian experience, or because they offer contrasting views and treatments of issues covered in the nine films I currently teach.

13. Jerry Williamson has noted the irony in the fact that in *Tobacco Road*, another major film also released in 1941, filmmakers applied some of the same hillbilly stereotypes to portray its characters as degenerates that were used in *Sergeant York* to "stoke the fires of patriotism in painting the young ne'er-do-well Alvin York as an ideal foot soldier in the nation's defense" (Williamson 2006, 1710).

References

Abramson, Rudy, and Jean Haskell, eds. 2006. *Encyclopedia of Appalachia*. Knoxville: University of Tennessee Press.

Arnold, Edwin T., Tyler Blethen, Amy Tipton Cortner, Anna Creadik, John Crutchfield, Silas House, John C. Inscoe, Gordon B. McKinney, and Jack Wright. 2004. "*APPALJ* Roundtable Discussion: *Cold Mountain*, the Film." *Appalachian Journal* 31 (Spring-Summer): 316–53.

Arnow, Harriette. 1954 (2009). *The Dollmaker*. Reprint, New York: Simon and Schuster.

Batteau, Allen. 1990. *The Invention of Appalachia*. Tucscon: University of Arizona Press.

Billings, Dwight B., Gurney Norman, and Katherine Ledford, eds. 1999. *Confronting Appalachian Stereotypes: Back Talk from an American Region.* Lexington: University Press of Kentucky.

Carnes, Mark C., ed. 1995. *Past Imperfect: History According to the Movies.* New York: Henry Holt.

Cold Mountain. 2003. Miramax Films. DVD 2004. Based on the novel by Charles Frazier. Directed and screenplay by Anthony Minghella.

Crawford, Martin. 2003. "*Cold Mountain* Fictions: Appalachian Half-Truths." *Appalachian Journal* 30 (Winter-Spring): 182–95.

Cunningham, Rodger. 1987. *Apples on the Flood: The Southern Mountain Experience.* Knoxville: University of Tennessee Press.

Deliverance. 1972. Warner Brothers. DVD Deluxe Edition 2007. Based on the novel written by James Dickey. Directed by John Boorman.

Dickey, Christopher. 1998. *Summer of Deliverance: A Memoir of Father and Son.* New York: Simon & Schuster.

Dickey, James. 1970. *Deliverance.* New York: Houghton Mifflin

Dollmaker, The. 1984. TV Film, CBS Fox. VHS tape 1992. Based on the novel written by Harriette Arnow. Directed by Daniel Petrie.

Ehle, John. 1971. *The Journey of August King.* New York: HarperCollins.

Foner, Eric. 2004. "Matewan." In Carnes, *Past Imperfect*, 204–7.

Foxfire. 1987. TV Film, CBS Hallmark Hall of Fame. DVD 2002. Written by Susan Cooper and Hume Cronyn. Directed by Jud Taylor.

Frazier, Charles. 1997. *Cold Mountain.* New York: Grove.

Grapes of Wrath, The. 1940. 20th Century Fox. DVD 2004. Based on the novel by John Steinbeck. Directed by John Ford.

Inscoe, John C. 1998. "Appalachian Odysseus: Love, War, and Best-Sellerdom in the Blue Ridge." *Appalachian Journal* 25 (Spring): 330–337.

———. 2004. Review of *Cold Mountain*, directed by Anthony Minghella. *Journal of American History* 91 (December): 1127–29.

———. 2008. *Race, War, and Remembrance in the Appalachian South.* Lexington: University Press of Kentucky.

Journey of August King, The. 1995. Miramax Films. DVD 2003. Based on the novel written by John Ehle. Directed by John Duigan.

Lee, David D. 1985. *Sergeant York: An American Hero.* Lexington: University Press of Kentucky.

Matewan. 1987. Cinecom Entertainment. DVD 2003. Written and directed by John Sayles.

Osborne, Robert. 2007. "Private Screenings: Jane Fonda." Turner Classic Movies. 28 March.

Sayles, John. 1987. *Thinking in Pictures: The Making of the Movie "Matewan".* Boston: Houghton Mifflin.

Sergeant York. 1941. Warner Brothers. DVD Two-Disc Special Edition 2007. Directed by Howard Hawks.

Shapiro, Henry D. 1978. *Appalachia on Our Mind: The Southern Mountains and Mountaineers in the American Consciousness, 1870–1920.* Chapel Hill: University of North Carolina Press.

Smyth, J. E. 2006. *Reconstructing American Historical Cinema: From "Cimarron" to "Citizen Kane."* Lexington: University Press of Kentucky.

Songcatcher. 2000. ErgoArts. DVD 2003. Written and directed by Maggie Greenwald.

Toplin, Robert Brent. 1996. *History by Hollywood: The Use and Abuse of the American Past.* Urbana: University of Illinois Press.

———. 2002. *Reel History: In Defense of Hollywood.* Lawrence: University Press of Kansas.

Whisnant, David E. 1983. *All That Is Native and Fine: The Politics of Culture in an American Region.* Chapel Hill: University of North Carolina Press.

Wild River. 1960. 20th Century Fox. DVD 2010. Based on the novels by William Bradford Huie and Borden Deal. Directed by Elia Kazan.

Williams, Cratis D. 1961. "The Southern Mountaineer in Fact and Fiction." PhD Diss., Columbia University.

Williamson, J. W. 1995. *Hillbillyland: What the Movies Did to the Mountains and What the Mountains Did to the Movies.* Chapel Hill: University of North Carolina Press.

———. 2006. "Feature Films." In Abramson and Haskell, *Encyclopedia of Appalachia.*

Wright, Jack, and John C. Inscoe. 1997. "Hollywood Does Antebellum Appalachia and Gets It (Half) Right." *Appalachian Journal* 24 (Winter): 192–215.

Young, Jeff. 1999. *The Master Director Discusses His Films: Interviews with Elia Kazan.* New York: Newmarket Press.

PART TWO

Appalachian Literature and Folktales

In and Out of the Classroom

FOUR

Building Bridges with Ron Rash's *The World Made Straight*: Results from One University and High School Partnership

ERICA ABRAMS LOCKLEAR

IT SEEMS TO ME THAT LIVING IN APPALACHIA and also teaching about Appalachia presents a complicated opportunity. On one hand, you are fully immersed in what sociologists would call a "case study." For instance, you can read about folkway food traditions like ramp festivals and then take a group of students to experience one of those festivals in April or May. But on the other hand, you must be very careful in making assumptions about what your students do and do not know about the region. Some of them are from Appalachia, but as scholars of the region know, that can mean a lot of things: someone from Western North Carolina (WNC) would have a markedly different experience than someone who grew up in Welch, West Virginia. And as various parts of the regions—WNC in particular—become more popular, many people move to the area from other places. A number of the students who take my Appalachian Literature class at the University of North Carolina at Asheville are not from Appalachia, and they take the course to learn about the region through its literature. According to institutional information about UNC Asheville's student body, in the 2009–2010 academic year, 55.3 percent of the student body was from WNC, while similar numbers accounting for students from Appalachia more broadly are not available (Office of Institutional Research 2009).

On the first day of class, some Appalachian Literature students arrive with preconceived notions about the Mountain South, and when I ask them to write about what they believe they already know about the region, they typically either admit that they know only stereotypes that they hope our class will disprove, or, more disturbing, they rely on stereotypes about the region as fact, making statements such as "I know education is not valued in the mountains." As a professor from WNC who grew up in a family that values education very much, reading statements like that one is difficult, but more problematic is how to approach them pedagogically. My initial, personal reaction is to scrawl on the page, "No! That is generalized and simplified and oftentimes wrong!" and leave it at that, but as any good teacher knows, real learning occurs in encouraging students to make their own discoveries that disprove previously held understandings. In other words, I can argue with my students about what they believe they know versus what I believe I know, or I can try to create a learning environment in which students begin to question the framework of their own understandings and then work to realign those frameworks based on their own individual discoveries. This is easier said than done.

As with any class, Appalachian Literature has a lot to accomplish. Ideally, we would have multiple semesters to consider how local color writing affected national perceptions of Appalachia, how more contemporary writers have dealt with the literary history of the region, and how current writers are still writing against the tradition established by authors like Mary Noailles Murfree and John Fox Jr. We would spend weeks discussing diversity in the region, including but not limited to Affrilachian writers like Frank X Walker and Crystal Wilkinson, and we would watch every pertinent documentary or film related to our reading material. But we are instead limited to one semester, and I am grateful to have that semester, since many universities (even those in the region) do not offer a class on Appalachian literature at all. So as with any class, we do the best we can, sampling bits of those items just listed, but all the while investigating how the literature we read dispels notions of homogeneity, backwardness, illiteracy, and a plethora of other misconceptions that have plagued the region for well over a century. To that end, we read as widely about the region as we can, but we also pay special attention to literature associated with WNC. It sometimes comes as a shock to students when they realize that any stereotypes they might hold about Appalachia also apply to them, since they are living and studying in the region, if only temporarily. And what better way to start questioning the foundation on which your beliefs about a particular place rest than to open the door and take a look around outside?

In an effort to prepare us to open that door, I assign as much literature written about WNC, or written by WNC authors, as I can without short-changing writing from other parts of Appalachia. One semester does not allow us to explore all that WNC has to offer in the way of literature, but we are typically able to read several poems by Jim Wayne Miller, sometimes we tackle Charles Frazier's *Cold Mountain* (1997), and twice I have taught Ron Rash's 2006 novel, *The World Made Straight*. My reasons for choosing Rash's novel are varied. First, I want students to have exposure to critically acclaimed contemporary Appalachian writers, and Rash certainly qualifies: to date he has been on the short list for the PEN/Faulkner Award twice; he has won the O. Henry prize not once, but twice; and mostly recently he was awarded the Frank O'Connor International Short Story Award along with $45,000. In 1994 he published his first collection of short stories, *The Night the New Jesus Fell to Earth*; and since then he has published four collections of poetry (*Eureka Mill* [1998], *Among the Believers* [2000a], *Raising the Dead* [2002b], and *Waking* [2011]); three additional collections of short stories (*Casualties* [2000b], *Chemistry and Other Stories* [2007], and *Burning Bright* [2010]); and five novels (*One Foot in Eden* [2002a], *Saints at the River* [2004], *The World Made Straight* [2006], *Serena* [2008], and *The Cove* [2012]), with another short story collection *Nothing Gold Can Stay* becoming available in the spring of 2013. In short, I want my students to know that Appalachian writers are thriving, and Rash illustrates that well for them.

Second, I choose *The World Made Straight* (2006) because it has a powerful local connection to WNC. The novel takes place in 1970s Madison County, an area just one county over from UNC Asheville's home county of Buncombe. It chronicles the story of Travis Shelton, a high school dropout who steals marijuana plants from Carlton Toomey, a man Rash depicts as a rough-and-tumble mountaineer with little patience for thieves. While reading the first few chapters, readers cringe as Toomey slices Travis's Achilles tendon as punishment for his crime, and we later empathize with Travis as he moves out of his parents' house and away from his verbally and sometimes physically abusive father to live with the community's drug dealer, Leonard Shuler. Readers also learn about Dena, a drug addict who has taken up with Leonard; as well as Lori, Travis's girlfriend who hopes to attend Asheville Buncombe Technical College after graduating from high school.

The novel manages to masterfully explore many popularly held notions about Appalachia, including communal rejection of those who pursue a formal education, women like Dena who are made victims of a patriarchal society but who also make poor life choices, and the increasing prevalence of drug use (both prescription and nonprescription) in Appalachia, particularly rural Appalachia. And yet Rash usefully complicates each of these themes, presenting exceptions to these supposed rules about mountain people. Although Travis's father disapproves of his efforts to earn his GED, as readers we understand that Travis values an education, and the symbolic importance of his drive up the mountain to a place notably named Antioch at the end of the novel does not go unnoticed by the careful reader. At the end of the book Dena manages to escape her situation, and although Rash does not tell us what happens to her, once readers realize that she is an abuse survivor, her drug addiction becomes more understandable, if no less problematic. Similarly, once readers understand that Leonard sells drugs out of his trailer because the lack of economic opportunity in Madison County makes it nearly impossible for him to earn money in any other way (especially after he was wrongly accused in a previous teaching position), readers become more sympathetic to his plight, if not more forgiving, especially when we discover that he is saving money to visit his child in Australia. Moreover, near the end of the novel and before his untimely death, Leonard stops selling drugs entirely, secures a job at the local library, and has plans to return to college for a degree in library science. In more ways than those described above, this book is an excellent one for teaching, especially because themes centered on education and the sometimes subsequent "getting above one's raising" that education can cause permeate the text, often striking a chord with students experiencing this same dilemma themselves.

Rash also skillfully weaves a secondary story into his main plotline, that of the Shelton Laurel Massacre. Several books describe the massacre and the events that led up to it, and using excerpts from these texts would certainly make sense when teaching *The World Made Straight* (e.g., Inscoe and McKinney 2000; Paludan 1981; Dykeman 1955; Trotter 1991). Thus far I have simply lectured on the massacre, and I also post links to our class Moodle site (described later in this essay), which students can access to learn more about the specifics of the event. Online resources have also proved helpful in contextualizing the event for students: Ron Rash is the Parris Distinguished Professor of Appalachian Cultural Studies at Western Carolina University, and the Mountain Heritage Center at Western Carolina has produced a short video about the massacre, as well as an interview with Rash about the incident and his decision to base his novel around it, both of which are available for viewing on YouTube. I also recently acquired *Massacre at Shelton Laurel*, a brief but difficult-to-find DVD written and directed by Jay Stone, that I plan to show the next time I teach *The World Made Straight*.

When lecturing on the event, I emphasize to students that during the Civil War, mountain communities were commonly in disagreement over secession, some supporting the Confederate cause, while others supported the Union. I then summarize the historical facts of the massacre, making clear that the lecture is meant only to contextualize the novel, and for a more detailed account, students should consult historical sources about the incident, texts that I make available. In short, I explain that in early January of 1863, during the height of the Civil War, a group of Union sympathizers living in the Shelton Laurel Valley of Madison County, North Carolina, were running low on salt because Confederate authorities in the county seat of Marshall had stopped the distribution of much-needed rations to Shelton Laurel (Inscoe and McKinney 2000, 118). A group of men from the area banded together and traveled to Marshall, raiding several stores as well as Col. Lawrence Allen's home. Reports indicate that the raiders beat his wife, forced his children (some of whom were sick with scarlet fever) to stand outside in winter weather, took the Allens' salt supply, and returned to Shelton Laurel. In response, under "ambiguous orders from General [Henry] Heth," Colonel Allen gathered men and traveled toward Shelton Laurel, as did Lieutenant-Colonel Keith, but from a different location; both Allen and Keith were commanders of the Confederate Sixty-Fourth Regiment (Inscoe and McKinney 2000, 118). As historians John Inscoe and Gordon McKinney explain, "Keith found and arrested fifteen men and boys (only five of whom, by some accounts, were among the Marshall raiders)," and these captures were made possible only by torturing some of Shelton Laurel's women, so they would reveal the whereabouts of their husbands, sons, and brothers (119). Two of the fifteen prisoners managed to escape, while the remaining prisoners were to be transported to Knoxville to a prison camp, but upon arriving in Shelton Laurel, Keith gave orders to kill the prisoners, including twelve-year-old David Shelton, and his troops obeyed. As Inscoe and McKinney explain, "After a quick and only partial burial of their victims, the troops returned to Tennessee, leaving family members to discover the grisly site the following day" (119). This violent incident marks a dark time in Madison County's history, and tensions surrounding the massacre are not altogether gone. The fact that Rash chose to build his novel around this historical event is significant, and I had to wonder after reading it for the first time how residents of Madison County would react to this novel.

When I first taught *The World Made Straight* in Appalachian Literature, we predictably talked about Madison County and its proximity to our location in Buncombe County, and we discussed the history of the Shelton Laurel Massacre, but I kept thinking to myself, *This is such a shame! We are so close to Madison County. We should be doing more with this novel. We should be talking with people who live there. We should be visiting the massacre site.* So the second time I taught the novel, I tried something new: we partnered with a high school English class in Madison County. I had long wanted to try to build community connections between the university and local high school students, but forming that relationship had proved to be a formidable task. The past year I had e-mailed several high school teachers in hopes that one of them would respond, but none did. The next year I tried a somewhat different approach, spending more time researching local high schools and the teachers who taught there. Madison County has only one high school, so I visited that website first and was pleased to find that the English department had its own web page, as well as some teacher profiles listed. I knew that the partnering teacher would need to feel comfortable using technology, and I was excited to discover Angela Sanderson, a teacher whose profile explained that she had previously worked as a technical writer and that she felt passionate about incorporating technology into her classroom. I also learned from her profile that she taught American literature and had a special interest in Appalachia. I sent her a cautiously optimistic e-mail explaining that I taught Appalachian literature at UNC Asheville, that we would be reading Ron Rash's *The World Made Straight*, which took place in Madison County, and I asked if she would be interested in forming some kind of partnership between our classes. Miraculously, that same night she sent me an enthusiastic response expressing interest in working together.

Over the next few months we worked hard to set up that partnership, and we soon discovered that we would each face challenges in doing so. When Angela asked for funds to purchase a set of books for her class, she was told that no funds were available because of the current economic situation and its impact on educational budgets. Not to be deterred, Angela wrote a grant to acquire funding to purchase books for her students, funds to support the field trips we were planning, and funds to travel to the Appalachian Studies Association Conference to present our work together; her grant was funded in full. Her success was both inspiring and motivating for me. Since the computer labs at the high school were often booked with other classes, Angela also planned to use computers in her own classroom, all machines that she had already purchased from personal funds. As for me, I knew what I wanted to do but not precisely how to go about doing it. Over the course of several weeks during the fall semester, I learned the university procedure for taking a class of twenty-five students on a field trip, I researched how to secure transportation for a group of that size, and I asked permission to create guest Moodle accounts for the high school students. I also started planning the visit I was hoping the high school students would make to our campus at the end of our partnership, and that involved securing funding for their lunches, reserving space for their presentations, and coordinating a campus tour and informational session about UNC Asheville.

After what felt like a great deal of planning on both ends, it happened: at the beginning of the spring semester I visited Angela's class to introduce myself, the project, and to get to know her students. Most every teacher I know feels nervous when encountering a new group of students, but I felt especially vulnerable in front of these high school students. What would they think of me or of this project? Would they even be interested? Before arriving that day I knew that the group was a regular class, not an honors class, and that there were seventeen boys and six girls. Angela had already told me that several of the students' reading ability was below grade level, and upon being told that they would begin the semester by reading a novel, more than one exclaimed that they had never read an entire book before. I also later discovered that only a handful of them had computer access at home, so my vision of them checking our Moodle site nightly was not a realistic one. And yet within the first five or so minutes of talking with the students, I was elated: they were excited that they were reading a book set in Madison County, an area that they knew well and one that most of them felt passionately about. They were equally excited to partner with college students, and when I told them that they could teach my students more about Madison County than we could learn from a book, they took that encouragement seriously and felt tasked to teach, rather than intimidated by older students. Perhaps the most memorable part of that visit was when one of Angela's students shyly but proudly told me that he had found one of his ancestors in the book. Even though he had been assigned to read only a small portion of the novel at that point, he had already read it in its entirety, and he quickly flipped to the page that listed his ancestor's name, literally beaming with pride.

As planned, her students spent roughly a month reading the novel, while my Appalachian Literature class spent two weeks. During those two weeks we used online discussion forums through Moodle to facilitate discussion with the high school students. Moodle, an acronym for Modular Object Oriented Digital Learning Environment, is a free, open-source software product that many universities, including UNC Asheville, use. Similar to Blackboard, it allows instructors to create courses online that can function either independently or as supplements to face-to-face time in a classroom. I use Moodle in the latter way, and in addition to posting course materials like the syllabus, reading assignments, and links for outside resources, we rely heavily on Moodle's discussion forum features. In the majority of my literature classes, I assign each student a "Moodle day," and on this day students are responsible for posting to the class discussion forum. Forums are organized based on week or author (depending on the course), and student posts are meant to catalyze in-class discussion. I ask students to provide author context, respond thoughtfully to the reading, speculate about possible essay topics in that reading, and make connections to other works we have read so far. I like this assignment for a few reasons: students who are typically quiet in class have a chance to share their thoughts with the entire class, but in a non-threatening way; I am able to thoroughly respond to each individual student, and I also use my responses to organize class discussion; these posts leave a written trail of discussion topics to which students can refer when studying for exams; and since I value Moodle participation as much as in-class participation, students often respond to posts, creating a virtual discussion group that carries over into our face-to-face interactions. The idea with our Madison High School partnership was that students from my Appalachian Literature class assigned to post on *The World Made Straight* would initiate discussion not only in our classroom, but in Angela's as well. I encouraged my students to ask direct questions to the high school students, and Angela allowed her students to devote a significant amount of class time to responding to my students' posts.

This portion of our partnership was both rewarding and challenging. It was gratifying to see responses from high school students in Madison County who were excited to share what they knew about the area with college students. I was also pleased to see that many of the high school students noticed and took issue with some of the negative stereotypes Rash portrays in the novel, but they also recognized the careful ways in which he overturns those same notions. My students were eager to see how the high school students reacted to the novel, and discussing those reactions added immeasurably to our class time. Despite these positive outcomes, the high school Moodle responses were not without their problems: several of Angela's students had trouble keeping up with their reading assignments, and many of the high school students' posts were short and oftentimes structurally or grammatically incorrect, sometimes to the point of hindering readability. Afterward, I also realized that I had overestimated what these high school students could do. I naively assumed that most of them would have computer and Internet access at home, which was not the case. Looking back, I am aware of my own privilege and ashamed that I made assumptions about access to technology that I take for granted. I also had not carefully considered the varying level of ability in her classroom, nor did I adequately prepare my students to encounter that kind of diversity. These realizations will help in planning next time.

Even so, the Moodle component of the partnership was worthwhile, and it is something I hope to do again in the future. After both classes finished the novel and concluded our online discussion of it, UNC Asheville students and I traveled to Madison High, where my students met the high school students face-to-face for the first time in the school's media center. Angela had thoughtfully prepared breakfast snacks for us, and our students mingled—albeit awkwardly at first—over doughnuts and juice. After a few minutes, conversations fell into place, and with a few exceptions, I was impressed by how well the students interacted with one another. As part of our last Moodle discussion about the novel, I had asked my students to post to our discussion forum any questions they would like to ask Ron Rash. Before our trip, I made a list of those questions, which I then handed out to students at the media center as they got to know one another during our visit. For the next twenty or so minutes, students were instructed to talk with one another about questions they wanted to ask Rash. Next, both sets of students had the rare and wonderful opportunity to participate in a teleconference about *The World Made Straight* with Ron Rash. He graciously gave us more than an hour of his time, during which he explained certain decisions he had made about the novel, the impetus for some of his character creations, and the ways in which his family reacted when he started writing and publishing fiction. University and high school students alike asked him questions that they had formulated together, and it was a fantastic experience. I was once again elated to see both sets of students highly engaged, and I was touched to learn that the mother of one of the high school students had read the novel and come to the media center to hear the teleconference.

After the teleconference, both sets of students traveled to nearby Marshall to see Colonel Allen's house, the site of the 1863 salt raid that presaged the Shelton Laurel Massacre, and to hear more about the incident from local historian Dan Slagle. A colleague at UNC Asheville recommended Dan to me as someone who knew much about the massacre, and when I wrote an extracurricular grant to secure funding for our field trip, I also requested funds to pay Dan for his time, as well as Rash for his willingness to teleconference with us. Everything was running smoothly, except for the fact that Angela and I were both nervously watching the skies, waiting for snow to start falling. That winter was particularly active in WNC, and the threat of impending snow that day almost canceled the entire trip. As we were standing on the steps of the Allen house, Angela received a call that the school was having an early dismissal, and we needed to hurry. So we ended the talk a bit sooner than we would have otherwise and headed to the French Broad Café for lunch. After lunch, the high school students had to return to their campus because of the early dismissal, but when the sun broke through the clouds as my students and I were standing in the restaurant parking lot, we decided to continue with our plans. With local historian Dan Slagle in the lead, we drove to Shelton Laurel and stopped at various sites of interest along the way, including the historical marker near the massacre site, the site itself, and the cemetery where victims of the massacre are buried. Because the cemetery is on private property we viewed it from afar, but if I plan a similar trip in the future, I hope to acquire permission to visit the site up close. My students responded very positively to the field trip, and the increase in comfort level in the classroom after the experience was palpable. I cannot speak for my students, but I felt as though we shared something special during the trip, and our rapport with one another for the rest of the semester was an easy, comfortable one.

The following week Madison High students were scheduled to travel to UNC Asheville to tour the campus, attend an informational session, eat lunch in the cafeteria with some of my students (courtesy of the Admissions Office), and present their final projects to my class. But the trip did not happen because Madison County schools were closed that day due to snow. If I have learned one thing from this experience, it is to never plan field trips in the mountains any time between November and April.

But our partnership did not end there. The theme of the 2010 Appalachian Studies Association Conference was "Engaging Communities," and Angela and I together gave a presentation about our partnership. The presentation was well attended, and it was validating to receive such a positive response to our work together.

Reflecting upon this experience, I now realize that it was a special and unique opportunity. Finding Angela was a fortuitous occurrence, and I was sad to learn that we can no longer partner together, since she left Madison High School and moved to Michigan. I am also fully aware that not all authors are as willing as Ron Rash to engage in such partnerships, and I predict that as he becomes even better known, he will have less time to do so. Even so, I am continually impressed by Appalachian writers' willingness to interact with students. One semester Gurney Norman enthusiastically answered some of my students' questions about *Divine Right's Trip: A Novel of the Counterculture* (1971); Silas House offered to do a teleconference with my students; and during the 2011 spring semester, Pamela Duncan met my students and me at a cemetery in Madison County that is featured in her first novel, *Moon Women*, and then accompanied us to Zuma Coffee in Marshall, where we had dinner together and enjoyed live bluegrass music. So I remain hopeful about future correspondence with authors.

Currently I am planning another high school partnership for the spring semester of 2013, and having already facilitated two such efforts, I hope that I can learn even more from students about how the experience has affected them. During the summer of 2011 I acted as a core faculty member in a National Endowment for the Humanities summer institute held at UNC Asheville called "Power and Place: Land and Peoples in Appalachia." Thirty teachers from fifteen states participated in the institute, where they learned to view Appalachia through an environmental history lens. During that time, I met a local high school teacher, Dawn Rookey, who teaches English at Owen High School in Buncombe County. In the spring semester of 2012, my Appalachian literature class and her junior-level high school students read Ron Rash's short story collection, *Burning Bright* (2010), and discussed it over Moodle. In particular, we focused on "Into the Gorge," a story about a man accused of illegally poaching ginseng. I had taught this collection once before, and students almost unanimously agreed that the charges leveled against the story's protagonist (Jesse) were unfair since his family had owned the land and harvested ginseng from it before it was sold to the Park Service in 1959. The story invites heated debate about land ownership, communal spaces, and resource rights, and as I predicted, it generated lively discussions on our class forum.

Whereas *The World Made Straight* allowed us to discuss the history of an important local event, among many other themes, "Into the Gorge" provides a welcome interdisciplinary opportunity for teaching. Every time I teach Appalachian literature I am shocked to learn that many students are not familiar with plants like goldenseal, bloodroot, and ginseng. In an effort to encourage students not only to view Appalachia through a literary lens—but also through an environmental one—I asked a faculty member in our Biology department, David Clarke, to help us with that task. David regularly teaches courses that are part of our interdisciplinary Appalachian Cluster, and he agreed to take my Appalachian Literature students on a nature hike on the Blue Ridge Parkway. Thanks to David, students learned about the properties of ginseng and how to look for it on the hike; they also were able to contextualize our previous discussions about the biodiversity of the Appalachians, a moving experience since we had just learned about mountaintop removal coalmining and its effects on biodiversity in the region.

At the conclusion of the last semester I included an essay question on the final exam that asked students to reflect on how the online discussions and subsequent hike broadened their understanding of the region. I had wanted to ask students to write about how interacting with high school students from the region—real people—challenged any stereotypical beliefs they may have had about Appalachian residents. Likewise, I wanted to know how discussing a common text with these students helped reshape or realign my students' understanding of the mountains, its literary history, and its environmental uniqueness. For various reasons, however, our interactions with high school students were fairly limited, so most students wrote about our hike, and those responses were illuminating. One thing I regret about the first partnership is that I was so focused on coordinating logistics that I unwittingly neglected to ask my students to reflect on the experience in writing. Doing so seems obvious now, but I missed an important opportunity to learn about how the experience changed their perceptions of the region and its people. Instead, I was left with assumptions, a conundrum that I plan to remedy next semester, when we partner with Madison County Early College students to read *The World Made Straight* once again.

Despite any oversights with the first iteration of a high school partnership, our interaction with Madison High School students taught me a lot of things. It reinforced my belief that literature does not happen in a vacuum, and when you live in the same region you are reading about, you should try to experience it in any way you can. And perhaps more importantly, this partnership taught my students and me that if you are reading literature about a particular group of people, when possible it makes a great deal of sense to ask those people what they think about the ways in which they are being depicted.

References

Duncan, Pamela. 2001. *Moon Women.* New York: Random House.

Dykeman, Wilma. 1955. *The French Broad.* Rivers of America 50. New York: Rinehart.

Frazier, Charles. 1997. *Cold Mountain.* New York: Grove.

Inscoe, John C., and Gordon B. McKinney. 2000. *The Heart of Confederate Appalachia: Western North Carolina in the Civil War.* Asheville: University of North Carolina Press.

Norman, Gurney. 1971. *Divine Right's Trip: A Novel of the Counterculture.* Frankfort, KY: Gnomon Press.

Office of Institutional Research. 2009. *The University of North Carolina at Asheville Fact Book, 2009–2010.* Asheville: University of North Carolina. http://www2.unca.edu/ir/factbook/factbook2009.pdf.

Paludan, Phillip S. 1981. *Victims: A True Story of the Civil War.* 1st ed. Knoxville: University of Tennessee Press.

Rash, Ron. 1994. *The Night the New Jesus Fell to Earth and Other Stories from Cliffside, North Carolina.* Columbia, SC: Bench Press.

———. 1998. *Eureka Mill.* Columbia, SC: Bench Press.

———. 2000a. *Among the Believers.* Oak Ridge, TN: Iris Press.

———. 2000b. *Casualties.* Columbia, SC: Bench Press.

———. 2002a. *One Foot in Eden.* Charlotte, NC: Novello Festival Press.

———. 2002b. *Raising the Dead.* Oak Ridge, TN: Iris Press.

———. 2004. *Saints at the River.* New York: Holt.

———. 2006. *The World Made Straight.* New York: Holt.

———. 2007. *Chemistry and Other Stories.* New York: Holt.

———. 2008. *Serena.* New York: HarperCollins.

———. 2010. *Burning Bright.* New York: HarperCollins.

———. 2011. *Waking.* Winston-Salem, NC: John F. Blair.

———. 2012. *The Cove.* New York: HarperCollins.

Stone, Jay. 2004. *Massacre at Shelton Laurel.* DVD. Haworth, NJ: Windfall Productions.

Trotter, William R. 1991. *Bushwhackers: The Mountains.* Winston-Salem, NC: John F. Blair.

FIVE

The Feast Hall, the Arsenal, and the Mirror: Teaching Literature to Students at Risk

JEFF MANN

I AM PRIMARILY A POET, only secondarily a teacher. So when I think about teaching—which I do rarely, since my pedagogy is more intuitive than consciously considered—I think in metaphor. The metaphors I choose can't help but reveal, to some extent, who and what I am.

The Feast Hall

When teaching literature, sometimes I feel as if I'm giving students much-needed food. It seems inevitable that a man like me, descended from a family of hearty mountain cooks and gourmands, would compare a poem to a biscuit, a short story to a big slab of country ham. The writing that has helped me survive—in particular, that by Appalachians, gay men, lesbians, and the confessional poets—certainly has felt like nourishment. And, to continue the culinary analogy, a soul without meaningful connections and affirmations is likely to feel starvacious, to use a coined word I'm fond of. Good writing can make those connections and allow those affirmations.

The Arsenal

As a liberal, an Appalachian, a gay man, and an environmentalist, I'm angered by much of what's going on in contemporary America, including rampant conservatism, mountaintop removal, and homophobia. Add to that my love of Greek, Roman, Nordic, and Celtic classics, plus an innate bellicose orneriness, and the other set of metaphors that occurs to me when I teach literature involves battle. Giving students resonant words they will cherish is like giving them armor, swords, and shields to protect their fragile individuality and self-esteem against an occasionally hostile world.

The Mirror

Finally, along with food and weapons, analogies natural to my personality, I also return with great regularity to a metaphor borrowed from poet and feminist Adrienne Rich. In her essay "Invisibility in Academe," she says,

> When those who have power to name and to socially construct reality choose not to see you or hear you, whether you are dark-skinned, old, disabled, female, or speak with a different accent or dialect than theirs, when someone with the authority of a teacher, say, describes the world and you are not in it, there is a moment of psychic disequilibrium, as if you looked into a mirror and saw nothing. (1986, 199)

When I teach, especially when I am addressing students in Appalachian Studies courses or the Gay and Lesbian Literature course I created at Virginia Tech, I am trying to save younger versions of myself from this lack of reflection, from the absences and omissions I encountered as a student, from hunger, helplessness, and invisibility. Such privations, if that is all you know, feel like one's natural state, one's deserved condition. One adapts, as cave salamanders have. One assumes that dark and wavering reflections are all there is, like Plato's chained prisoners in his "Allegory of the Cave." So much of what I do as a teacher is shaped by what I once experienced as a student. Forgive, then, a few pages of my past.

West Virginia History, 1972–1973

When I was in the eighth grade, I took a full school year's course in West Virginia history. I had a very good teacher; I absorbed fact after fact. *Harper's Ferry is the lowest point in the state. West Virginia became a state on June 20, 1863. Arch Moore is the governor. There are two sizable Indian mounds in the state, at South Charleston and Moundsville.* Et cetera, et cetera. Enflamed with one of my first grand ambitions—to achieve the coveted Golden Horseshoe award—I studied like mad, took the Golden Horseshoe Test, and—one of my first rapturous successes—made the top score in the county. This meant that I got to go to the state capitol in Charleston, West Virginia, have my shoulder sword-tapped by the state superintendent of schools, and become a Knight of the Golden Horseshoe. Hooray! *Sir Jeff* . . . it sounded good.

As I returned to Summers County triumphant, full of youthful hubris, I knew more about West Virginia than I ever had before or ever would again. However, I did not know enough to realize that I had never heard of Matewan or the Paint Creek/Cabin Creek strikes, Sid Hatfield's assassination, the Battle of Blair Mountain, the ruinous environmental effects of mining, the War on Poverty, or the economic consequences of absentee land ownership.

No Hillbillies Here, 1973–1977

In high school I eagerly took to literature just as my parents expected. I was one of the few students in the ninth grade to love Shakespeare's *Romeo and Juliet*, and in study hall I read *Dracula*, *The Iliad*, and *The Odyssey* just for fun. Emily Brontë's *Wuthering Heights* provided me with an early role model: one day, with luck, I'd be as smoldering, complex, passionate, and irresistible as Heathcliff. By the tenth grade I was devouring *Julius Caesar* in English class, and, inspired by a Latin course, my pleasure reading was composed of historical novels about Rome. Eleventh grade was American lit, and I was right in my element, since my father had already got me hooked on Emerson and Thoreau, Dickinson and Whitman. By the twelfth grade, I'd realized I was gay, so my enthusiasm for *Hamlet*, *Macbeth*, and Robert Frost was mixed up with more pleasure reading, Mary Renault's historical novels about ancient Greece, which are full of men loving men.

All fine material, all authors to be admired and reread throughout my adulthood-to-come. But no Appalachian authors. There I was living in Hinton, West Virginia, a small mountain town along the New River, and the teachers at Hinton High School didn't expose me to mountain writers' works (except one Jesse Stuart story I didn't really take to). Well, the faculty was no doubt under pressure to teach classics, and I loved classics. I loved just about every writer I was introduced to. Gay/lesbian writers I had to, of course, furtively discover on my own. Appalachian writers, well, even if I would have known of them, I wouldn't have been much interested anyway. Appalachia had no culture. Mass media had made that clear. It was a backward place that young intellectuals like me wanted to flee as soon as possible.

Only one event caused me briefly to rethink these certainties. During my ninth-grade year, the Appalachian poet Muriel Miller Dressler read at my high school. I had never heard a live poet read, certainly not a West Virginia poet writing about West Virginia. She read her poem "Appalachia," mentioning the ways in which mountain folks establish their family graveyards on hilltops (2000, 105–6). *Well, yes*, I thought. *Just like ours, the Ferrell family cemetery up at Forest Hill.* Something clicked, some deep and nourishing recognition. That part of me shaped by the mountains, by Appalachian culture, that part of me I was not even at that point aware of, felt itself mirrored. I harassed my English teacher till she tracked down and lent me a copy of Dressler's poem, which I, without access to easy photocopying, wrote out in longhand. I had to have my own copy to study and reread.

Country Boy at College, 1977–1981

It was my second semester at West Virginia University. I hated dorm life—all those immature boys I had to pass for straight around—so I hung out at my lesbian friend Carolyn's a lot, in her tiny apartment in Sunnyside, Morgantown's student ghetto. That semester her roommate Allen was taking an Appalachian literature course. Allen and I were both gay, and we both were from southern West Virginia, so I felt a certain kinship with him. Why he would want to take such a course confused me, however. Maybe because his daddy was a coal miner. I picked up the class textbook, *Voices from the Hills* (Higgs and Manning [1975] 1996), and browsed through it. Other than Jesse Stuart, I recognized none of the names in the table of contents. Well, I knew I was fairly well read. These writers were not known to me; therefore, they must not have been important. How's that for a faulty syllogism? I wanted to take courses in modern poetry and Shakespeare, read writers like W. B. Yeats and John Keats. I had no time for Appalachian literature.

My senior year, and I was almost done with degrees in English and Nature Interpretation. I had a friend from South Charleston, Robin, who matched me in several Southern traits, including the way we said "I," which had branded us as Southerners in the linguistics course we were taking together. She was reading *Years That Answer* by Maggie Anderson (1980). "Maggie's from West Virginia, and she went to school here at WVU," Robin explained. By this point, deeply gripped by Sylvia Plath's work, I had started fooling with the idea of writing poetry seriously, so it was a relief to know that someone from West Virginia could make it as a poet. I browsed through *Years That Answer* and started getting that click-click-click of recognition I had with Muriel Miller Dressler's work. Gardening, lots of gardening and vegetable poems. Green beans, cucumbers, melons. The arts and crafts fair at Ripley, West Virginia. Queen Anne's lace. Yep, yep. All the great themes of classic literature I'd been gobbling up for years, but also details specific and relevant to West Virginia. And to think that Maggie Anderson studied under a professor of mine, Winston Fuller, from whom I was taking a great class, Contemporary American Poetry. The gap between the ambitious nobody I was and published poets like Maggie narrowed just a tiny bit.

"Country Roads, Take Me Home," 1982–1989

My first semester in the English graduate program at WVU, fall 1982, I sat in on a poetry workshop taught by Winston Fuller and finally met Maggie Anderson. She read from her work and signed my copy of her book. If she represented Appalachian literature, well, that field was starting to look more valid, more appealing to me, despite my mainstream literary ambitions and interests. Maggie's poems expanded my ideas of what art could be made from, where inspiration could be found. When I read Maggie, my country roots seemed like something to be proud of rather than to be ashamed of, though, as a gay man, I couldn't imagine a successful love life anywhere except an urban area.

In fall 1985, I landed a part-time position teaching freshman comp at George Washington University in Washington, DC. Finally I'd gotten away from the mountains and all those homophobic rednecks. But the city was one obnoxious annoyance after another. Rude people who did not display the Southern manners I was accustomed to. Noise. Traffic. Everything took too long or moved too fast or cost too much. Hearing John Denver's "Take Me Home, Country Roads," on the radio made me teary-eyed. The gay community did not welcome me with open arms, unbuttoned shirts, or unzipped pants; I was too plain, poor, somber, and shy to be an erotic hit. It took a virulent case of homesickness to make me realize that I was a country boy and an Appalachian, despite my sexual orientation and literary enthusiasms. I read my first Appalachian novel, Thomas Wolfe's *Look Homeward, Angel* (1929), and I took the title's advice. I was back in the mountains by Christmas, and in the mountains I planned to stay. Cities, I had decided, were fit only for visiting, not living in.

There was a horrible year of teaching part-time at both Waynesburg State College in southern Pennsylvania and Fairmont College in northern West Virginia. I was a "gypsy instructor" with no money, car troubles, and too many frigging comp papers to grade. Then I ended up back at WVU teaching more comp and the deadly dull Business English. Folks around the department were talking about Breece D'J Pancake a lot. I picked up a copy of his stories and saw how well fiction could be spun from the mountain-familiar. Hell, I even recognized that very curve in the road on Gauley Mountain that Pancake mentions in "Time and Again" (1983, 83–88). Another recognition-click: exciting to see the world you knew reflected in good fiction.

Soon after, Winston Fuller, then a colleague, invited me to join a literary supper club that included Maggie Anderson, Winston, and their spouses. What an honor to socialize with someone whose writings I so admired! That first evening, gathering at the Middle Eastern restaurant Ali Baba's, I met another West Virginia poet, Irene McKinney, and soon thereafter was buying and reading her books. Being gay had seriously problematized my Appalachian identity—so much of gay life was urban, so much of Appalachia was colored by homophobic brands of Christianity—but reading Maggie, Irene, and Breece Pancake helped considerably. Their work gave me that feast hall, that arsenal, that mirror.

Those at Risk, 1989 to the Present

In the summer of 1989, I finally left WVU to teach English at Virginia Tech in Blacksburg, Virginia: better money, and closer to my hometown and family. It didn't take me long to meet Alice Kinder, another instructor in the VT English Department. Those with similar accents gravitate together fast. She was in-your-face proud of her mountain background and even referred to herself as a hillbilly. Pretty soon she had convinced me that personal experience was more important than any knowledge of scholarship, that I didn't need to have had a course in Appalachian Studies to talk about mountain life. "You haven't studied it, but you've lived it," she urged. *Well, yes,* I realized—thinking about my father's gardens, my grandmother's mountain cooking, my aunt's tales and sayings, johnny house, and coal bucket—well, yes, I had lived it. Alice and I started giving presentations on Appalachian culture at Elderhostels in the region: Mountain Lake Resort and Smith Mountain Lake 4-H Camp. I read articles in the Foxfire book series to supplement or refresh my experiential knowledge, looked up old ballads, learned about the oral tradition, mountain tools, and foodways. When, thanks to Alice's recommendation, I was assigned to teach Humanities 1704/Introduction to Appalachian Studies—a welcome escape from teaching detested freshman comp—I dove wholeheartedly into books about the mine wars, novels by Denise Giardina and Lee Smith, poetry by Robert Morgan and James Still. As Giardina's character Carrie Bishop says in *Storming Heaven*, "There is enough to study in these hills to last a lifetime" (1987, 89). I regretted only that my studies in this regard started so late, as, almost twenty years after first flipping with disinterest through Allen's Appalachian lit textbook *Voices from the Hills* (Higgs and Manning [1975] 1996), I taught Appalachian Studies using that very same textbook.

So, full circle, the past student has become the present teacher (though the teacher, like anyone with an active mind, intends to keep learning all the way to the grave's muddy brink). This particular teacher is most interested in teaching students at risk. As a gay man and as an Appalachian, I have often felt dismissed, threatened, mocked, or ignored. To return to the metaphors with which I began, I have felt starved, which is to say without sustenance; vulnerable, which is to say without armor; and invisible, which is to say a monster or cipher without any accurate or discernible reflection in the mirror. Students who share these unpleasant experiences, those who are members of embattled minorities, most concern me, whether they are lesbian/gay/bisexual/transgendered, Appalachian, or members of ethnic minorities. I have found myself in a marginalized position of some sort just about my entire life, and it's the students in that same difficult position who engage my heart. They feel, to a greater or lesser extent, like members of my clan, and we mountaineers are known for our passionate loyalty to our clans, however they might be defined.

Teaching Appalachian Literature and Gay and Lesbian Literature for the English department and Appalachian Studies for humanities has been my way of trying to reach such students. A goodly number of the pupils in the Appalachian classes are mountain-raised, and about half of the students in gay/lesbian lit classes I've taught have been LGBT kids. When I teach them about Denise Giardina or Maggie Anderson or Sappho or Cavafy, I'm giving them some of what they need to fight, stay strong, and live their lives in defiant independence.

LGBT kids just about everywhere feel pretty much at risk and besieged, and this fact shouldn't surprise anyone. Appalachians, however, are not always recognized as a minority group, much less one that is oppressed and harassed. My years of teaching at Virginia Tech, however, have more than convinced me that queers and hillbillies are two of the few groups left about whom one may make jokes with relative impunity. Since this anthology focuses on Appalachia, I'll stick at this point to how important it is for teachers to spread the word that Appalachia, rather than being a backward and benighted place, is possessed of a valuable, unique, and rich culture all its own.

Virginia Tech has a widely varied student population. A majority of the students are from what residents of that region call NOVA; that is, Northern Virginia, which is to say the upper-middle-class suburbs of Washington, DC. These students know little about rural life, and many of them are not pleased to be stuck in a "cow town" in Southwest Virginia for several years. In dramatic contrast, other VT students are locals: students from the mountainous areas of Virginia, and, to a much lesser extent (due to high out-of-state tuition), West Virginia. These two groups of students, the NOVA crew and the locals, are discernibly different, in accent and dress. Each recognizes the Other. Hostilities sometimes ensue.

In all of my classes, not just the Appalachian-themed ones, I make it clear to students that I am a mountain man. (I also make it clear that I'm gay, but that's another "kettle o' feesh," as my aunt used to say.) What this often means is that Appalachian students warm up to me fast, even if some of them are initially hesitant because I'm so casually open about my unconventional sexual orientation. They feel safe with me, and so they tell me stories they aren't likely to share with other professors.

Where Are You From?!

"*I was in another class the other day, and not only did my professor make fun of the way I talk, but another student asked me if he could record me on his tape recorder. He said I sounded 'cute.'*"

"*Me and some Giles County buddies were invited to a frat party a few weeks back. Great, we thought. Girls to flirt with, and free beer too! We were there only about half an hour when the frat guy who'd invited us came up to us, sort of embarrassed, and said, 'Sorry, boys, but you're gonna have to leave.' 'Why?' I ask, pissed off. 'Because my frat brothers think you talk funny.' I threw my beer bottle against the wall and we left. I've had a grudge against Virginia Tech ever since.*"

"*My daughter Nicole was on the Blacksburg town bus the other evening. She and some other girl were the last ones who hadn't gotten off. So Nicole is talking to the driver—they graduated from the same high school—and the other girl looks at them and listens for a while and then rolls her eyes and says, like she can't believe what hicks*" *they are, 'Where are you from?!' And Nicole, God bless her, doesn't miss a beat. She just turns right around and says, 'I'm from here. Where are you from?!'"*

I've gotten a few tastes of this kind of casual and thoughtless mockery myself (though my age, my carriage, and my bulk have probably spared me from a lot more, and for that, I'm grateful, since I'm easily offended and have a terrible temper). Once, in the late 1990s, some gay friends of mine and I entered a Mexican restaurant in Rehoboth Beach, Delaware. When the young maître d' saw my West Virginia T-shirt, he made some remarks about brothers copulating with their sisters. Taken completely aback by such bad manners, disbelieving, by the time I convinced myself that he had actually said what he'd said, the opportunity to tell him something along the lines of "You are cordially invited to go fuck yourself" had passed.

Others' scorn is something I can shrug off fairly easily. I'm in my early fifties, have occasionally encountered homophobia, have heard many jokes about West Virginians and hillbillies, and have had many years to develop in response a strong sense of self, pride in my regional origins and my sexuality, and a rebellious determination to live my life as unconventionally as I please. I roll my eyes at such ignorance, mutter to myself, "Consider the source," or, when in less-forgiving moods, exude a bristling hostility that says, "You'd better just shut up and pass by. Do what's best for both of us and just pass by." But like most young people, college kids are not yet so strong. Appalachian students at Virginia Tech are like most self-conscious youths: they want to belong, they want to be liked, they want to avoid being the brunt of jokes. So many do what Cinderella's sisters did in the Grimm brothers' version of the tale. They cut off parts of themselves in order to fit. They try to assimilate. They change their dress or try to modify their accents. And they take courses in Appalachian literature and Appalachian Studies, hoping that, in those classrooms at least, they can be themselves, feel legitimate, and see mountain life reflected accurately.

"A Lot More Trouble to Roll Out Steel . . ."

The strength to say who you are, to grow as you will, respectfully but determinedly to refuse the pressures to assimilate and to conform—how does a teacher help a student find that strength? Here, in what space this essay has left, are a few rich and complex meals, sharp swords, sturdy shields, and glittering looking glasses I use to help Appalachian students develop pride and self-esteem and to teach non-Appalachian students how worthy of respect this region is:

1. "Appalachian Values" by Loyal Jones ([1975] 1996), a short essay included in *Voices from the Hills*, is a fine place to start. So many students, both flatlanders and hill kids, have heard a good deal from mass media about how flawed and backward Appalachian culture is, so Jones's essay is a healthy corrective. Furthermore, inviting mountain-bred students to talk about the ways in which they see such values as attachment to land and to family, self-reliance, and hospitality in their own backgrounds starts up lively discussion fast. I encourage honest response by first telling a few anecdotes that illustrate the ways in which I see in myself those values Jones lists: I'm a stoic fatalist, I don't like to be beholden, I like to do for myself, I remain in this region in order to remain close to my family. Mountain kids inevitably feel that thrill of recognition and always leave that day's class meeting feeling pretty good about being from the hills.

2. Every day, I point out to my classes, all of us must create some compromise between the persons we want to be and the persons the world wants us to be. What better work to discuss this conflict, the need to be ourselves versus the ache to belong, than Harriette Arnow's ([1954] 2009) *The Dollmaker?* Students resist reading the novel in its very long entirety, but "Adjusting," Arnow's ([1975] 1996) excerpt included in *Voices from the Hills*, is an effective way to start a class discussion of assimilation and the social pressure to conform.

The novel's protagonist, Gertie Nevels, at a school open house, encounters her son Reuben's teacher, Mrs. Whittle, who is clearly, to use one student's succinct summary, a "bitter old bitch," and who serves as the clear embodiment of that societal voice that demands that we abandon our individuality and "adjust." Mrs. Whittle mocks Gertie's dialect, complains about Reuben's sullen attitude, and explains condescendingly, "That is the most important thing, to learn to live with others, to get along, to adapt one's self to one's surroundings."

"'The trouble is,'" Mrs. Whittle goes on to accuse, "'you don't want to adjust—and Reuben doesn't either.'" Gertie's is one of the great individualist responses in literature: "'That's part way right. . . . But he cain't hep th way he's made. It's a lot more trouble to roll out steel—an make it like you want it—than it is biscuit dough'" (Arnow [1975] 1996, 274). It's at this point that, if reading the excerpt out loud, I try politely to suppress my natural response, a rapturously shouted, vigorous "*Hell,* yes!"

3. Harriette Arnow and James Still are often mentioned together as two monumental mid-twentieth-century Appalachian writers, so it's easy to segue from *The Dollmaker* ([1954] 2009) to *River of Earth* ([1940] 1978). Most NOVA students are from middle-class and upper-middle-class backgrounds and have very little sense of what poverty is like, so it's a revelation for them to read a novel in which the characters are so poor that the next meal is often of uncertain origin. Students who have known poverty, on the other hand, are going to admire and relate to the strength with which the Baldridge family stubbornly endures.

4. I often use James Still's poem "Heritage" to depict the ways in which natives of the Appalachian region have such a passionate attachment to place (another of the values that Jones mentions). "I will never leave these prisoning hills," swears the speaker (and note the concise way Still suggests ambivalence even in this paean of praise) (Still 1986, 82). This poem always gets me a little wet-eyed when I read it out loud, so I often use a bit of comic relief afterward by telling my students a joke, "Hillbillies in Heaven," from Loyal Jones and Billy Edd Wheeler's *Laughter in Appalachia*, the basic gist of which is that hillbillies in heaven need to be kept chained up, or else "they'd go home every weekend" (1987, 30).

5. The coalfield novels of Denise Giardina are not only amazingly written, powerful, and unforgettable, but they can serve as a series of wonderful illustrations of those values that Loyal Jones mentions, from the self-reliance displayed by many of the characters in *Storming Heaven* (1987) to the stubborn attachment to place, the characters' refusal to leave the dying coalfields, in *The Unquiet Earth* (1992). Most useful of all, however, is how Giardina, gracefully and without heavy-handed didacticism, portrays the ways in which Appalachians learn contempt for themselves through the false and exaggerated images of mass media and the ways in which poverty in Central Appalachia is caused by greedy outside interests, absentee landowners, and the rapaciousness of the coal industry—the Colonialism Exploitation Model, as some Appalachian Studies scholars call it. Students are full of stories about television shows and films that depict mountain folks as morons, and those from the coalfields can certainly relate to tales of unemployment and out-migration. There are, predictably, some heated debates between students from mining backgrounds and students who are passionate environmentalists. I do my best to remain neutral, so as not to alienate the former group, but I'm guessing that my environmental sympathies show through.

6. Appalachian folk culture is what I most relish about my region: the dialect, proverbs, stories, legends, superstitions, and foodways. Jan Harold

Brunvand's *The Study of American Folklore* is a wonderful way to put Appalachian folk culture in a larger context. Brunvand's descriptions of oral, customary, and material culture are exceptionally clear, and they encourage students from other areas of America or other countries to share their own region's customs, place-names, foods, and ghost stories. In such a context— almost anthropological—it's easy to convince students to take pride in the uniqueness of their native cultures and to look at difference and diversity as enriching, exciting, and delightful, not threatening. I even pull out a few details of gay folklore just to remind them of how every subculture, whether occupational, regional, or sexual, has its own myths, jargon, and oral tradition. Teaching Lee Smith's novels *Fair and Tender Ladies* (1988) and *Oral History* (1983) is an effective way of examining the specifics of Appalachian folk culture while also introducing the students to moving and poignant story lines. (I must add that Ivy Rowe, the protagonist of *Fair and Tender Ladies*, is a fine role model for anyone resisting convention and societal expectations.)

7. As a writer, I often feel ghettoized as either a gay or an Appalachian author. Many mainstream readers and publishers assume that writers like me who depict the experiences of sexual or cultural minorities have nothing of value to say to them, so we are dismissed to the Regional Writers or Gay/Lesbian sections of the bookstore (if we're lucky enough to be published at all), and our work is discussed only in Appalachian Literature or Gay/Lesbian Literature courses (again, if we're lucky). I resist this pigeonholing by bringing the work of Appalachian writers, as well as LGBT writers, to my creative writing classes. Neither group of writers is represented to any extent in creative-writing textbooks, so I simply ransack my personal library and begin many classes by reading poems or brief prose passages by any of the fine authors mentioned above. Mountain writers deserve wider recognition, I passionately believe, and if I can't do anything about my own publications' ghettoization, I can certainly take advantage of my position as a professor to spread the word about my fellow Appalachian writers. For instance, I tell my pupils that Maggie Anderson's "Long Story" is a gripping illustration of narrative poetry (1992, 21–23); and Irene McKinney's "At 24" is delicious in its sharp tone and insistence on personal freedom from gender-role expectations (2004, 91).

Other professors, those enamored of mainstream writers without minority identity or status, are welcome to sing their praises and encourage students to emulate them. I prefer the privilege of supporting members of my own clan, whether they be Appalachian or LGBT, writers or students. What I admire most are lives and words like Arnow's steel: courageous, complex, marginalized, and at risk; refusing to be passively shaped like malleable biscuit dough; troublesome, rough-edged souls who are defiantly themselves.

References

Anderson, Maggie. 1980. *Years That Answer*. New York: Harper and Row.

———. 1992. *A Space Filled with Moving*. Pittsburgh: University of Pittsburgh Press.

Arnow, Harriette. (1954) 2009. *The Dollmaker*. Reprint, New York: Simon and Schuster.

———. (1975) 1996. "Adjusting." In Higgs and Manning 1996, 263–74.

Brunvand, Jan Harold. 1968. *The Study of American Folklore*. New York: Norton.

Dressler, Muriel Miller. 2000. "Appalachia." In *Wild Sweet Notes: Fifty Years of West Virginia Poetry, 1950–1999*, edited by Barbara Smith and Kirk Judd, 105–6. Huntington, WV: Publishers Place.

Giardina, Denise. 1987. *Storming Heaven*. New York: Ivy Books.

———. 1992. *The Unquiet Earth*. New York: Norton.

Higgs, Robert J., and Ambrose N. Manning, eds. (1975) 1996. *Voices from the Hills: Selected Readings of Southern Appalachia*. 3rd. ed. Dubuque, IA: Kendall Hunt.

Jones, Loyal. (1975) 1996. "Appalachian Values." In Higgs and Manning (1975) 1996, 507–17.

Jones, Loyal, and Billy Edd Wheeler. 1987. *Laughter in Appalachia: A Festival of Southern Mountain Humor*. Little Rock, AR: August House.

McKinney, Irene. 2004. *Vivid Companion*. Morgantown, West Virginia: West Virginia University Press.

Pancake, Breece, D'J. 1983. *The Stories of Breece D'J Pancake*. New York: Holt, Rinehart and Winston.

Rich, Adrienne. 1986. *Blood, Bread, and Poetry: Selected Prose, 1979–1985*. New York: Norton.

Smith, Lee. 1983. *Oral History*. New York: Penguin.

———. 1988. *Fair and Tender Ladies*. New York: Ballantine.

Still, James. (1940) 1978. *River of Earth*. Lexington: University Press of Kentucky.

———. 1986. *The Wolfpen Poems*. Berea, KY: Berea College Press.

Wolfe, Thomas. 1929. *Look Homeward, Angel*. New York: Scribner's.

SIX

I Hear Appalachia Singing:
Teaching Appalachian Literature in a General
Education American Literature Course

LINDA TATE

> It's a funny thing: Though I have spent most of my
> working life in universities, though I live in Chapel Hill
> and eat pasta and drive a Toyota, the stories that present
> themselves to me as worth the telling are most often those
> somehow connected to that place and those people. The
> mountains that used to imprison me have become my
> chosen stalking ground.
>
> —Lee Smith

> I don't mean I went home literally—I'd been going back
> for holidays and summer visits all along—I mean I went
> home inside; I began to pay attention to all those voices,
> to the language and people I grew up with. In doing so, I
> abandoned the larger culture's belief that such voices had
> no place in art, had, in fact, nothing to say.
>
> —George Ella Lyon

LEE SMITH OFTEN TELLS THE STORY of the day she left
her home in the mountain community of Grundy, Virginia, to attend Hollins
College. While she was waiting for her father to return from his Ben Franklin

dime store and drive her to school, she sat on the front porch while her mother and aunts talked interminably about whether her mother had colitis. Smith could not wait to leave home!

Later that year, working her way through the fiction books in the college library, Smith came across James Still's ([1940] 1978) novel *River of Earth*. She was taking classes with such luminaries as R. H. W. Dillard and Louis Rubin, and though she had dreamed since childhood of being a writer, she was earning only Cs on the short stories she submitted, stories, as she says, "about stewardesses living in Hawaii, about evil twins, executives, alternative universes" (Smith 1998b, 279).

But then Smith came across Still's novel. "At the end of the novel," she recalls, "I was astonished to read that the family was heading for—of all places!—Grundy!...I read [the] passage over and over. I simply could not believe that Grundy was in a novel!... *River of Earth* was as real to me as the chair I sat on, as the hollers I'd grown up among" (1998b, 279–80). Through reading *River of Earth*, Smith realized that her real material was her upbringing in the quickly disappearing traditional world of the Appalachian Mountains. At the end of her first year of college, she finally earned an A when she wrote a story about women sitting on a porch talking about colitis.

"It was real important to me," says Smith, reflecting on that crucial moment in her development as a writer. "I understood then that that was the best story I had been able to write that year, and I understood that that was my material, that was real and that was true, whereas this other stuff was all made up" ("Lee Smith" 1996).

Since the day she discovered her hometown in a novel, Lee Smith has worked hard to preserve traditional Appalachian culture and stories. She's done so in the fiction she's written. She's done so in her teaching, nurturing the voices of other mountain writers and storytellers. And she's done so in the example she's set for how to inspire and pass on this love of home, community, place. Though she's gone on to make her adult life in the Chapel Hill area of North Carolina, Smith's success as a writer has come through her imaginative return home. Smith's life is a parable that tells students it is possible to live in the modern world *and* maintain a connection to the past, to the traditional, to home.

Lee Smith's 1960s experience at the private Hollins College is in many ways a far cry from the lives of the twenty-first-century students at my state university. And yet, despite obvious economic differences and obvious generational differences, I believe that Smith's time at Hollins shares fundamental similarities with my students' enrollment at a public university, Shepherd University, in the new millennium. My students find themselves, as Smith and her classmates did in the 1960s, in a time of real flux, poised at the intersection of the past and the present.

Moreover, my students are pursuing their educations at the geographic edge of the region, Shepherdstown, West Virginia, not in the mountains but near enough to them to draw many students from the region. Many, if not most, of the students from the mountains see their move to this border region as a positive step away from their Appalachian roots and look forward to the educational opportunities they'll have closer to urban centers outside the mountains. At the same time, while my students—many of them first-generation college students—deservedly look forward to greater economic advantages than their parents and grandparents enjoyed, they and their home communities would benefit from their ability to maintain rich connections to family and place. Many of them, however, do not perceive the value of remaining connected to the past or to the place that has been home, and the faculty who teach them face the key challenge of showing these students that being Appalachian is not a limitation, as many outside the region would have them believe, but a real source of groundedness in a rapidly changing world.

In a very real way, my students—much like Lee Smith and her classmates—are poised with one foot in an older, traditional world and one foot stepping into a new, postmodern, fast-paced world. But while Smith pursued her education at a time and in a place where a creative, liberal arts education was valued, my students are overwhelmingly pursuing professional degrees. As they make their way through the state university, checking off required courses in a number of disciplines, their real focus is on earning their degrees in education, nursing, and business. Though the state university prides itself on having a general education program with a strong liberal arts emphasis, the reality is that the vast majority of these students are much more focused on getting the professional credentials they need to move into the contemporary world. How, then, to reach these students, determined as they are to move beyond what they see as a confining background to the professional world of the American middle class? Is it possible to give them the tools they'll need to succeed in that world to which they aspire *and* give them an appreciation for and a connection to home?

This is the environment in which I teach Survey of American Literature, a required general education course, the classic "dread" course that students approach either apathetically or, in many cases, with outright disdain. Many students across the United States view such courses (particularly those not in their major fields of study) negatively, and it is a challenge for many instructors to generate student enthusiasm for these courses. This is very much the case at the university where I teach: many of the students don't have a family experience of college attendance (and thus don't have personal knowledge of the value of a well-rounded liberal arts education) and instead are quite focused on getting the professional training they need as quickly as possible. It is hard indeed for them to understand what literature has to do with anything they wish to pursue in life. As faculty, how can we convey to them that something so seemingly inconsequential as storytelling can have relevance to them as they hurry to earn professional degrees and make their way in the work world? How can we engage these students who are eager to get their curricular tickets punched and move on to their "real" courses? How, in short, can we convince them that the stories of the past can be valuable to them as they launch themselves into a new world?

In shaping my Survey of American Literature course, I am guided by bell hooks's *Teaching to Transgress: Education as the Practice of Freedom*, in which hooks emphasizes the need for "excitement" in higher education. She writes:

> *Excitement* in higher education was viewed as potentially disruptive of the atmosphere of seriousness assumed to be essential to the learning process. To enter classroom settings in colleges and universities with the will to share the desire to encourage excitement, was to transgress.... This excitement could co-exist with and even stimulate serious intellectual and/or academic engagement. (1994, 7)

And excitement, hooks asserts, involves seeing students "in their particularity as individuals" (1994, 7): "As a classroom community, our capacity to generate excitement is deeply affected by our interest in one another, in hearing one another's voices, in recognizing one another's presence" (8). It is this level of excitement and engagement—this emphasis on students as individuals—that I wish to bring forth in my classroom.

Though the course I've developed meets the fundamental requirements of a conventional American Literature survey (as designated by the shared reading list in my Department of English), it departs from the canonical "high literature" approach common to survey courses of the last half century and instead returns to the ancient underpinnings of literature: storytelling. Using as a course framework Walt Whitman's proclamation that "the United States themselves are the world's greatest poem" and that the "genius of the United States" lies in the common people themselves, I begin and end the course with celebrations of stories and poems told and sung by everyday Americans.

I open the course with a brief excerpt from Whitman's (1855) "Preface to *Leaves of Grass*" (McQuade et al. 1999, 1152–65), and with his celebratory poem "I Hear America Singing." I follow the Whitman passages with an English-language transcription of the traditional Seneca tale, "The Story-Telling Stone." The students and I talk about the ancient human urge to tell stories about our lives and the Senecas' understanding that tales are so fundamental to human existence that they emerge from stones, from the earth itself. We then spend the semester exploring a range of American voices, reading the work of those who have traditionally been designated as "major" American writers (e.g., Benjamin Franklin, Ralph Waldo Emerson, Henry David Thoreau, Nathaniel Hawthorne, Herman Melville, Emily Dickinson, Mark Twain, Ernest Hemingway, Arthur Miller, and others); *and* hearing the voices of others who have also told key parts of the American tale (e.g., Anne Bradstreet, Frederick Douglass, Harriet Jacobs, Zitkala-Sa, Charlotte Perkins Gilman, Kate Chopin, Langston Hughes, Tomás Rivera, N. Scott Momaday, Alice Walker, Maxine Hong Kingston, and others). The course comes to a close with a wide-ranging celebration of diverse American voices. We return to Whitman's celebration of the United States as the world's greatest poem and listen as Langston Hughes ("I, Too, Sing America") and Julia Alvarez ("I, Too, Sing América") add their verses to Whitman's "I Hear America Singing."

But ultimately we turn to stories and songs much closer to home: the stories and songs of Appalachia. Closing the course with the Appalachian Renaissance gives me the opportunity to help these students see the relevance of literary and cultural study for their own lives—and even if the activities of this last week don't convince students that they want to continue reading on their own, they are nevertheless left with the understanding that their own cultural background is worth preserving and paying attention to, something worth valuing as they move into the new world of the twenty-first century. It is powerful to watch students sit up in their chairs a little straighter, pay keener attention, linger after class to look at the extra books I've brought in, ask about the old-time music that is playing before and after class, and visit with me to tell stories about their grandparents.

The students are not totally unprepared for this discussion. The previous unit ends with the literature of the Great Depression, with an excerpt from John Steinbeck's *The Grapes of Wrath* (1939) and an excerpt from James

Still's *River of Earth* ([1940] 1978). In that unit, we discuss the fact that working people—even working people from the Appalachian region—can be the subject matter of great literature. But now we turn to literature that is even closer to home and even more recent in its publication—and as I talk about the Appalachian Renaissance and Appalachian culture, I make clear repeatedly that traditional music and storytelling and family bonds are not relics of the past but are shared folkways that still live and breathe in many mountain communities. I choose my examples deliberately so that at some point during the week most of the students will recognize their own families, communities, and personal experiences.

I open the week's lessons with a brief discussion of the many stereotypes and pejorative labels that have been applied to people from the mountains, from those that emerged when mountain people were "discovered" at the end of the nineteenth century to current media portrayals of people from the region. At first, many of the students laugh knowingly as I recount the negative images of the region. Then I remind them that the majority of them come from areas that the federal government—via the Appalachian Regional Commission—deems as being part of "Appalachia." This is a shock to the many students who did not grow up in coal-mining communities or in mountain hollers. Those who grew up east of the Blue Ridge Mountains, on the flat Piedmont that signals the beginning of the descent to the Atlantic Ocean, are stunned to learn that, as far as the United States government is concerned, they are, in fact, Appalachian. These stereotypes, these pejorative labels, are being used to describe *them*. Many of these students, like other students throughout and on the edges of the region, have handled these cultural slights by distancing themselves from the region, by joining—either overtly or subtly—in the jokes and prejudices of those who are not from the mountains. At first, the students might talk about *Deliverance* or *The Beverly Hillbillies*, but as I begin to stress that they are among the people being described, they begin to grow uncomfortable, knowing that these portrayals don't mirror their own lives.

After setting this context, we begin to talk about the efforts of writers, artists, musicians, scholars, and others to correct this inaccurate view of the region's people. We talk about the folk music revival and cultural preservation efforts such as the Foxfire series. We talk about Appalachian Studies programs at universities and the many, many writers emerging from the region. And we talk about all of the cultural celebration going on at this particular university—the course in Appalachian culture, the music and literature festival, the writer-in-residence program.

Our focus then turns to the writer who has served as the region's key literary figure for the last thirty years: Lee Smith. In preparation for class discussion, the students have read an early chapter in Smith's novel *The Devil's Dream* (1992). They've read the narrative of "Old Man Ira Keen" and learned the story of Kate Malone, a tale he tells in the song "The Preacher's Son," and in his subsequent narrative about the song. This will be the focus of our literary discussion—but Smith's entire life story will serve as the real text for the week's discussion. For it is her journey from small-town Southwest Virginia to Hollins College, from discovering the work of James Still to finding her own voice, from using her own writing to preserve the stories of Appalachia to nurturing the work of other storytellers, writers, and songwriters from the region that becomes the final focus of this course. Smith's work, and indeed her entire life, is a perfect choice for this last week: the fiction itself is superb; the central message of the selection underscores the idea that the need for creative expression is a deep human urge common to all cultures; and the story of Smith's life—from her girlhood in an ordinary Virginia town to her nurturing of other voices—makes clear that *any* of the students in this class also could choose to express themselves creatively.

I open the discussion of Smith's work with a six-minute clip from the "Lee Smith" episode of the *Signature: Contemporary Writers* video series. The clip serves multiple purposes: it introduces Lee Smith to the students and provides enough biographical information about her so that students can get their bearings; it establishes the core theme of leaving home and returning again, physically or imaginatively; and it introduces the literary text we'll be discussing, *The Devil's Dream* (1992). In this segment, which begins at 22:39 and ends at 28:35, University of North Carolina Southern Studies scholar Fred Hobson and Smith herself discuss this fundamental moment in a human being's development. Inevitably, a number of students in the class recognize themselves in these descriptions of the young person leaving home.

The clip opens with Hobson's description of Smith and the steps she needed to take to embrace her Appalachian heritage: "I think to really appreciate the culture, to really let herself be re-immersed into the culture, to approach it without a certain critical slant, she had to get away, she had to gain an affection through distance" ("Lee Smith" 1996). From there, the video moves to Smith's oft-repeated telling of the day she left for college and her subsequent discovery that the seemingly mundane details of life in Grundy—colitis conversations and all—could be the stuff of serious literature.

The second portion of this clip focuses on *The Devil's Dream* (1992). Here, the video features excerpts from Katie Cocker's opening narrative, the narrative that immediately precedes the selection the students have read. By using this portion of the video, I am able to give students more exposure to the novel while also keeping the length of their reading assignment manageable (always a key consideration in a general education course)—and at the same time, I am able to underscore the idea that it is a fundamental part of human development to leave home and then find a way to integrate an understanding of home into the adult psyche. As Katie says, given voice in the video by a stage production actress and by Smith herself in a reading from the novel, "I have to admit, there was a time when all I wanted to do was get out of that valley. I was just dying to get away from home. . . . It took me a long time to understand that not a one of us lives alone, outside of our family or our time, and that who we are depends on who we *were*, and who our people were" (Smith 1992, 14). This passage reinforces one of the central ideas I want students to take away from this lesson: while it is natural to want to leave home, there is also value in preserving a link to the past.

This first video clip concludes with footage of Smith driving in Grundy, pointing out the many national fast-food chains that have come even to this small town in Appalachia. As she drives through Grundy, she talks about her recognition that the cultural uniqueness of the region is in danger of disappearing and her subsequent idea for her landmark novel, *Oral History* (1983). When Wendy's and Long John Silver's came to town, she says, she realized "that I had to start writing about this area and that I had to write down all these stories that my dad had told me and my uncle Vern and Ava and my aunt Kate and everybody else because I could see sort of the beginning of the end in a way. When those fast-food chains came in, somehow that made me realize that modern life was gonna come even here" ("Lee Smith" 1996). Smith then describes her decision to write *Oral History*: she structured the novel, with its story of one mountain family over the course of one century, so that she could show the changes in the land, the people, the language, the economy. "Unless we set it down, we really work to preserve it," Smith says, "we're in danger as a culture of losing that which makes us most unique" ("Lee Smith" 1996).

After this six-minute video clip, I begin to talk with the students about the narrative strategy that Smith employs in many of her novels: the focus on one mountain family over a long period of time. As she tells the story of the Bailey family, she simultaneously tells the story of mountain music—from its roots as "old-time" music to its discovery by recording executives at the Bristol Recording sessions, from the creation of bluegrass and finally to rockabilly and Dolly Parton–esque pop country music. In short, the novel traces the evolution of country music from "primitive," backwoods culture to Nashville commercialization.

We then move into a discussion of the excerpt the students have read: "Old Man Ira Keen," the novel's first full chapter. I provide a bit of context for the chapter: I tell students that the novel opens with a brief segment about Katie Cocker and her decision to record a family album at Opryland. The novel then proceeds to tell the story behind each of the songs on the album and, in doing so, tells the story of the musical Bailey family and the parallel story of country music. The first "song" on the album is "The Preacher's Son," a ballad written by Ira Keen, now an old man. I explain that Old Man Ira Keen is speaking to a "songcatcher," a Cecil Sharp figure who has come to the mountains to collect old ballads and tunes. In his narrative, Ira Keen describes his creative process and then goes on to tell the real events behind the short ballad. This seventeen-page chapter serves a fourfold purpose: (1) it opens the story of the Bailey family (the central narrative line for the novel); (2) it establishes the historic cultural roots of mountain music (with its emphasis on music-making in the home, including ballad-singing and fiddle-playing); (3) it describes the creative process of mountain artists such as Ira Keen; and (4) it underscores the deep human need for expression and the physical and psychological devastation that can occur when this fundamental urge is denied, as is the case when Kate Malone is forbidden by her husband to play the fiddle—what he calls "the voice of the Devil Laughing" (Smith 1992, 23).

Students love Ira's storytelling, and the Recorded Books unabridged audio recording of the book does an especially good job of bringing his storytelling to life. The opening segment of the chapter (which lasts about a minute in the audio recording) beautifully expresses the creative process. Ira says,

> A song don't just spring outer nowhere, ye know, hit'll grow in yer mind like a honeysuckle vine just a-wrappin itself around all the times and all the people and places that is yer life.... A song will grow up in my mind unawares, and one day I'll just pick up this here dulcimore and hit'll be there whole and good, and springin to the tongue.
>
> ...And let me tell you one thing, there ain't nothin in the world to compare with the feeling that comes over you then, hit's like, Well, *this* is what happened, I see it all clear now, this is who done what, and who said what, and how it fell out in the end.... Hit ain't often we are given to see.
>
> Seems to me hit'll come to me in a song most likely, that is iffen hit comes atall. (Smith 1992, 17)

This passage makes clear that creative expression is available to all human beings, that giving narrative form to our experiences is a fundamental component of developing deeper understanding.

Balanced against Ira's powerful account of how he has come to write such ballads as "The Preacher's Son" (the lyrics for which are included at the beginning of the chapter) is the story of young Kate Malone. One of the musical Malone family, Kate marries the hard-shell Baptist preacher, Moses Bailey. As Ira tells the story of Kate and her children, who play the fiddle despite Moses's commandment that they not do so, he shows the strong human need for creative expression and the violence that can erupt when that need is denied. Ultimately, the music itself is destroyed, as Moses smashes the fiddle; the family is destroyed, as Moses beats Kate and the children and as the eldest son, Jeremiah, runs away and is killed; and Kate herself is permanently destroyed, as she loses her mind from this terrifying and soul-killing experience. This powerful story gives us as a class the opportunity to talk about this same thread we've seen throughout much of the material we've read in the course—the deep human desire to read, write, tell stories, and share one's human experiences. Students recall the Senecas' emphasis on storytelling as the bedrock of human existence; recall all that Frederick Douglass went through to learn to read and the power he experienced when he was finally able to write his own story; the lengths Emily Dickinson went to so that she could craft her private poetry in her Amherst bedroom; the psychological devastation Charlotte Perkins Gilman's unnamed narrator experiences in "The Yellow Wallpaper" when she is not allowed to write.

This emphasis on storytelling—in written words and in song—provides a natural segue into the second clip from the *Signature* video. I begin this clip at 32:42 and end it at 42:04. This ten-minute segment focuses on Smith's role as a teacher, as a nurturer of other creative voices in the mountains. For, ultimately, what is most significant about Smith's work is not just the beautiful fiction she writes nor even her commitment to preserving the culture of the region; what is most crucial is the role she plays in ensuring that all human beings have access to creative expression. The very opposite of Moses Bailey, who physically silenced the voices of those around him, Smith actively listens for voices that have not been heard and then works hard to facilitate their expression.

This segment on Smith-as-teacher begins with a focus on several young women who were her students at North Carolina State University, where she taught writing for nearly twenty years. From there, the video moves on to focus on Smith's work with two older women, Lou Crabtree and Florida Slone. Crabtree is the author of *Sweet Hollow* (1984), a collection of short stories; and Slone is a songwriter from Knott County, Kentucky, who had not yet learned to read and write at the time she began working with Smith at the Hindman Settlement School. "One of the things I have enjoyed doing most over the years," says Smith in the video, "is working with people, particularly people who really have stories to tell and have not yet told them. . . . One of my greatest experiences . . . has been to try to encourage people to write their stories and then to try to send them out, to try to help them get published" ("Lee Smith" 1996).

This video clip features short excerpts from an interview with Crabtree as well as a segment in which Crabtree reads from her work. Crabtree talks about the deep importance of writing her stories: "Lee taught us to write about our life and the things that we thought and the things that were, and now I am able to take some of those bad things and put them in a new light just because of the writing about it" ("Lee Smith" 1996). Smith herself reflects on the profound lessons she learned from Crabtree about the necessity of writing and creative expression, underscoring the sense that Smith is a woman of great humility, whose own work as an artist grows the more she works with and nurtures the voices of others. "Talking with [Lou Crabtree] . . . and seeing her life," Smith says, "I began to understand what the writing itself meant to me. . . . It's the writing that signifies. And Lou made me understand that. Lou made me understand a lot of things."

The final segment of this video clip focuses on Smith's work at the Hindman Settlement School in Knott County, Kentucky. Ironically, Hindman is the school where James Still spent most of his life—and it was here that Lee finally met and became close friends with the novelist who had inspired her when she was a first-year Hollins student searching for her voice and her material. Working with Still, who died in 2001, Smith has become one of the driving forces behind the Hindman Writers Workshop, an annual weeklong event that brings together established, emerging, and developing writers from throughout the Appalachian region in an egalitarian, supportive environment.

When she won the Lila Wallace-Reader's Digest Foundation Award for 1995–1997, Smith decided to use the money to work in an adult literacy program at Hindman. It was through this initiative that she met Florida Slone, a Knott County songwriter who had never learned to read and write. Smith describes Slone as a woman who has been "a remarkable artist for her entire life." Much like Old Man Ira Keen, Slone has written songs to mark significant events in her life. "Now," says Smith, "she's just learned to read and she's just learned to write as an adult." Working together, Smith and Slone wrote the songs down and put them in poetic form. Once Slone had mastered this skill, says Smith, she "stayed up all night writing down all the songs she could think of" ("Lee Smith" 1996).

The last few seconds of the video clip are perhaps the most powerful—and by this point, my often restless American Literature students are quiet and intensely focused. They are *listening* to Florida Slone tell her story. Slone says:

> Really, if it wasn't for Lee and the settlement school down here, there's a lot of songs I'd never be able to put 'em on paper 'cause when I was growing up I didn't get to go to school. I had to work and hoe corn and plant a garden and milk the cows and feed the hogs and stuff like that. . . . Well, when you don't have education, why, I thought the world wasn't too big, you know. After they learned me to read and write a lot of it, then I still didn't know how to write my songs down right, you know, I didn't know how to verse 'em out nor nothing. So Lee, she came and so we started out and she got me started on 'em. Well, I'm still writing songs and things, and Lee has been a real big help because I'd've never had 'em without her. And I wish there were more people in Knott County that were like Lee Smith because she's got a heart and she reaches out to people and she helps 'em. ("Lee Smith" 1996)

Florida Slone's voice is humble yet extremely powerful: many students hear their mothers and grandmothers in her simple, direct account, and virtually none are rustling their papers, trying to signal that it's time for class to end. As I move into the final activity of this unit (and thus the closing activity of this course), the students are right there with me, eager to hear another voice from this region they call home.

The final mountain voice I share with the students is that of George Ella Lyon reading her poem "Where I'm From." Like Smith, Lyon understands that stories, especially family stories, provide a deep foundation for self-understanding. For Lyon, voice—the way we speak—is core to this sense of self-identity. If we deny the "speech [we] were born into," she says, we will "foster the false impression that culture happens somewhere else . . . , that culture is a commodity that we buy or travel far to see rather than something that comes *from* us and speaks *to* us" ("Voiceplace" 1998, 168). This will lead us to the faulty conclusion that stories and "the people who tell and hear them" are found only in urban America, not in Appalachia or other rural areas (168).

Just as Lee Smith tells the story of discovering in college that her small hometown of Grundy could be the focus of literature, so too George Ella Lyon describes the day in her Indiana University MFA class when she realized through reading the work of Ohio poet Michael Allen that a poet could write about "Sunday dinner at his grandmother's, about growing corn, about everyday things that he knew as well as his face" (Lyon 1998, 169). In the same way, other Appalachian writers like Jeff Daniel Marion and Lee Howard gave her "courage and a new direction": "I found out there was a whole passel of people out there writing down how their grandmother talked and why she talked like that and why her farm was taken away from her. I found out there was an entire tradition of Appalachian writing. . . . I found out I had a culture" (169–70).

At this point, the students have heard the tale of Lee Smith discovering her hometown of Grundy in the pages of James Still's novel. They've heard Katie Cocker talk about the desire to get away from home and the need we all have to find out where we're from. They've listened to Ira Keen describe the deep human need for creative expression. They've been captivated by Lou Crabtree and Florida Slone, ordinary Appalachian women who tell of everyday hardships in their stories and songs. They've nodded in recognition at George Ella Lyon's description of her Sunday school upbringing and the overflowing box of old family photos.

Now, after a semester of hearing the voices of the common people who together comprise Walt Whitman's great poem that is the United States, the students are invited to add their lines to the poem, to make their voices heard as they, too, sing America. Having just listened to a one-minute online recording of Lyon reading her poem, students now sit quietly and pen their own lives, writing their own "Where I'm From" poems. A number of them—many of whom have never written a line of poetry before—craft beautiful verses, and before they move on to exams and the next steps in their professional training, they celebrate home and family. Thus, together, we bring to life bell hooks's encouragement "not merely to share information but to share in the intellectual and spiritual growth of our students" (1994, 13).

Sitting with my students on that last day of class, listening as they scratch the lines of their lives into their spiral-bound notebooks, I sense with them the promise that they'll take home, family, community, and region with them into their new worlds to come.

Note

Epigraphs: Lee Smith (1998b, 280); George Ella Lyon (1998, 170).

References

Alvarez, Julia. n.d. "I, Too, Sing América." http://iipdigital.usembassy.gov/st/english/pub
lication/2008/06/20080625200016eaifaso.5940515.html#axzz2Dea6abcx.

Crabtree, Lou. 1998. *The River Hills & Beyond.* Abingdon, VA: Sow's Ear Press.

———. 1984. *Sweet Hollow.* Baton Rouge: Louisiana State University Press.

Dyer, Joyce, ed. 1998. *Bloodroot: Reflections on Place by Appalachian Women Writers.* Lexington: University Press of Kentucky.

Gilman, Charlotte Perkins. (1892) 1999. "The Yellow Wallpaper." In McQuade et al. 1999, 1735–45.

hooks, bell. 1994. *Teaching to Transgress: Education as the Practice of Freedom.* New York: Routledge.

Hughes, Langston. (1932) 1999. "I, Too, Sing America." In McQuade et al. 1999, 2226.

"Lee Smith." 1996. *Signature: Contemporary Writers.* Vol. 5. Directed by Tom Thurman. Lexington: Kentucky Educational Television.

Lyon, George Ella. 1993. "Where I'm From." *George Ella Lyon: Writer and Teacher.* http://www.georgeellalyon.com/where.html.

———. 1998. "Voiceplace." In Dyer, *Bloodroot*, 168–74.

McQuade, Donald, Robert Atwan, Martha Banta, Justin Kaplan, David Minter, Robert Stepto, Cecelia Tichi, and Helen Vendler, eds. 1999. *The Harper Single Volume American Literature.* 3rd ed. New York: Longman.

Smith, Lee. 1983. *Oral History.* New York: Penguin.

———. 1992. *The Devil's Dream.* New York: Putnam's.

———. 1998a. *The Devil's Dream.* Unabridged audio recording. New York: Recorded Books.

———. 1998b. "Terrain of the Heart." In Dyer, *Bloodroot*, 278–81.

Steinbeck, John. (1939). *The Grapes of Wrath.* New York: Viking Press.

Still, James. (1940) 1978. *River of Earth.* Lexington: University Press of Kentucky.

"Story-Telling Stone, The." N.d. In McQuade et al. 1999, 18–20.

Tate, Linda, ed. 2001. *Conversations with Lee Smith.* Jackson: University Press of Mississippi.

Whitman, Walt. (1891-1892). "I Hear America Singing." In McQuade et al., 1999, 1166.

———. (1855) 1999. "Preface to the 1855 Edition of *Leaves of Grass.*" In McQuade et al. 1999, 1152–65.

SEVEN

"Way Back Yonder" but Not So Far Away: Teaching Appalachian Folktales

TINA L. HANLON

From Oral Tradition to the Classroom

Jack and the Wonder Beans by James Still opens by placing Jack and his poor mother "way back yonder," but they are also in "their homeseat . . . here on Wolfpen Creek" (where Still lived in Knott County, Kentucky). "Or around about" (Still [1977] 1996). As Still's introduction demonstrates, the words of storytellers, written or oral, draw us in to worlds that fascinate because they are always remote and familiar at the same time, fantastical but also realistic, timeless and yet timely as they reflect our deepest fears and wishes. Most people know ancient stories about Jack's encounters with giants and giant beanstalks, but many do not recognize, as James Still did, the value of regional and local variations of traditional tales. Still's classic novel *River of Earth* ([1940] 1996) is much more likely to be assigned in college courses than *Jack and the Wonder Beans*, yet Still said that the latter book "has a chance of greater longevity than any of my other works. All my powers and my gifts, such as they are, came together in those few pages. The news that some children are sleeping with this book and that their elders are reading it with some delight tickles me" (1979, 124).

Like Jack, Mutsmag (a poor girl who outwits a giant and a witch), and other folk heroes, teachers who introduce Appalachian folktales into college courses must be resourceful and self-reliant to overcome three potential obstacles. First, written literature is likely to be taken more seriously than tales from oral traditions. Second, unless the course focuses on folklore, Appalachian Studies, or cultural diversity, stories from the Appalachian Mountains are likely to be overlooked or considered less worthy of study than better-known, mainstream American and world literature, including literary fairy tales by famous writers such as Washington Irving or Hans Christian Andersen. And third, modern Americans tend to associate these forms of storytelling with childhood, thus considering them too trivial for adult study. Adults may enjoy listening to storytelling as light entertainment at folk festivals or on the radio, but not view it as serious subject matter for college study.

Fortunately, many late twentieth-century cultural and academic developments have worked against these biases, including the coming-of-age and growing prestige of research in folklore, popular culture, Appalachian Studies, and children's literature. Scholars now recognize that the Appalachian oral tradition is one of the richest in America. Over the past millennium oral tales have been brought to the Appalachian Mountains by Native Americans and then Europeans and Africans, and the stories of Asian and Hispanic immigrants will probably get more attention in the future. Thus folktales portray diversity within the region and link it with larger traditions of world folklore and literature.

Types of folktales encompass, or overlap with, many kinds of stories from oral traditions: legends associated with real places or people, realistic anecdotes and family stories, jokes and riddles, tall tales, animal fables, creation myths, pourquoi tales about the origins of particular phenomena, and other tales with magic or supernatural elements. Talking animals are prominent in some Native American and African American traditions, while magic helpers as well as monstrous and evil adversaries represent the conflicts that ordinary humans experience in many folktales, including those brought to Appalachia by Scots-Irish immigrants and other Europeans from the eighteenth to the twentieth centuries. These magic tales, also called fairy tales, wonder tales, or märchen, often blend Old World folktale motifs with elements of regional American culture and dialect. By the strictest definition, the term "folktale" applies only to a story being told and heard through a natural oral tradition. Yet in our literate, multimedia society, most of us encounter folktales in fixed modern forms such as writing or films. The storytelling revival that has grown since the 1960s has inspired not only the work and pastimes of many professional and amateur storytellers carrying on the oral tradition, but an explosion in the production of folktale retellings and adaptations in books, films, and drama. Traditional ballads and other types of folk narratives also influence new types of performances and books. The National Storytelling Festival occurs annually in Jonesborough, Tennessee, a historic Appalachian town, and graduate students at nearby East Tennessee State University can earn a degree in storytelling.

For students not specializing in folklore or storytelling, folktales can be integrated into a wide variety of courses. I have taught Appalachian folktales in undergraduate courses in children's literature, American literature, composition, a special topics course called World Folktales and Literature, and team-taught courses in environmental science, as well as Appalachian literature. A wealth of resources is available in every medium for student projects on Appalachian folktales, from colorful books and recordings designed for the enjoyment of all ages to scholarly criticism and collections with detailed notes on sources and storytelling methods, as well as unpublished tales in archives. The Digital Library of Appalachia contains a growing collection of print, audio, and video recordings from archives of Appalachian colleges, which students can access online (http://www.aca-dla.org).

Whether students are natives of Appalachia or not, they benefit from gaining a deeper appreciation of the region's heritage. One Ferrum College graduate who studied Appalachian culture and performed with the Jack Tale Players at Ferrum now teaches Appalachian folktales at a Montessori school in her home state of California. Students in the Hollins University summer graduate program in children's literature, who came from many different states and two other continents, were especially fascinated by the Appalachian tales we studied in one segment of Traditions and Adaptations in Literature for Young Children in 1998; later I was asked to teach the course with a thorough emphasis on Appalachian children's literature. Several of the Hollins students branched out from their study of Appalachian folktales and literature to develop similar research and teaching projects in other regions and write their own folktale adaptations.[1]

Advantages and Pitfalls of Teaching with Folktales

The many benefits of using folktales in college courses, including short assignments in general studies classes, are summarized below in three groups of advantages and related pitfalls. Some of the obstacles already introduced—misconceptions about marginalized rural cultures, popular entertainment, and children's culture—can become advantages as students move from enjoying stories that are familiar and entertaining to deepening their critical perspectives on folklore and regional culture. The pitfalls, typical difficulties that may require some extra attention, can lead to valuable learning experiences, helping students move beyond negative stereotypes and oversimplified depictions of the region and develop a variety of academic skills.

1. Folktales are typically short, memorable, and fun. It is easy to distribute copies of short tales to a class, or assign tales available online, discuss them during a class period, and compare a variety of examples relating to different topics. They can serve as springboards for discussion and writing assignments in a variety of courses, without taking time for extensive reading assignments. Almost every type of literary and cultural analysis has been applied to folk narratives, so short or familiar pieces from oral traditions can be used to introduce longer works of literature (many of which have mythological or folkloric roots or themes), as well as topics in history, social science, environmental science, and fine arts.

Folktales are entertaining, and viewing illustrated versions, film adaptations, and storytelling performances—either live or on video—adds variety and enjoyment to class assignments. Folk narratives are also memorable, using patterns of language and plot that make them easy to retell or sing and dear to the hearts of tellers and listeners.

2. Folktales are found in endless variety in every culture, illustrating cultural diversity as well as links between different cultures and between oral and written traditions. Every culture has long traditions of oral storytelling, folksinging, and joke-telling. Students can learn about cultural diversity within Appalachia and discover links with cultures outside the region, as well as finding allusions to familiar folk heroes, songs, and sayings throughout popular culture. Some Appalachian folk heroes, such as John Henry and Davy Crockett, are known throughout the nation. Others will intrigue students if they trace connections between particular regional tales they study and stories or songs they know.

Because there are so many variants of most folktales—often with different titles and character names, one of the pitfalls is getting the details mixed up in our heads when we discuss them. If you review three versions of "Mutsmag" for tomorrow's class, will you remember by morning which ones show the heroine stealing back the king's horse from the giant? Students must learn to read and listen carefully when they encounter variants of the same tale. In reports they need to identify the particular versions of folktales they discuss and cite them accurately. Students may need extra instructions for documenting oral, audiovisual, and unpublished sources or picture books. Adapters, retellers, translators, and illustrators should be recognized in fully documented papers.

Because folktales link oral and written literatures of the world, including them in college courses helps us overcome some of the biases ingrained in modern education and scholarship, where the written word and the individual creative artist have been privileged over audiovisual and communal methods of communication and cultural exchange. Folktales remind us that all literature developed from oral traditions, and that most people throughout human history have had no writing system to record their languages and stories. It can be difficult to break students of the habit of referring to the original source or author, or the "real" or "correct" version. Usually there is no known original version or writer. In a medieval literature class at Ferrum College, John Bruton introduced Appalachian folktales because "Jack and Old Fire Dragon" has similarities with *Beowulf* and other northern European hero tales, and because studying variants of the same tales from a living oral tradition close to home helped students understand the transmission of stories in ancient literature.

Another pitfall related to the cultural diversity of folktale traditions is that students may think tales from unfamiliar cultures are bizarre or pagan. In a Cherokee legend about the origin of corn, curious boys who discover the secret of their mother or grandmother, Selu, learn that the corn falls right off the sides of her body, until their spying leads to her death and the necessity of working the fields to grow corn. The boys within some versions of the tale view this source of food as unsavory until they accept the gifts of the Corn-Mother, and readers of folktales must learn to accept the underlying wisdom of stories that seem bizarre on the surface. Every culture has strange, nonrealistic stories in its mythology and folklore, but there is a natural tendency to take for granted a story we grew up with—whether it's about a whale swallowing Jonah, frogs turning into princes, or a cow jumping over the moon. Sometimes we need to remind students to show respect for the culture that produced the folklore and avoid using biased language when discussing unfamiliar and familiar stories or poems. Since folklore is often written down or retold using features of vernacular dialects, not in standard English, it's also important to be patient with tales retold in different dialects and styles of language, as it usually takes just a little time to become accustomed to the rhythms of an unfamiliar voice in speech or writing.

Moreover, although some of the culturally specific details and language in folktales from different times and places may seem strange and unfamiliar, the straightforward narrative style of most oral tales quickly reveals one of the most intriguing phenomena in human experience: the similarities in stories from all over the world with universal themes and familiar, recurring motifs. For example, there are obvious historical connections between the Appalachian "Ashpet" and the German "Ashputtle," which European settlers in Appalachia would have known, but why are stories with similar "Cinderella" motifs also found in ancient African and Asian traditions? Or, is it a coincidence that African Americans and Native Americans in eastern North America tell so many tales with a rabbit as the predominant trickster hero? Because folktales represent human experience through symbols and archetypes, theories about the universal elements in world folklore and myth can lead to fascinating debates about how to interpret particular tales. They provide excellent examples of the complex interplay of realism, fantasy, and symbolism in folklore and literature.

One more pitfall can accompany our enjoyment of folktales from different cultural traditions. That is, the widespread popularity of folklore adaptations, multicultural literature, and historical fiction in recent decades can result in over-emphasizing folkways of the past to represent cultural diversity. In the field of children's literature, there are not enough books for younger readers that portray Native Americans or other Appalachians living in cities as well as rural areas and working in ordinary jobs in contemporary life. Some books give overviews of Cherokee customs or Appalachian traditions using only the past tense. The multitude of stories about grandparents passing on folklore and traditional crafts to their families can be heartwarming, but we must not let students assume, for example, that all Appalachians make quilts and live in remote hollows where everyone is a farmer or a miner, as well as a gifted storyteller or a ballad-singer.

3. Folktales unite children and adults, enhancing transitions from childhood to adult life, and from popular culture to academic subjects and skills. Short works from folklore can provide springboards as students move from writing about childhood experiences to more complex types of analysis. They need to learn, as an important part of their heritage, that Disney versions and other widely available children's books and movies do not adequately represent the larger body of folklore that people of all ages have enjoyed for centuries. Some students know this subconsciously, but school assignments can help them recognize the significance of folktales in their own experience. For example, one Virginian wrote a thoughtful and enjoyable essay in a freshman composition about memories associated with a version of "The Three Pigs" his grandmother told to him and his brothers.

One pitfall of these advantages is that, because so many people associate folktales and fairy tales with childhood, they may assume that the content should be only entertaining and innocent, or, conversely, that the tales should always teach lessons to children. Older children and adults who don't experience folktales or picture books thus lose touch with exciting parts of their own culture. Most folktales, ballads, nursery rhymes, and jokes were originally told or sung by adults to other adults or mixed audiences (long before the Romantic concept of childhood innocence came along). Students may be shocked by the gory details and "adult themes" in many traditional tales, but of course, these are the very elements young people enjoy if they get beyond modern American misconceptions about fairy tales as children's stories. Many current storytellers, dramatists, and filmmakers endeavor to entertain the whole family, just as traditional storytellers have done around the home or campfire for generations. Among other benefits of teaching with folklore, what more worthy goal is there for general studies courses than to prepare young adults to share good stories with the children in their lives in the future?

Another pitfall of associating folktales with strong memories and enjoyment is that deep emotional ties to literature from childhood can make us reluctant to analyze it objectively, to critique our favorite stories, or to learn other versions. It takes some time to realize that we can retain nostalgic preferences while also appreciating the larger social implications, variations, and methods of interpreting traditional stories and poems. Personal memories that evolve into academic interests can motivate students to pursue high-quality research and writing projects. Two undergraduate students in teacher education at Ferrum College, who had seen the Jack Tale Players perform in their elementary schools, were excited about the opportunity to do research on Jack tales for their Children's Literature project, and even interview the founder and director of the Jack Tale Players, Rex Stephenson. Michelle Vincent conducted research in folklore archives at the Blue Ridge Institute for this project and wrote in her research paper, "It is really important for children to see folktales outside of Walt Disney because the true folktales give children a better account of history" (Vincent and Hanlon 2005). Later this enthusiastic student was awarded a summer scholarship to continue her archive research and develop teaching materials and a conference presentation on folktales from Southwestern Virginia.[2]

Studying Contemporary Approaches to Transmission and Adaptation of Folktales

In courses where folktale and fairy-tale traditions are studied in some detail, Appalachian folktales can illustrate most of the current approaches to retelling and adapting traditional tales in different media. The following list of seven contemporary approaches to folktales, which can be varied according to your class's needs and interests, uses variants of "Mutsmag" and other examples to illustrate some of the discussion topics and debates that arise when analyzing the complex relationships between oral traditions and adaptations. After studying any of these types of folktales, students who collect folklore from their own families and communities, or write, illustrate, adapt, or dramatize tales in creative projects, often deepen their understanding of the traditions as well as they do through traditional research papers.

1. The faithful retelling of old tales is an oral tradition continued by many recent and living storytellers. It's fun to take a class to a performance or storytelling festival, or invite a storyteller to class, but audio and video recordings can supplement or substitute for watching live performances. *Telling Tales*, a series of films produced by Kentucky Educational Television in 1989, with downloadable teacher's guides available on the KET website, includes "Mutsmag," told by Anndrena Belcher (1989), and some Jack tales, among other multicultural tales. "Mutsmag" is also retold by Michael "Badhair" Williams on his video *Tell Me a Story*, volume 5 (1986); and by Charlotte Ross on the video *The Jack Tales Festival 2002*.

Transcribed oral tales are available in many published collections of Appalachian folktales and in archives and more general anthologies. Richard Chase's *The Jack Tales* and *Grandfather Tales*, published in the 1940s, are still two of the most popular folktale collections in North America. "Munsmeg," one variant of "Mutsmag" that Chase collected in Southwestern Virginia for the Virginia Writers Project of the Works Progress Administration, is archived in the James Taylor Adams Collection and reprinted on the AppLit site.[3] Another version, "Polly, Nancy, and Muncimeg," appears in Leonard Roberts's 1959 collection of Kentucky folktales. Several of his books, as well as collections by Marie Campbell ([1958] 2000) and Ruth Ann Musick ([1970] 1989), record Appalachian tales with similar motifs, and give notes on the oral sources of their folktales.

"Mutts Mag," recorded orally by the distinguished Appalachian scholar Cratis Williams in 1981, was published in a posthumous book of his writings, *Tales from Sacred Wind: Coming of Age in Appalachia* (2003). Williams's son and daughter recall hearing him and Richard Chase tell this tale and others when they were young. Williams attempted to imitate the voice of his grandmother, who learned the tale from her mother. His account of his grandmothers' difficult lives helps us imagine how satisfying Mutsmag's triumph over the giant would have seemed to them. They traced their family's storytelling back to the early nineteenth century in Southwestern Virginia, but Williams acknowledged that by 1981 his memory could have been influenced by sharing tales with Chase and reading Chase's *Grandfather Tales* (1948). Thus, as recent scholarly debates have recognized, even though folktale collectors ever since the Grimm brothers in nineteenth-century Germany have longed to trace a pure oral tradition within a particular culture or family, evidence shows that influences have drifted back and forth between oral storytelling and printed versions of popular tales for generations.

2. Many storytellers and editors have been actively revising the "canon" of popular folktales and fairy tales by searching out old stories that were neglected by mainstream society but appeal to modern values. Feminist scholars have been especially interested in this approach to folktales, along with writers and educators striving to establish a better representation of cultural diversity in oral and written tales that are widely known.[4] As in the broader traditions of folktales and fairy tales in the Western world, Jack and other male characters with the most active and heroic roles are more famous than female characters such as Mutsmag. However, as the family history of Cratis Williams and the folktale collections mentioned above demonstrate, both women and men have told tales about heroic females for many generations.[5] The strong women in Appalachian folktales are often spunkier and more independent than their counterparts in European folktales, who appear so often in recent feminist anthologies, such as Mutsmag's British predecessor Molly Whuppie. That is just as true—sometimes more true—in Chase's collections from the 1940s as it is in newer adaptations that incorporate specific revisions to highlight the strengths of female characters or reflect other modern values. *Grandfather Tales* (Chase 1948) made "Mutsmag" and other tales of strong women, such as "Whitebear Whittington," "Catskins," and "Gallymanders! Gallymanders!," widely available more than six decades ago. With a frame story about neighbors sharing tales, *Grandfather Tales* devotes almost as much attention to female storytellers and characters as to males.

Marilou Awiakta's storytelling and writing appeal to contemporary values by explaining traditional Cherokee culture in relation to attitudes toward nature and modern technology (see Grace Toney Edwards's chapter, "Teaching the Poetry and Prose of Marilou Awiakta," in this book). She also emphasizes that Cherokee traditions value women as strong leaders, maintaining a harmonious balance in gender relations and seeking individual spiritual growth. Her book *Selu: Seeking the Corn Mother's Wisdom* (1993) is an innovative blend of poetry, essay, and retellings of traditional tales such as "Selu," on the origin of corn, and the story of Selu's husband, Kanati, the First Man, a hunter. These tales and other Cherokee legends have become available in a wide variety of collections, illustrated books, recordings, and websites since the 1980s.

3. Folktale adaptations have grown in abundance and artistic variety since the development of modern picture books and children's theater in the Victorian period, and the advent of film adaptations in the twentieth century. Now that we have so many adaptations of Appalachian folktales in different media, their diversity of styles, approaches, and interpretations works against tendencies to stereotype stories and people from the region. Ray Hicks's collection of three Jack tales includes a CD of the legendary storyteller's oral retellings, the texts edited by Lynn Salsi, a glossary of dialect expressions, and illustrations by Owen Smith in a style reminiscent of the Midwestern regionalist painter Thomas Hart Benton. With more than one picture-book adaptation of well-known Appalachian tales such as "Jack and the Bean Tree," "John Henry," "The Three Pigs," and "Whitebear Whittington," we have varied opportunities for comparing oral and written retellings as well as for analyzing the relationships of words and pictures. If students compare related tales from outside Appalachia, they can trace traditional motifs recurring with variations in visual as well as verbal details. For example, links between "Jack and the Robbers" and famous illustrations of the German tale "The Bremen Town Musicians" (with the animal companions standing on top of each other) are dramatically suggested in Owen Smith's tall color illustration of Jack and two animals riding on the donkey (Hicks 2001, 31).[6] It is also interesting to compare different visual images of the folk hero Jack in the many illustrated Jack tale books that are now available. He is usually a lanky adolescent striding across the American landscape to seek his fortune, but in Paul Brett Johnson's picture books such as *Fearless Jack* (2001), he is a younger boy, a Tom Sawyer type, with a dog at his side whose expressions react to each incident.

Variants of "Mutsmag" include "Muncimeg" in Gail E. Haley's illustrated collection from North Carolina, *Mountain Jack Tales* (1992). One of Haley's energetic wood engravings shows Muncimeg straining tenaciously with the physical and emotional effort of pulling a sack of gold away from the sleeping giant (97). Kentucky storyteller Anne Shelby expanded the domain of this self-reliant folk heroine by producing a play about her and then featuring her in a 2007 book, *The Adventures of Molly Whuppie and Other Appalachian Folktales*—the first collection devoted primarily to Appalachian folktales about strong women. In addition to blending the British Molly Whuppie with Muncimeg in the title story, Shelby revised Kentucky Jack tales collected by Leonard Roberts so that Molly, "clever, brave, and strong," has a dominant role in most of the book's fourteen lively tales, which retain the flavor and language of traditional folktales while reflecting modern values. Omitting most of the harsher violence in old tales, for example, sparing her readers from having to walk over corpses and seeing people "unnecessarily beating one another to bloody pulps with clubs and things," Shelby depicts the siblings of Molly and Jack as sometimes jealous, competitive, and stingy, but not vile or murderous (2007, 86). Molly maintains her independence by tricking boorish boys in "Molly and the Unwanted Boyfriends" and never receives marriage for herself or her sisters as a reward, but she does marry Jack after rescuing him from a rich giant.

Students can also read "Mutsmag" on the AppLit website, an adaptation by R. Rex Stephenson with illustrations by Virginia schoolchildren who saw Stephenson's Jack Tale Players perform his new dramatization in 2000. A college student working in a computer lab cropped and formatted the children's drawings, adding a few interesting animated effects such as Mutsmag's mother floating up to heaven when she dies. Blending in some motifs from other stories, Stephenson expanded traits that make Mutsmag less dependent on magic help than her predecessors and more reliant on her own wits and resourcefulness, as well as gifts inherited from her dying mother. Her self-assertion grows when she outwits a gang of robbers and makes her sisters beg for help after the robbers tie them to a tree. The drawings submitted by teachers of kindergarten through third grade reveal that children were most fascinated by this scene of sibling rivalry in which Mutsmag talks back to the mean sisters while they are helpless. Images in the drawings also demonstrate that the story theater method of dramatization, in which actors use their bodies to create different characters and objects such as the tree, is effective in stimulating the children's imaginations. Stephenson's ending, in which Mutsmag chooses her own reward—a box of gold rather than marriage to the love-struck prince—is a wonderful compromise between variants of this tale with the traditional ending of royal marriage and those with monetary rewards but no marriage. Undergraduate and graduate students who read Stephenson's adaptation have written essays comparing "Mutsmag" with "Hansel and Gretel" and analyzing the language and the heroine's character traits of self-reliance and resilience.[7]

Mutzmag is a live-action film in the series *From the Brothers Grimm* by Virginia filmmaker Tom Davenport, whose insightful approach to folklore and film traditions produced innovative alternatives to the Disney animations that so many Americans associate with fairy tales. Davenport's Mutzmag, played by a North Carolina student, settles down in a nice house of her own near the home of the kind king and queen after ridding the neighborhood of the cannibalistic giant and witch. While Stephenson's Jack Tale Players create a two-headed giant in "Mutsmag" with one actor on the shoulders of another, in Davenport's film one large man plays the giant. Some students say he isn't scary enough and others think he is more frightening because he is more realistic. The film's visual effects emphasize the gothic horror of the dangers the heroine faces, but, as Sappho Charney discusses in an essay on "power and violence in *Mutzmag*" (1993), her quiet heroism and role as narrator assure viewers that Mutzmag will survive. Davenport provided a wealth of background material on adapting folktales and on the making of his low-budget films, appealing especially to students who may want to make their own films.

4. A fourth approach to retelling, revising, or adapting folktales is transplanting tales from one cultural context to another, as Davenport did when he began his series by setting folktales from the Grimm brothers, such as "Rapunzel" and "The Frog King," in the American South at different periods of history. Barry Moser's trilogy of picture books based on European folklore, *The Tinderbox* (1990), *Polly Vaughn* (1992), and *Tucker Pfeffercorn* (1994), fulfilled his dream of setting fairy tales in the mountain landscapes of his native Tennessee. *Tucker Pfeffercorn* is a brilliant feminist adaptation of "Rumpelstiltskin," with a coal miner's widow being oppressed by a ruthless coal boss rather than a greedy king. Becky Mushko transplanted the same tale to the Blue Ridge landscape of her home in Southwestern Virginia. In *Ferradiddledumday* (2010), she weaves images of plants and animals lyrically into the plot, with the rhythms of the seasons flowing through the story as naturally as the magic of the old fairy tale. The heroine, Gillie, is like older folk heroines, such as Snow White, when her innate virtues are reflected in her unity with nature.

In a more unusual example of "transplantation," *The Tale of Willie Monroe* (1999), Alan Schroeder and illustrator Andrew Glass adapted a Japanese tale of three strong women as an Appalachian tall tale about a gullible muscleman and two much tougher and cleverer women. Another artist and writer influenced by Appalachian folktales, Elizabeth Dulemba, has illustrated two bilingual picture books, moving "Jack and the Bean Tree (or Beanstalk)" to the desert Southwest in *Paco and the Giant Chile Plant* (Polette 2008) and retelling a humorous Appalachian tale with Hispanic characters in her (2009) book *Soap, Soap, Soap*, which is available with embedded Spanish phrases throughout and a glossary. In debates about the authenticity of revised or transplanted tales, some readers resist adaptations that change what they perceive to be the original tale—or at least the version they grew up with. Yet, in oral traditions, tales change with every retelling and move from place to place along with people who tell them, so using modern values or technologies to make the tales reflect one's own personality or society does not necessarily violate storytelling traditions. It's logical for Moser's *Polly Vaughn* (1992) to criticize hunting and gender stereotypes in ways that older versions of the traditional ballad would not, while others might interpret the tragic story of Polly's accidental death in the woods differently.

5. Writing satires, or "fractured fairy tales," is another fascinating trend in adaptations of folktales and fairy tales. Satires such as the zany *Stinky Cheese Man* (Scieszka 1992) and other books by Jon Scieszka and illustrated by Lane Smith have become increasingly popular, although they tend to parody the outdated themes and unrealistic elements of more generic and mainstream fairy tales rather than folktales from specific regions or minority cultures. There is a rich tradition of humor in Appalachian folktales, and some fear that farcical stories from inside the culture may perpetuate negative hillbilly stereotypes as much as jokes or satires by outsiders. But mocking human nature and foolish behavior is an ancient part of storytelling traditions around the world. One of Appalachia's most popular comical tales about fools and noodleheads, "Old Dry Frye," appears in Chase's *Grandfather Tales* (1948) and more recent reprints and retellings. With motifs that can be traced back to the Middle Ages, it exposes a series of neighbors who make up new stories about a corpse to get rid of it and avoid blame for the death of Old Dry Frye, a stereotypical country preacher who eats so much fried chicken at people's houses that he chokes to death on a bone.

Bits of more contemporary types of satire appear in other recent retellings and adaptations of Appalachian tales. Stephenson's dramatization of "Ashpet" spoofs a traditional Cinderella motif when the prince, searching for Ashpet, makes the audience laugh by approaching their feet with jokes about the awkward and smelly business of trying a shoe on different girls. Stephenson added some farcical details to "Mutsmag," including the dumb "democratic one-eyed gang" of robbers and Mutsmag's loud singing of "Froggy Went A-Courting" to keep her sisters awake in the giant's house. And Stephenson's 2006 adaptation of "Two Lost Babes" satirizes contemporary eating habits when two witches try to fatten up lost children with piles of junk food. Thus some Appalachian storytellers play up humorous elements more than others, or add some modern jokes, but they seldom subvert the structure or themes of older tales as thoroughly as many postmodern satires of fairy tales do. One exception is Bev Futrell's song "Little Omie's Done Got Wise" (2001), performed by the Reel World String Band from Kentucky, which mocks Appalachian legends and ballads in which women are gullible murder victims, such as "Pretty Polly," "Polly Vaughn," and "Little Omie Wise."

6. Another approach linking folktales with literary traditions is writing original stories that combine motifs from traditional tales, as writers of literary fairy tales from Hans Christian Andersen to Jane Yolen have done. Authors of new stories may be creating spin-offs of well-known tales—writing new Jack tales, for example, or filling in perceived gaps in folklore traditions by developing new kinds of heroes, or blending old motifs in original, contemporary ways. *Look Out, Jack! The Giant Is Back!*, by Tom Birdseye and illustrated by Will Hillenbrand (2001), is presented as a sequel to "Jack and the Beanstalk," with wacky humor about a gluttonous giant eating piles of Southern food. Anne Isaacs's award-winning picture book *Swamp Angel* (1994) depicts a new tall tale heroine, with Paul O. Zelinsky's innovative illustrations on backgrounds representing different varieties of wood. As gigantic and powerful as Paul Bunyan or Pecos Bill, incredible Angelica Longrider becomes "the greatest woodswoman in Tennessee," wrestling with a monstrous bear until they stir up enough dust to create the Smoky Mountains.

In Jane Yolen's story "Snow in Summer" (2000), which has been published in collections of contemporary fairy tales for adults, some dialect in the dialogue, place-names, and other details place the story in Appalachia. Less gullible than the traditional Snow White, Summer narrates her own story and gets revenge when her evil stepmother comes after her. Instead of marrying a prince or anyone herself, she gets her father married off to a nicer, nurturing woman, her dead mother's friend who had taught her stories all her life, while Summer takes refuge with seven fatherly miners; she not only keeps house but tells "stories of magic and mystery" that keep them and herself alive.

7. Studying Appalachian folktales can show students how folklore is often woven into longer works of literature, where it provides culturally specific background details, sheds light on particular characters or events, represents themes symbolically, or contributes to experimental narrative techniques. Yolen expanded both the realistic and magical elements of her short story in her (2011) novel, *Snow in Summer: Fairest of Them All*. The setting, called Addison, is based on her husband's family home of Webster, West Virginia, in the 1930s and 1940s. Cousin Nancy, who calls Summer "Molly Whuppie" at one point, provides rowan seeds, briars, and Summer's own caul to ward off

the evil magic of the stepmother who victimizes Summer and her father for years. Other magic helpers include a white owl, which Summer views as the angelic presence of her dead mother, and the miners' pet bear, who commits fantastical acts of loyalty and rescue. As a novel, Yolen's story has become an even more intriguing blend of European wonder tale and realistic American regional fiction.

"Old Dry Frye", "Whitebear Whittington," and an unusual version of "Mutsmag" appear in *Fair and Tender Ladies* (1988), Lee Smith's compelling realistic novel about the life of Ivy Rowe in the mountains of Virginia; several folktales that storytellers recount during her childhood influence Ivy throughout life. Study of James Still's novels *River of Earth* ([1940] 1996) and *Sporty Creek* ([1977] 1999) can be enhanced by discussing his combination of gritty modernist realism and elements of folklore. For example, Uncle Jolly is a trickster character who wanders through the lives of the child narrators, his nephews, in both novels—a folk hero who is more perceptive and wisely influential than his comical exterior suggests (Hanlon 2007, 178–80). In Laurence Yep's young adult novel *The Star Fisher* (1991), a teenage protagonist tells her sister an Asian folktale that helps in her search for her own identity as a Chinese immigrant moving to West Virginia. Sharyn McCrumb's ballad novels, such as *The Ballad of Frankie Silver* (1998), are also named after traditional folk narratives that lie at the core of each book's fascinating blend of Appalachian history and contemporary fiction (see Whited [2003]).

A more experimental kind of fantasy appears in Virginia Hamilton's (1983) novel, *The Magical Adventures of Pretty Pearl*, and a crop of innovative twenty-first-century books. Hamilton created a new African goddess who comes to America to help former slaves and befriend Cherokees in hiding after the Trail of Tears. *Pretty Pearl* combines Appalachian history and traditional African American folk heroes, including John Henry, in a powerful young adult novel about persecution and migration in the post–Civil War Southern mountains. Sally M. Keehn expanded and transformed British folk narratives into two fantastical novels set in rural Appalachia. Both have colorful, willful heroines narrating their strange and comical coming-of-age quests, seeking personal and communal reconciliation after the Civil War and long-standing family feuds and love triangles. *Gnat Stokes and the Foggy Bottom Swamp Queen* (Keehn 2005) remakes "Tam Lin" in eastern Tennessee, where a twelve-year-old attempts to rescue a boy kidnapped seven years earlier by Zelda the Swamp Queen. *Magpie Gabbard and the Quest for the Buried Moon* (Keehn 2007) is based on an English folktale about the moon coming to earth. These novels unfold in a wild blending of Appalachian folkways, tall-tale exaggeration, love charms, magical creatures and transformations, detached undead body parts, prophesying kettles, magic rings, religious satire, symbolic songs and poems, and historical and literary themes such as the influence of a new schoolteacher and the new novel *Little Women* (Alcott [1868]) at the end of *Gnat Stokes*.

Charlotte Jane Ellington used a whole collection of legendary tales to shape a realistic historical novel about the adopted daughter of Cherokee leader Nancy Ward. *Dancing Leaf* (2007) retells twelve Cherokee legends, introducing each chapter with a tale that establishes the focus of Dancing Leaf's coming-of-age experiences and her reflections on the oral tales, until she plans to record her traditions in English and Sequoyah's new Cherokee writing system. The legendary monster Uktena, for example, relates to her nightmares about the mother and brother she lost when white men invaded her village. Unlike so many previous books about the Trail of Tears, *Dancing Leaf* is set before that period of mass forced removal; it deals not only with pressures on Cherokee people in their eastern Appalachian homelands to assimilate and move west, but depicts Cherokees and some white characters who were succeeding in coexisting peacefully with respect for traditional Cherokee culture and self-governance.

George Ella Lyon's *Gina. Jamie. Father. Bear.* (2002) alternates between two points of view, linking the quests of a contemporary high school girl; a boy who lives in another dimension, in an ancient or timeless world of folktales such as "Whitebear Whittington"; and their troubled fathers. Gina's psychic experiences explore the unfathomable relations between past and present, life and death, the worlds of dreams and everyday consciousness. In Candice Ransom's novel *Finding Day's Bottom* (2006), a Virginia grandfather tells the child narrator three traditional Appalachian folktales about clever girls and describes a mystical place called Day's Bottom. It grows out of his psyche and imagination in a different way than the regional folktales passed down for generations, showing that he understands how people of all ages need both reality and fantasy, and how the child with a more literal belief in his imagined place needs time to accept the reality of her father's accidental death. Thus the authors of recent Appalachian fiction are finding new ways to reflect on the enduring value of folktales as they explore a variety of postmodern historical and psychological perspectives with innovative combinations of realism, folklore, humor, and fantasy.

One student who studied Appalachian folktales in an introductory literature course and watched a Jack Tale Players performance wrote that she recommended this experience to others because "it will bring them to appreciate their heritage more." Bringing stories from "way back yonder" closer to home for students to develop this kind of appreciation is the goal of teachers and storytellers. Rex Stephenson, a professor of drama who has adapted Appalachian folktales for more than thirty-five years, summed up the multiple dimensions of the folktale tradition's appeal by observing, "Far from being minor amusements, folktales put us in touch with the values of people. They affirm the creativity of people and show the power of stories in transmitting cultural principles."[8]

Notes

1. For example, in "Mutsy of the Sea" (2009), Shelby Mahan, from California, transformed the Appalachian Mutsmag into a folk hero who surfs on the West Coast. On AppLit, http://www2.ferrum.edu/applit/texts/MutsyOfSea.htm.

2. "James Taylor Adams: Biography by Michelle Vincent" is a web page created for this project, on AppLit, http://www2.ferrum.edu/applit/authors/adams.htm.

3. Typescripts of folklore and other papers collected by James Taylor Adams of Wise County were given to Clinch Valley College (now University of Virginia's College at Wise) and later copied for the Blue Ridge Institute archives at Ferrum College. AppLit contains reprints of some tales from this collection, as well as bibliographies and study guides on folktales. Variants of all tales mentioned in this essay are listed in AppLit's Annotated Index of Appalachian Folktales, http://www2.ferrum.edu/applit/bibs/tales.

4. See articles by Kay Stone (1975; 1986) and Nina Mikkelsen (2000) for examples of feminist criticism with discussion of Appalachian folktales.

5. Charlotte Ross notes in *Encyclopedia of Appalachia* (2006) that written records of a story related to "Mutsmag" go back to 1100 in Scotland.

6. See illustrations at "The Annotated Bremen Town Musicians" on Heidi Anne Heiner's website, SurLaLune Fairy Tales. This site is an excellent source for comparing tales from different traditions and related resources. The animals in "The Bremen Town Musicians" have no human leader like Jack in "Jack and the Robbers."

7. Stephenson's illustrated story and related resources, including performance photographs and video clips, are all linked at "Introduction to *Mutsmag* by R. Rex Stephenson," on AppLit, http://www2.ferrum.edu/applit/texts/mutsmag_story/mutsback.htm. The archive "Munsmeg" and Stephenson's "Mutsmag" script are also published in *Crosscurrents of Children's Literature* (Stahl, Hanlon, and Keyser 2006), in Part 3, "Oral and Written Literary Traditions."

8. Stephenson quotation recorded on publicity materials of the Jack Tale Players, Ferrum College, no date.

References

Alcott, Louisa May. 1868. *Little Women*. Boston: Robert Brothers.

AppLit: Resources for Readers and Teachers of Appalachian Literature for Children and Young Adults. Edited by Tina L. Hanlon. Ferrum College. http://www2.ferrum.edu/applit.

Awiakta, Marilou. 1993. *Selu: Seeking the Corn-Mother's Wisdom*. Golden, CO: Fulcrum.

Belcher, Anndrena. 1989. "Mutsmag." In *Telling Tales* series. Lexington: Kentucky Educational Television. Videocassette. Downloadable Teacher's Guide. http://www.ket.org/education.

Birdseye, Tom. 2001. *Look Out, Jack! The Giant Is Back!*. Illustrated by Will Hillenbrand. New York: Holiday House.

Campbell, Marie. (1958) 2000. *Tales from the Cloud Walking Country*. Reprint, Athens: University of Georgia Press.

Charney, Sappho. 1993. "'No Chalkmark on the Mantel': Power and Violence in *Mutzmag*." In *The Antic Art: Enhancing Children's Literature Experiences through Film and Video*, edited by Lucy Rollin, 39–46. Fort Atkinson, WI: Highsmith Press.

Chase, Richard. 1943. *The Jack Tales: Folk Tales from the Southern Appalachians*. Boston: Houghton Mifflin.

———. 1948. *Grandfather Tales: American-English Folk Tales*. Boston: Houghton Mifflin.

Davenport, Tom, dir. 1992. *Mutzmag: An Appalachian Folktale*. Delaplane, VA: Davenport Films. Videocassette and DVD.

Digital Library of Appalachia. Appalachian College Association Central Library. http://www.aca-dla.org.

Dulemba, Elizabeth O. 2009. *Soap, Soap, Soap / Jabón, Jabón, Jabón*. McHenry, IL: Raven Tree Press.

Ellington, Charlotte Jane. 2007. *Dancing Leaf*. Johnson City, TN: Overmountain Press.

Futrell, Bev. 2001. "Little Omie's Done Got Wise." On *The Coast is Clear*. Reel World and Les Campbell. Lexington, KY: Reel World String Band. Compact disc.

Haley, Gail E. 1992. *Mountain Jack Tales*. New York: Dutton.

Hamilton, Virginia. 1983. *The Magical Adventures of Pretty Pearl*. New York: Harper and Row.

Hanlon, Tina L. 2007. "'Read my tales, spin my rhymes': The Books for Children." In *James Still: Critical Essays on the Dean of Appalachian Literature*, edited by Ted Olson and Kathy H. Olson, 174–89. Jefferson, NC: McFarland.

Heiner, Heidi Anne. 2012. SurLaLune Fairy Tales. Last updated 12 September. http://www.surlalunefairytales.com.

Hicks, Ray. 2001. *The Jack Tales*. As told to Lynn Salsi. Illustrated by Owen Smith. New York: Callaway.

Isaacs, Anne. 1994. *Swamp Angel*. Illustrated by Paul O. Zelinsky. New York: Dutton.

Johnson, Paul Brett. 2001. *Fearless Jack*. New York: McElderry.

Keehn, Sally M. 2005. *Gnat Stokes and the Foggy Bottom Swamp Queen*. New York: Philomel.

———. 2007. *Magpie Gabbard and the Quest for the Buried Moon*. New York: Philomel.

Lyon, George Ella. 2002. *Gina. Jamie. Father. Bear.* New York: Atheneum.

Mahan, Shelby. 2009. "Mutsy of the Sea." On AppLit, http://www2.ferrum.edu/applit/texts/MutsyOfSea.htm.

McCrumb, Sharyn. 1998. *The Ballad of Frankie Silver*. New York: Dutton.

Mikkelsen, Nina. 2000. "Strange Pilgrimages: Cinderella Was a Trickster—and Other Unorthodoxies of American and African-American Heroic Folk Figures." In *A Necessary Fantasy?: The Heroic Figure in Children's Popular Culture*, edited by Dudley Jones and Tony Watkins, 24–50. New York: Garland.

Moser, Barry. 1990. *The Tinderbox*. Illustrated by Barry Moser. Adapted from the story by Hans Christian Andersen. Boston: Little, Brown.

———. 1992. *Polly Vaughn: A Traditional British Ballad*. Boston: Little, Brown.

———. 1994. *Tucker Pfeffercorn: An Old Story Retold*. Boston: Little, Brown.

Mushko, Becky. 2010. *Ferradiddledumday: An Appalachian Version of Rumpelstiltskin*. Illustrated by Bruce Rae. Blumo Bluff, VA: Cedar Creek Publishing.

Musick, Ruth Ann. (1970) 1989. *Green Hills of Magic: West Virginia Folktales from Europe*. Reprint, Parsons, WV: McClain.

Polette, Keith. 2008. *Paco and the Giant Chile Plant / Paco y La Planta de Chile Gigante*. Illustrated by Elizabeth O. Dulemba. McHenry, IL: Raven Tree Press.

Ransom, Candice. 2006. *Finding Day's Bottom*. Minneapolis: Carolrhoda Books.

Roberts, Leonard W., ed. 1959. "Polly, Nancy, and Muncimeg." In *Up Cutshin and Down Greasy: Folkways of a Kentucky Mountain Family*, 119–23. Lexington: University Press of Kentucky.

Ross, Charlotte. 2002. "Mutsmag." On *The Jack Tales Festival 2002*. Blowing Rock, NC: Dianne Hackworth. Videocassette.

———. 2006. "Storytelling, History of." *Encyclopedia of Appalachia*, edited by Rudy Abramson and Jean Haskell, 1267–68. Knoxville: University of Tennessee Press.

Schroeder, Alan. 1999. *The Tale of Willie Monroe*. Illustrated by Andrew Glass. New York: Clarion.

Scieszka, Jon. 1992. *The Stinky Cheese Man and Other Fairly Stupid Tales*. Illustrated by Lane Smith. New York: Scholastic.

Shelby, Anne. 2007. *The Adventures of Molly Whuppie and Other Appalachian Folktales*. Illustrated by Paula McArdle. Chapel Hill: University of North Carolina Press.

Smith, Lee. 1988. *Fair and Tender Ladies*. New York: Ballantine.

Stahl, J. D., Tina L. Hanlon, and Elizabeth Lennox Keyser, eds. 2006. *Crosscurrents of Children's Literature: An Anthology of Texts and Criticism*. New York: Oxford University Press.

Stephenson, R. Rex. 2004. *Grandmother Tales: Mutsmag and Ashpet, Traditional Tales from the Blue Ridge Mountains*. Charlottesville, VA: New Plays for Children. Reprinted by Woodstock, IL: Dramatic Publishing, 2012.

Still, James. 1979. "An Interview with James Still." *Appalachian Journal* 6 (Winter): 121–41.

———. (1940) 1996. *River of Earth*. Reprint, Lexington: University Press of Kentucky.

———. (1977) 1996. *Jack and the Wonder Beans*. Illustrated by Margot Tomes. Reprint, Lexington: University Press of Kentucky.

———. (1977) 1999. *Sporty Creek*. Reprint, Lexington: University Press of Kentucky.

Stone, Kay F. 1975. "Things Walt Disney Never Told Us." *Journal of American Folklore* 88, no. 347, Women and Folklore (January–March): 42–50.

————. 1986. "Oral Narration in Contemporary North America." In *Fairy Tales and Society: Illusion, Allusion, and Paradigm*, edited by Ruth B. Bottigheimer, 13–31. Philadelphia: University of Pennsylvania Press. Reprinted in Stahl, Hanlon, and Keyser, *Crosscurrents of Children's Literature*, 253–65.

Vincent, N. Michelle, and Tina L. Hanlon. 2005. "Studying the Oral Tradition with Folktales in the James Taylor Adams Collection: Final Report for Lee B. Ledford Scholarship." Submitted to the Appalachian College Association. Ferrum College.

Whited, Lana. 2003. "'Based on a True-Story': Using *The Ballad of Frankie Silver* to Teach the Conventions of Narrative." In *From a Race of Storytellers: Essays on the Ballad Novels of Sharyn McCrumb*, edited by Kimberley M. Holloway, 33–50. Macon, GA: Mercer University Press.

Williams, Cratis D. 2003. "Mutts Mag." In *Tales from Sacred Wind: Coming of Age in Appalachia*, edited by David Cratis Williams and Patricia D. Beaver, 72–83. Jefferson, NC: McFarland.

Williams, Michael "Badhair." 1986. "Muts Mag." In *Tell Me a Story*. Vol. 5. Barr Entertainment. Videocassette.

Yep, Laurence. 1991. *The Star Fisher*. New York: Puffin.

Yolen, Jane. 2000. "Snow in Summer." In *Sister Emily's Lightship and Other Stories*. New York: Tor. Reprinted in *Black Heart, Ivory Bones*, edited by Ellen Datlow and Terri Windling, 90–96. New York: Avon, 2000.

————. 2011. *Snow in Summer: Fairest of Them All*. New York: Philomel.

PART THREE

The Novel in Appalachia

EIGHT

Teaching Modern Appalachia in Wilma Dykeman's *The Far Family*

PATRICIA M. GANTT

> That word—"region"—has imprisoned a rich and spacious segment of our country more oppressively than have the high mountains which are its characteristic feature.... The frustration with such stereotyping is that it sets the work apart from the mainstream of human experience [and] separates [it] into a kind of museum piece, an artifact rather than a living reality.
>
> —Wilma Dykeman, 27 May 1984

> Wilma Dykeman has demonstrated that the "identity crisis" of modern America ... [extends to] Appalachia— and the answers may be as abundant there as anywhere on this confused continent.
>
> —Lois Philips Hudson, 1966

I TEACH AT UTAH STATE UNIVERSITY in Logan, Utah— quite a distance from the blue hills of my North Carolina birth. My students, most of whom are planning to be secondary teachers, have probably never traveled east of the Missouri, much less the Mississippi. Certainly none of them has any familiarity with the French Broad, that river so intimately a part of Wilma Dykeman's fiction. Yet I have found that Dykeman's novels are so accessible to this audience that I have successfully used them multiple times in classes focusing on folk narrative, foodways, and material culture; teaching literature; and young adult fiction.

The first of Dykeman's novels that I taught to this western audience was her best-known, *The Tall Woman* (1962). It was such a resounding success with my folk narrative class that many listed it as the high point of the semester. One student suggested it to her mother for selection by her book club, and numerous others wanted to know why they had not heard of Dykeman before and whether she had written other works.

In a subsequent semester of a course in teaching literature—a required offering for secondary English majors—the majority of my students were "repeats." Having taken the course in folk narrative, they suggested that we study another Dykeman novel. Building on their enjoyment of *The Tall Woman*, I decided to include its sequel, *The Far Family* (1966). By so doing, I could include techniques for studying a novel or play that not all students had read, as well as the usual authorial background, cultural contexts, themes, and stylistic techniques (language, genre, characters, etc.) that they would need to know how to approach with any work. Students signed up for one to two aspects of the novel that they would be responsible for tracking throughout our study and converting into classroom activities. (Note: Each of their selections is italicized throughout the rest of this text.) At the end of our analysis, they would add their findings to a file others could access for use or adaptation in their classrooms or further projects.

The first obstacle to our study—that not all students had read the previous Dykeman novel—was disposed of quickly. From their prior knowledge, those who had read *The Tall Woman* volunteered to provide information to the others. They did so by presenting key scenes, delineating characters and themes, and so on, using PowerPoint and small-group exchanges. One technique is something I call Traveling Teacher, in which an individual rotates among small groups, teaching a new aspect of a work until she or he has made the full circle of the classroom. Finally, we discussed the need and usability of such approaches for those *times when students have read different works*: poems focusing on a common theme (e.g., nature), separate acts of a play that time constraints don't allow the class to study as a whole, or individualized readings.

Next, we set up the *background of the novel and its author*, using the following analysis: The publication of *The French Broad* (1955) and *Neither Black nor White* (with James Stokely; 1957), along with their subsequent acclaim, placed Wilma

Dykeman in frequent demand as a speaker on Appalachian history and contemporary Southern problems. With the appearance of *The Tall Woman*, she received even more requests for articles and speeches. Besides establishing a readership, Dykeman had won the full confidence of her publishers—Holt, Rinehart and Winston—who had produced both her histories and *The Tall Woman* and were eager to see more of Dykeman's writing. (My own students' request for more paralleled that of Dykeman's contemporaries.)

Increasingly, time to write became difficult for Dykeman to find—particularly time to write fiction, which took her longer than writing non-fiction.[1] As she later told Bernadette Hoyle: "Sometimes I write six or seven hours in one day, [but] sometimes I go six or seven days and write one hour." Even when her sons, Jim and Dykeman Stokely, were small, she tried to write every day, "perhaps a book review or just the outline of a new idea," but often motherhood or speaking engagements took precedence over writing. "It's never," Dykeman says, "that you want fewer boys or interests; it's just that you want more time and greater energy" (Hoyle 1954). Despite her complicated schedule, Dykeman began a sequel to *The Tall Woman*. Called *The Far Family*, it carries Lydia McQueen's family into the twentieth century, allowing Dykeman to introduce Appalachia as part of the mainstream of American experience, the second of the contextual frames through which she wishes the region to be viewed. It also shows Dykeman experimenting with style and expanding several themes (e.g., values of racial equality, family unity, and environmental stewardship) already explored in her fiction and nonfiction, but continuing in importance to her. One does not need to be familiar with *The Tall Woman* to appreciate its sequel fully.

In *The Far Family* Dykeman again writes a *multigenerational story* of a large family with mountain roots. In this novel she asks her readers to consider questions that cannot be isolated to one region: How should we respond to the demands of our loved ones? How can we set priorities that enable us to meet responsibilities without diminishing our own or someone else's humanity? What will we do—or refuse to do—under pressure? How can we use the physical resources of our homeland without destroying them? What do we owe our society and our world? Dykeman's literary investigation of these *universal matters*, according to Lillian Smith, "restores faith in the [contemporary] novel as something more than a yawp and a juvenile scream" (1966).

The *setting* for *The Far Family*[2] is the 1960s in fictional Nantahala County, somewhere in the Appalachian Mountains of Western North Carolina, and centers on the Thurston siblings—Ivy, Frone, Phoebe, Clay, and Kin; their mother, Martha; and Phil, Ivy's son, a United States senator. Most of the Thurston brothers and sisters live far from their Thickety Creek beginnings, and assemble reluctantly to decide whether they can help Clay, who is caught in "one pure damned mess" (*Far*, 14). Hawk Williams, a black man, has been killed on a hunting trip, and Clay is implicated in the murder. Too drunk to remember what happened, Clay can deny nothing. The family gathers at the home of their sister, Ivy Thurston Cortland, through whose *voice* Dykeman tells much of the story.

Unlike their McQueen grandparents, the Thurstons are "a cumbersome load" to one another; they appear to share few values (*Far*, 30). Their homes are located far apart, and the brothers and sisters seldom visit. Even Ivy, to whom the idea of home is precious, has for years used her farm as a base for worldwide travel; she is as familiar with Paris as with her native Appalachia, and has returned to North Carolina only recently. With all their differences, Ivy welcomes her family, and rejoices in "the links of a long chain reaching back and forward, holding them all—visible and invisible—together" (106). She offers them reminders of the emotional wealth they share from their mutual past, and tries to minimize the ways they have grown apart.

Ivy, seen in the last chapter of *The Tall Woman* as a baby already resembling Lydia McQueen, continues in her adult years to be like her grandmother in her dedication to family and her concern for protecting the land. Whether digging in her beloved garden, stacking lavender-scented sheets in the linen closet, or skillfully building a fire, she takes pleasure in hard work: "The wrinkles around her mouth and eyes came from ready laughter and openness to weather. Her hands had enlarged and toughened with every chore she undertook" (*Far*, 12). Ivy shares the commonsense values and practical skills one finds in many of Dykeman's heroic females, from Miss Kinzaida of "Summer Affair" (1951) to Lydia McQueen and Aunt Tildy in *The Tall Woman* (1962), but, unlike them, she has extensive formal education.

In this novel Dykeman does not remain exclusively within the consciousness of one principal character, as she had done in "The Prison" (1948b) and *The Tall Woman* (1962). Instead, she focuses on several people who represent three generations of Thurstons—the past (Martha), the present (Ivy and Clay), and the future (Phil). Martha, at the time of Clay's trouble, is elderly and bedridden, but many sections depict her as a dynamic young wife and mother. Ivy and Clay offer transition, since both their childhoods and their adult lives contribute to the novel. A few of the segments told through Phil's perspective deal with his life in Washington, where he jostles for political power and tries to balance a complicated romantic life; others take place among the assembled Thurstons, where Phil "had never felt more powerless" (*Far*, 202). He is torn between helping his uncle, whom he knows slightly and likes less, and advancing his own career. The young senator has several worthy projects lined up in Washington, and fears that by siding with Clay he will lose the black constituency he has worked hard to win. Phil sees Hawk Williams's murder as "a time bomb with the pin pulled," and wonders why "every family seemed to have some fool like Clay to throw a hitch into the machinery . . . why couldn't he just crawl off somewhere and [destroy himself] quietly, without any mess?" (28–29). These considerations allow students to consider both *tone* and the topic of *social tension*.

The most convincing voices in Dykeman's fiction continue to be those of *female characters*; the reader is consistently privy to their thought processes. Dykeman skillfully inscribes her women's comments with *subtext*, as when Ivy, sharply aware of the tension among family members, enters the living room they occupy in strained silence. She goes immediately to the fireplace and pokes at the small log fire: "I like a little open fire this time of year," she says. "It keeps off the chill" (*Far*, 31). Ivy senses the need for a comment—nearly any comment—and makes one that gives her brothers and sisters a focus besides themselves, and can invite memory: "Far as I can tell," Ivy's sister Frone replies, "you've always liked an open fire any time except maybe July fourth" (32). As memory begins to flow, tensions ease. Dykeman can make gestures carry considerable meaning, too, without the need for words: Ivy, shocked to learn that Clay must be tested by a psychiatrist, reveals her distress by dropping, then quickly picking up, one of the chrysanthemums she is arranging. Often Dykeman uses her female characters' silences to send messages. Ivy, challenged, may simply not answer, but in no way does her silence convey acquiescence (33). She may discreetly let a silence fall, unburdened by a need for constant speech (36). Frone and Ivy communicate nonverbally through an articulate volley of looks, such as they exchange when their brother Kin enters, seemingly oblivious of Clay's crisis, talking at length about his latest wildflower garden (39). A female character may also be given the summative word, following an unresolved debate. Aunt Tildy, sitting unobtrusively in a corner, is patching a shirt and listening as Martha and Tom argue at length about what Martha considers extravagance: Tom wants the outward show of wealth a new barn, a house, and an imported stud bull will give him among the men of Thickety Creek, but Martha is distraught at the price they have had to pay for this show—the "richest piece of their bottom land," lost to Cass Nelson (109). Tildy sides with

Martha for retention of family land and against senseless innovation and pretense by snorting: "Menfolks! . . . They've always got to be out resurrecting the world when they've got more problems at home than they can say grace over" (110). It is clear where authorial sympathy lies.

Although Dykeman creates a broader selection of male than female characters in *The Far Family*, her ability to write in male voices is not so convincing as it is in female ones. Phil is the least believable of the *male characters*; he can say all the right words—glossing over trouble where needed or redirecting others' comments into a pleasanter vein, but the reader has little sense of what Phil is like. One does not come to "know" him the way even a marginal character like Miles Austin becomes known, a real-estate broker who thrives on turning undeveloped mountain land into malls and golf courses; or Hugh Moore, Clay's lawyer, who, "clever but never intelligent," flaunts his "influence and grubby knowledge" (*Far*, 77, 79). Passages in which Phil recalls conversations with the two romantic interests in his life, Sherry Austin and Ann Howard, are notably lifeless. Leslie L. Banner says the contemporary sections of this novel are "bland and predictable without the support of the narrative interest which is inherent in an imaginative recreation of the past" (1984, 136). Banner's broad indictment of the modern sections of *The Far Family* is extreme, but does have some validity, especially in scenes where Phil's voice dominates.

The lack of consistent credibility in male voices does not mean, however, that Dykeman has created unsympathetic male characters. Nor does it indicate that she fails to give them dimension—especially Clay, whom Lillian Smith has described as "one of the most complex and interesting characters in contemporary fiction" (1966). Ivy's troubled brother, whose sensitivity and haunted introspection alternate with heavy-handedness, is realistic—and realistically frustrating for his family to cope with. Dykeman confided in W. D. Weatherford that she "tried to balance the destructive personality of Clay, who has lost his roots and appreciation of the earth in our machine civilization, with the constructive influence of Ivy."[3] Clay's self-destructiveness is evident long before his (perhaps suicidal) death. Like Clay, Leck Gunter, the old-timer Ivy encounters at the airport when she goes to pick up Phil, is believable; this section and the later one when Gunter visits Phil to encourage government programs that can "help us help ourselves" are gems (*Far*, 209). In Gunter's character, Dykeman is on home territory; he is a mountain man, like those she interviewed for *The French Broad* and created in earlier fiction, as with "Summer Affair's" Dock Styles (1951). By the time Dykeman wrote *The Far Family* (1966), she had written successfully from a male perspective in

"The Prison" (1948b), and had created compelling male characters in *The Tall Woman* (1962)—Lydia's brothers Paul and Robert, for example, or the enigmatic Doc Hornsby—but the Thurston men more closely resemble Dykeman's lesser portrayals, such as "Summer Affair's" Ben Williams or *The Tall Woman's* static, brooding Mark McQueen. Her disparity in depicting males and females is a flaw in the novel Joseph Wood Krutch otherwise praises as "an absorbing book by a skillful storyteller."[4]

In *The Far Family*, Dykeman not only presents the action through *multiple perspectives*, but departs from the straightforward chronological development of her previous fiction. To do so, she uses *interchapters* and recalled incidents, interweaving past and present through alternating time sequences. Chapter titles ("Today," "Yesterday," "Today and Tomorrow," for example) indicate Dykeman's time sequence. Although Dykeman does not alternate with absolute rigidity, most odd-numbered chapters depict present events (news of Williams's murder and Clay's subsequent hearing, Phil's political aspirations, Ivy's attempts to reconcile family differences, etc.), while even-numbered ones depict the past (events from Martha's marriage to Tom Thurston, Clay's childhood, Ivy's schooling and her memories of Hudson Cortland, her late husband, etc.). Richard Walser praises Dykeman's use of interchapters, saying "these views into the past lend credence to the varied reactions of the brothers and sisters," who are all "immediately distinguishable personalities" (Walser 1966).

The interchapter technique was an innovation for Dykeman, a means of showing characters with a strong sense of "time and the onflowing of time. It doesn't cut off and you can't discard the past and you can't forget the future" ("Dykeman" 1973). Dykeman's skill in *blending present with past* and the deft way she incorporates memory or discusses its function are strengths of *The Far Family*. She opens the novel with a vibrant *sense of place* "perceived through the senses, but . . . maintained in memory as well, serving as a matrix between the past, the present, and the expectation of tomorrow" (Gage 1989, 4). Language and the interplay of chronological settings work together to establish a bittersweet tone in this passage, set in Ivy's consciousness:

> Always in autumn she thought of the farm. No, she did not think of it; she felt it again. The bitter smell of damp fallen leaves, the sight of purple farewell-summer blooming in a random field, the cry of a blue jay high in the noon sky—any of these or a dozen other sensations could bring the farm into the present; breathe the land to life again; dim the smell of gasoline, the sound of motors, the gleam of chrome and glass.

> Even in Paris once, not long ago, walking along the Boulevard Haus-mann, she had stirred a rustle of leaves under her feet and suddenly she heard Papa in the September corn rows of the Sandy Field: "You girls step lively now. Lay by all the fodder we can against a hard winter." (*Far*, 11)

This lyrical recollection draws the reader in with its strong, accessible *sensory imagery*—the blue jay's cry and the acrid aroma and rustle of fall leaves. Further, it initiates an organic connection between the unnamed "she" (Ivy) and the land, a bond that indicates Ivy's function as authorial voice. The allusion to a Paris visit suggests that Dykeman casts her second novel far beyond *The Tall Woman*'s Thickety Creek, at least in recalled experience. Present and past, each with a distinct culture and language, begin their variation here as well: in the middle of Paris, on a street frequented by smart café society, the speaker recalls her mountain beginnings, and being told to "step lively" so as to "lay by" sufficient corn ("fodder") to feed their farm animals.

Several times in *The Far Family*, scenes involving the preparation or consumption of food are *springboards for memory*. Aware of the connection between sharing food and *storytelling*, Dykeman frequently writes scenes that take place in kitchens or around dining tables; she says people gather in this way to share "memories—not just food."[5] Images of sharing food figure repeatedly in Dykeman's work. Jackie and Bert ("The Breakdown" [1948a]) meet Amelia Morris in a diner and exchange life stories over breakfast. The breakfast table is the scene of tension in "The Prison" (1948b), as the unnamed husband's family tries to convince him to take the new job as executioner. Lydia McQueen's community marks most of its *rites of passage*—births, religious gatherings, and deaths especially—by bringing food to share, and telling stories while they prepare and eat what they have brought.[6] *The Far Family*'s Ivy Cortland uses food in an attempt to bring her family together in spirit:

> As the family surveyed the platters and bowls and serving dishes heaped with steaming food, they realized what their sister had done. "Ivy," Frone said, "it's been years since I've had corn pudding!" Her severe face softened as she dipped a serving spoon into the luscious golden crust. "Do you remember how Papa always called corn old two-in-a-hill? How he liked corn and hot biscuits for breakfast?" . . . Kin had taken a helping from one of the long casseroles. "Sweet potatoes." He looked gratefully at Ivy. "You never forgot." (*Far*, 82)

Ivy uses remembered dishes to remind her family that, in spite of sharp differences and present trouble, they are allied by a common past. Soon the Thurstons are relaxed and easy with one another: "They sat at the table and pealed forth laughter as they remembered .... their over-all allegiance to each other remained. And Ivy had used their common memory of big meals together to remind them of the old strong bonds" (*Far*, 84–85). At least for a while, food and memory combine to smooth out family differences and soothe Thurston pain.

More than spurs to memory, scenes at the table are Dykeman's means of inserting images of an international context, the last of the frames Dykeman specifies as important to a consideration of Appalachia. Over dessert at the country club, executives seeking European ties for mountain industries speak of a trip to Holland and Italy, where cheap labor is plentiful (*Far*, 280). In one recalled meal, Ivy is a child in her mother's lap, listening to her uncles relate experiences in Japan and the Philippines during World War II. Uncle Burn tells the children, who are not interested in his political observations on the bombing of Nagasaki, about "a place where bananas and coconuts would cost nothing only to eat them"; Ivy and the others are "lost for a moment in thought of the luxury of unlimited bananas ... rich to the taste, smooth and strange as the tropic lands where they grew" (45). Later, when "tropic lands" are less exotic to the Thurstons, such places enter the conversation again, as Phil discusses his recent travels on a congressional fact-finding mission to third-world countries. He describes the worst moments of the trip—also related to food, although this time a lack of it—among "half-starved people" with "scrawny legs and bloated stomachs and cavernous eyes" (86). He concludes with an observation that, regardless of how little other countries may understand about American culture, "some of our mistakes abroad today" have been more than "foolish" (86). Phil's political experience opens the family dialogue to international issues.

Interchapters set at the turn of the century, as well as memories various family members share while gathered at Ivy's, display the best qualities of Dykeman's earlier work: *The Far Family* is filled with examples of her skill with *description*, her fondness for comparisons to nature, and her rounded depictions of mountaineers. Strong images abound, as when Hawk Williams, fatally shot, "slump[s] down like a rag doll with all the stuffing emptied out" (*Far*, 21). Like the biblical Martha, Martha Thurston is a meticulous housekeeper; Dykeman exemplifies this fastidiousness in "clear lamp chimneys glistening from the soapy water" they are washed in (56). Slaughtering a hog, the

Thurstons scrape its feet "until they were pink and dainty and would cook to a sweet gelatinous mass" (84). Ivy's sister Phoebe, staring out the window and brooding, sees "a moon like a burnished brass boat swimming on the jagged frozen waves of the dark mountains" (233). The sky seems to Clay "a leaden-colored blotter" as his worries increase (316). He has lost his job to "a lousy machine"; his wife has divorced him; and he is accused of a murder he was too drunk to deny (11). The narrator describes Clay as being "full of bourbon whiskey and homesickness for a time that never was" (12).

Clay is further associated with the *image* of an arc, which Dykeman uses to frame *The Far Family*. Early in the book Ivy recalls an occasion when she and her siblings were children and their uncle Burn had given them silver dollars. Possessing actual cash is unusual to them; they are used to raising what they need or bartering for it. One night, as they all sit on the porch steps and watch fireflies "dot the lawn with light," Clay tosses his silver dollar into the air again and again (*Far*, 16). Warned to be careful, he defiantly flicks his dollar into the air once more, and the coin "arc[s] out beyond the men, far beyond the circle of light from the windows . . . into the edge of the yard where snowball bushes and red rambler roses [grow], out into the darkness" (17). Clay cannot find his coin. The next day, everyone looks, but the money is gone. Ivy asks herself, "How could he have just sat there and thrown it away?" (18).

This incident, clearly based on the biblical parable of the talents, is emblematic of Clay: he throws away his gifts carelessly. Later, at the hearing, Homer Bludsoe confesses to Hawk Williams's murder, committed in retaliation for a brutal beating Williams had given Bludsoe's daughter. Free of one of his burdens, Clay rushes to his car, which makes him "feel alive and purposeful and full of authority" (*Far*, 314). Negotiating a sharp mountain turn, Clay takes a chance, just as he has before with his silver dollar. The car jumps the pavement, "arc[ing] out beyond the roadside weeds and laurel bushes" to carry Clay to his death in the chasm below (320). Each time Dykeman combines Clay and an arcing object, there is loss—this time, the more dramatic waste of a man's life.

Dykeman says the passage in which the silver dollar arcs into the darkness is the only one her editors ever tried to change. They felt it was not necessary to the book, but Dykeman did. She wanted to set up the arc image and repeat it at the end of the novel as a frame; this sort of attention to detail pleases her. Dykeman insisted on retaining the scene, and Holt, Rinehart went along with her. She calls this the only instance of "attempted editorial interference" in her work.[7]

As she had previously done in her fiction and nonfiction, Dykeman uses metaphors of nature as a staple of description in *The Far Family*. These comparisons sustain nature as an important presence—almost a character itself—in the novel, and again indicate Dykeman's authorial sympathies with character and situation. A sweater Ivy's Paris concierge wears is "the color and texture of dried walnut hulls," a memory of Ivy's mountain home (*Far*, 11). Ivy describes joy first as something to "hold and taste like a ripe wild berry," then as a gift "delicate as cobwebs" (12–13). Kin, the brother who lives closest to traditional mountain ways, is "as sturdy, ponderous and long-enduring as a locust post" (38), while Aunt Tildy is "as determined as rain" (121). The sawmill, which, *ironically*, makes the Thurstons wealthy as quickly as it creates "raw gaping scars" across mountain forests, sounds "as insistent as a great fly droning over the valley" (177, 167). News in Thickety Creek spreads quickly, "like green on the hillsides" in spring (191). As in Dykeman's other writings, a reversal of nature imagery, or the disaffinity of a character for nature, underscores the narrator's negative view. Manipulative socialite Sherry Austin, never aligned with nature, is "hard and realistic as asphalt" (126). After she revives her old intimacy with Phil, Sherry reveals that some years before, she had aborted their baby without telling Phil she was pregnant; at the time, Phil had neither power nor money, commodities Sherry finds essential.[8] By contrast, Ivy is part and parcel of nature, her name derived from the native ivy that "clings to the mountains" and "comes in the cutover places and covers up the scars with blooms in spring" (1962, 304). Like the stubborn little plant she is *symbolically* named for, Ivy is a healer whose constancy can be relied on.

Knowledge of mountain culture, evident from Dykeman's earliest writing, suffuses this second novel. She once again reveals a mastery of mountain *dialect and idiom* that gives texture to her writing: people tipsy on Bludsoe liquor "raise a ruckus" (*Far*, 185); a considerable distance is "a pretty far piece" (247); when Ivy wants to marry a man from outside their community, her decision "stirs up a commotion" (267). Dykeman laces her characters' memories of Thickety Creek (before the sawmill brings the outside world in to stay) with titles and lines of traditional ballads ("The Twa Corbies" or "Go Tell Aunt Rhody"); she implies characters are forsaking traditional patterns of living by changing their musical references to selections from *popular culture* ("Little Brown Jug" or "The Merry Widow Waltz").[9] Added realism comes in Dykeman's characteristic insertion of *folk beliefs*, such as the cry of a screech owl, which Martha Thurston is sure signifies "bad luck in store" (166). Such connections invariably signify in Dykeman's fiction, whether early or late.

Dykeman weaves her careful description, knowledge of the mountains, and alternating time sequences into a novel that also addresses an important theme of Southern fiction—race relations. *The Far Family* is a vehicle for civil rights themes, explored here in various attitudes expressed about the murder of Hawk Williams. Almost a decade earlier, *Neither Black nor White* (1957), Dykeman's investigation of *contemporary racial attitudes* in the South, had won a Hillman Award as the nation's best book on race relations. Long before she wrote the Bludsoes, a family with African American ancestry, into *The Tall Woman* (1962), Dykeman had also created a short story based on the experiences of a black mother who visits her daughter in Chicago. For her novel with a civil rights theme, Dykeman therefore combines research and imagination.

Oliver Jones designates Dykeman's choosing this theme as "a bold experiment" for 1960s Southern fiction (1989, 27). He states that Dykeman's white characters "either exemplify or refute the *stereotypes* discussed in the nonfiction," and "have attitudes toward blacks that range from blatantly racist to idealistic" (27). Her black characters, Jones feels, are rounded and believable, "neither saints nor savages, but realistic and representative" (27). That she includes them at all is noteworthy. Many of her literary contemporaries dealt with racial conflict by steadfastly writing it out of their fiction, leaving the African American South in domestic positions, in the margins of their novels, or not represented in their work at all.

When she wrote *The Tall Woman*, Dykeman depicted the Bludsoes as victims of prejudice. They are objects of fear and suspicion in Thickety Creek, whose white citizens falsely accuse them of every major crime occurring in the novel. The Bludsoes are guilty of nothing except selling corn whiskey and an understandable preference for keeping to themselves. On many occasions, Bludsoes act as silent judges; they reward Lydia McQueen's acts of kindness and tolerance with anonymous favors (for example, when Mark is away, they do Lydia's hog butchering for her). The Bludsoes are responsible for giving Lydia's character a measure of increased dimension, for they reveal her very human fallibility, not noticeable elsewhere in the novel. She thinks they are behind the outliers' raid; she is clearly wrong, and comes to know it.

In *The Far Family* the Bludsoes reappear, and one of them, Homer, eventually emerges as Hawk Williams's killer. Williams and Bludsoe contrast markedly, a difference Dykeman uses to indicate the variation possible in any group. Williams, despite being the victim of violence, is a man held in contempt by blacks and whites alike: Lorna Williams, Hawk's wife, admits, "Nobody around here to miss anything from Hawk but slaps by those big leather hands he had on him" (*Far*, 148). Although a murderer, Bludsoe discloses a strong sense of ethics; he does not have to save Clay by confessing to Williams's murder. If Clay were prosecuted for the crime, he could not refute his accusers. Bludsoe does confess, however, because, as he says, "I can't let no other man pay my debts" (302). Dykeman meant Bludsoe's sacrificial honesty "to show the personal heroism of a simple man."[10] She wrote to W. D. Weatherford that she "should have had someone point up his heroic and courageous act a little more clearly in the book," regretting that she had not made the positive aspects of Bludsoe's character more obvious.[11]

The Far Family's most telling portrait of race in the 1960s is in Dykeman's depiction of Naomi Henderson, the slender woman who cooks and cleans for Ivy and helps her care for her invalid mother, rather than in Bludsoe and Williams, whose violent clash forces the Thurstons to assemble. As Oliver Jones (1989) has noted, Dykeman provides few details about Naomi. The reader is not aware of Naomi's last name until late in the novel, when it is revealed in an aside by Ivy. The Thurstons call Naomi by her first name, as they do most other black characters, despite her invariably addressing them by title and surname (*Far*, 28). She and Ivy have a long-standing relationship marked by mutual unfailing courtesy and kindness, but Ivy makes many assumptions: Naomi, for example, is expected to take on Ivy's responsibilities for Martha whenever Ivy goes out; unaided, Naomi prepares lunch for all the Thurstons because, as Ivy explains when Frone offers to help, "She doesn't like anyone with her in the kitchen" (309). In Ivy's assumptions about Naomi, as in Lydia McQueen's about the Bludsoes, Dykeman points out how insidious racism can be, infecting the lives of the best intentioned. Even a character as exemplary in other ways as Ivy has internalized some of the prejudice of her place and time.

The closing chapters of the novel suffer to some degree from the blatant antiracist monologues Dykeman gives Homer Bludsoe to deliver at Clay's hearing. Questioned about his reasons for shooting Williams instead of going through the judicial system for justice, Bludsoe bursts out: "Don't none of you know anything? All that's tearing apart this world today between black and white, and you still don't see?" (*Far*, 300). According to Richard Walser, the book's conclusion is "hampered by unnecessary rhetoric and melodramatics," but these flaws comprise, Walser adds, "minor faults in an exciting, excellent work of fiction."[12] *The Far Family* allows Dykeman's readers a look at the complexity of black-white relationships across the United States, and argues steadily for increased tolerance and an end to old inequities. Its labored conclusion to the Williams murder case does not majorly offset the value of what Dykeman set out to do in having her novel address contemporary racial issues.

To her exploration of modern social tensions, Dykeman adds an ecological theme. *The Far Family* would hardly be a Dykeman novel if it did not touch on her concern for proper use of the earth. Her work through the decades challenges her readers to be stewards of the land, and cautions them to avoid the "twin hazards of chauvinistic boosterism and impatient despair" which can undercut their efforts for regional progress (Dykeman 1977,41). Pollution, clear-cut timbering, and unchecked development are environmental dangers confronting the Thurstons. These problems were just coming to notice in the mountains at the time depicted in Dykeman's first novel, where Lydia McQueen dies after drinking water from a tainted spring. In *The Far Family*, though Ivy is the main speaker for *environmentalist causes*, Martha and Phil join her in working to protect the land.

Martha Thurston is the daughter most like her mother, Lydia, not only in physical appearance but in her philosophy. She dominates the even-numbered chapters of *The Far Family* just as Ivy Cortland does the others. When her husband, Tom, zealous about making money and reputation in Thickety Creek, builds a sawmill and slices down trees all around them, Martha protests: she is certain the scars he leaves on the land are not worth whatever money they provide. Like many other mountain women in Dykeman's literary landscape, she turns to the Bible for guidance. Finding a passage instructing man to multiply and replenish the earth, she says to her daughter:

> I want your papa to read that verse. It doesn't mean just multiplying your own kind, I know it doesn't. It means to replenish the earth of all you wrench from it, multiply the fruits instead of just subtracting them. Oh, I feel somehow that this timbering of his is all wrong. He can't just take from the land and never give back. (*Far*, 163)

Martha's protests are wasted on Tom. By the time their children have grown, people whose prime concern is for their bank accounts rather than any responsibility for the environment have proliferated. Where a meadow ringed with trees once stood, Ivy Cortland goes to meet her son at the airport. Mountain ways and values have almost been left to memory; many now see them as antithetical to the brand of "*progress*" they seek for Nantahala County.

At the airport Ivy encounters Leck Gunter, an old-time mountain man who in this passage serves, with Ivy, as guardian of the land. He seeks an interview with Phil, hoping to persuade the young senator to enact legislation protecting the mountains while there is still something left to protect. Gunter bemoans the destruction that men like Miles Austin have already brought to the county, with their unquenchable thirst for more and more country clubs and industrial parks. The old mountaineer attests to the dilemma all modern people must deal with when he says, "We stirred up a strange beestand before we knew the price of the honey" (*Far*, 24). Neither Gunter nor Ivy wants to return to the previous century; one result of the dubious progress both of them worry about is its "honey," after all. They know, too, the difficulty of maintaining a delicate balance between the land and the practical needs of the people it must sustain. Something else they see, as Austin and his cronies do not, is that more is not synonymous with better. Both Ivy and Gunter are determined to exert their energies to protect the natural resources of their Appalachian homeland. Dykeman uses Gunter again later to voice the complexity of land-use issues. Establishing his ties with the Thurstons by recalling that he once worked for Tom, Gunter tells Phil, "[Ivy's] papa had his big sawmills [in Thickety Creek], kept half of us in the valley in good jobs" (207). His memory of the financial security the lumber business provided counterpoints Martha's protest to Tom.

Encouraging her son to write legislation mandating careful use of mountain resources, Ivy tells him the only way to repair the destruction that has already come to Appalachia is with a "new dimension for life," which she defines as "hardcore optimism, the tough faith that life is worth preserving" (*Far*, 334). She advocates preserving the vigor of nature as an antidote to those with "tough wizened hearts . . . and big, lazy tender minds" who have put personal gain above their obligation to succeeding generations (334). When Phil leaves for Washington, he affirms his responsibility to his mountain heritage: "If I can know my family . . . well enough, maybe I can understand people on the other side of the world, too" (333). He further determines to promote wise use of regional and national resources. The novel ends on this note of promise.

Because of the critical response to Dykeman's first three books, *The Far Family* was reviewed widely. Reviewers in Massachusetts, Illinois, Colorado, and North Carolina agreed on Dykeman's ability to create "rounded, recognizable characters caught up in a situation with some relevance to the kinds of lives we live" (Walser 1966). Writing for the *Chicago Tribune*, author and activist Lillian Smith expressed her view that the book was a "new kind of regional novel" with a "skilled avoidance of stereotypes" and concern for "the deep meanings that events of our times have for all of us" (1966). This avoidance of stereotypes, along with a sophisticated treatment of regional problems, marks all of Dykeman's mature work.

The Far Family is satisfying Dykeman fiction, both for her popular audience and for the literary critic. It offers the faithful reader some favorite Dykeman hallmarks and characters, while introducing several satisfying stylistic innovations. The author courageously tackles sensitive racial themes and, avoiding pat solutions, speaks out for increased human understanding. Her purpose in writing the novel was to show "the interrelationship of all life—forest and factory, man and woman, Negro and white, earth and air and beast, the poor and proud and the affluent and influential" (Bone 1966, 713). In this book Dykeman places her confidence in the public's desire for more than a recasting of her first, very successful novel. She asks her readers to discard narrow notions of Appalachia as a peculiar part of an isolated, rural past, peopled exclusively by stereotypes. Such views are to Dykeman "artificial barriers by which people cut themselves off from the understanding of the wholeness of life" (Bone 1966, 713). While questioning several contemporary definitions of social and environmental progress, *The Far Family* presents the people and problems of the Southern Appalachians in a fresh national and international context of modernity.

For my students, whose class reports, essays, and student activities served as culminating activities for our study of Dykeman's modern novel, our explorations had dual significance. Not only did our work enable them to discover the literary and thematic devices embedded there, but it helped my group of novice teachers to prepare for a shared future in which all of us would benefit—just as Wilma Dykeman urges her readers to do in this saga of the Thurston family. Through their work with her novel, Appalachia reached out to the Rockies.

Notes

1. Dykeman is always meticulous about details, and says she can toy for months with a character's name before arriving at one with the precise connotation she likes (Dykeman, interview by author, 14 March 1992).

2. Hereafter cited in text as *Far*.

3. Wilma Dykeman to W. D. Weatherford, 15 March 1966, Weatherford Papers.

4. Walser Papers.

5. Wilma Dykeman, interview by author, Winston-Salem, North Carolina, 14 March 1992.

6. Dykeman intentionally departs from depicting a rite of passage as a food/memory-sharing ritual in *The Tall Woman* in Lydia McQueen's final illness with typhoid fever. She

wished to show McQueen's "impact on the community by having them stop by with memories alone"; the possibility of McQueen's loss shocks Thickety Creek out of its accustomed pattern of taking food to the home of the deceased (Dykeman interview, 14 March 1992).

7. Wilma Dykeman, interview by author, Asheville, North Carolina, 10 March 1989.

8. Close female-male relationships form an important part of each of Dykeman's novels, but she does not depict scenes of physical intimacy in any detail. When she does introduce intimate scenes, as in the ones between Sherry Austin and Phil Cortland, or the one Ivy overhears between Martha and Tom Thurston, she typically depicts sex used as a weapon: Sherry wants proximity to social power as a Washington wife; Tom suggests his wife "invite him to a party" as a reward for his support in her claim to the McQueen family home (*Far*, 47).

9. Dykeman provides insight into characters through differences in the songs they select: Martha, firmly religious, wants Phoebe to sing "Beulah Land" or "No Dark Valley"; Tom, who avoids religious ceremony whenever possible, prefers "Shanghai Rooster Got No Comb" (*Far*, 132). Literary choices, too, are encoded with insights about incident or character. Ivy, falling in love with an older man, Hudson Cortland, wants to read *Jane Eyre*; Dykeman signals his suitability for Ivy by making Thoreau's *Walden* his favorite book.

10. Dykeman to Weatherford, 15 March 1966.

11. Ibid.

12. Richard Walser, 27 March 1966, Walser Papers.

References

Banner, Leslie L. 1984. *The North Carolina Mountaineer in Native Fiction.* PhD Diss., University of North Carolina. Ann Arbor, MI: University Microfilms International, 1986.

Bone, Larry E. 1966. Review of *The Far Family*, by Wilma Dykeman. *Library Journal* 91 (1 February): 713.

Borland, Hal. 1962. "Lover of the Land." Review of *The Tall Woman*, by Wilma Dykeman. *New York Times Book Review* (1 July): 18.

Dykeman, Wilma. 1948a. "The Breakdown." *Southwest Review* 33:260–65.

———. 1948b. "The Prison." *Prairie Schooner* 22:203–9.

———. 1951. "Summer Affair." *American Magazine* 152 (3): 42–45, 130–33.

———. 1955. *The French Broad.* New York: Rinehart.

———. 1962. *The Tall Woman.* New York: Holt, Rinehart and Winston.

———. 1966. *The Far Family.* New York: Holt, Rinehart and Winston.

———. 1977. "Appalachia in Context." In *An Appalachian Symposium: Essays Written in Honor of Cratis D. Williams*, edited by J. W. Williamson, 28–42. Boone, NC: Appalachian State University Press.

Dykeman, Wilma, and James Stokely. 1957. *Neither Black nor White.* New York: Rinehart.

"Dykeman: Writer Resents Regional Label." 1973. *Louisville Courier-Journal and Times.* 29 April.

Gage, Jim. 1989. "Place in the Fiction of Wilma Dykeman's *The Tall Woman*." *Iron Mountain Review* 5, no. 1 (Spring): 3–7.

Hoyle, Bernadette. 1954. "An Asheville Author Talks Shop." *Raleigh News and Observer*. 15 August, sec. 4: 5.

Hudson, Lois Philips. 1966. Richard Gaither Walser Papers, 4168. 3 June. Wilson Library, University of North Carolina.

Jones, Oliver K. ("Chip"). 1989. "Social Criticism in the Works of Wilma Dykeman." Master's thesis, University of North Carolina.

Smith, Lillian. 1966. Review of *The Far Family*, by Wilma Dykeman. *Chicago Tribune*, 17 June, B12.

Walser, Richard. 1966. "Strong People in Family Saga." Review of *The Far Family*, by Wilma Dykeman. *Raleigh News and Observer*, 31 July.

Walser, Richard, Papers. 4168. Southern Historical Collection, Wilson Library, University of North Carolina, Chapel Hill.

Weatherford, W. D., Papers. 3831. Southern Historical Collection, Wilson Library, University of North Carolina, Chapel Hill.

NINE

Fred Chappell's *I Am One of You Forever*
as a Subject for Literary Analysis and an Alternative
Image of Mid-Twentieth-Century Appalachia

RICKY L. COX

SET IN WESTERN NORTH CAROLINA AROUND 1940,
Fred Chappell's *I Am One of You Forever* (1985)[1] is the first in a series of four
short novels centered on the immediate and extended family of Jess Kirkman,
the book's narrator and central character. Despite occasional reminders that
the story is being told by a grown-up Jess in early middle age, the point of
view is primarily that of Jess as an observant, thoughtful boy between ten and
twelve years old, who is equally at ease hoeing corn and reading prose transla-
tions of Homer. Jess narrates the three succeeding novels as well, which carry
the reader through the deaths of both parents. Although at times limited to
relating stories in which he plays no part, he functions throughout the four
books as the keeper and interpreter of this fictional family history.

In addition to its virtues as a depiction of the Appalachian region, *I Am
One of You Forever* is a rich and rewarding novel for thesis-driven literary analysis by college-level writers. Thanks to an unusual structure and an array of
easily perceived and delineated themes, a book that is complex enough to challenge the most perceptive graduate student is also easily divided into coherent
pieces, in sufficient size, shape, and variety to be accessible and appealing to
the least confident of college freshman writers. It can be argued, for example,
that the book is actually a collection of short stories and not a novel at all,

despite the front cover statement to that effect. It is undeniably a story of coming-of-age and maturation, but just *who* is maturing, young Jess or the men with whom he spends most of his time, is a matter of opinion. Thanks to a string of elaborate practical jokes and regular bits of comic dialogue, *I Am One* is at times hilarious, but it is also a deeply sad story, due not only to the death of a beloved central character, but also to the overtly empty or simply unexplained lives of a string of visiting relatives. Even the pronoun references in the title, which appears to be Jess's answer to a question asked of him in the last sentence of the book, may be debated by readers. *I Am One of You Forever* is both simple and complex in its use of plot and in its development of characters, both adolescent and adult in its outlook and appeal, and both conventional and experimental in its themes and structure.

The second portion of this essay contends that *I Am One of You Forever* offers to teachers and readers an image of mid-twentieth-century Appalachian life and people that may serve as complement or counterpoint to the darker, better-known pictures drawn by writers like James Still in *River of Earth* ([1940] 1996), set in Eastern Kentucky around 1930; and Harriette Arnow in *The Dollmaker* ([1954] 2009), which takes place in Eastern Kentucky and Detroit during World War II. Each of the ten positive attributes described in Loyal Jones's ([1975] 1996) post–War on Poverty essay "Appalachian Values" may be identified within the characters and relationships of *I Am One*, albeit in forms broadened or diluted, depending upon one's perspective, by formal education. At the same time, Chappell offers an illuminating contrast to novels like the two named above, which depict families at the mercy of an industrial-based economic system they can neither control nor comprehend, and divided within themselves about whether to cling to the old ways or embrace the new. Apart from the immediate threat of World War II, the future is open-ended for Chappell's surprisingly modern Kirkman family, whose understanding of the encroaching outside world and chances of success within it are enhanced by formal education (both parents are college graduates) and brightened by economic resources that are, while modest by today's standards, considerable compared to those of the Baldridge family in *River of Earth* and the Nevels family in *The Dollmaker*.

Writing About I Am One of You Forever

For lack of a better organizing principle, this discussion of topics for literary analysis begins with the cover, and from there mirrors the sort of guided randomness that characterizes many class discussions. One idea leads to another, but as will be seen, the same illustrations may be used to develop distinctly different theses, so class discussions of *I Am One* are deliberately and naturally somewhat circular, regularly revisiting scenes or characters from a different perspective. Unless otherwise noted, all these topics have been handled successfully and often creatively at least once, some many times, in thesis-driven analytical papers of between three and five typed pages by freshman composition and American literature survey students.

THE COVER

The initial reassurance or relief students may derive from the relative brevity (184 pages) of *I Am One of You Forever* is enhanced by a cover that, like the book behind it, is both simple and complex. The front of the 1987 Louisiana State University Press paperback edition, which has to date been readily available, suggests a sampler quilt, with sixteen blocks depicting farm tools, buildings, and animals in silhouette, as well as stylized floral patterns that appear to be traditional quilt squares. A grapevine stencil edges the top and bottom of the front cover and extends across the spine and back cover. The dominant red and dark green give the whole thing the inviting, wholesome look of a pastoral-vineyard-themed Christmas wrapping paper. The first time I used this book in a freshman composition course, an accountant in her forties who had returned to school to study art and was herself an avid quilter, found a literal, metaphorical, or symbolic connection between each "block" of the cover and some aspect—setting, action, or character—of the book. The grapevine border she explained as subtle but ever present, set apart from the other images but also enclosing them, in the way that alcohol is a constant though not always conspicuous presence in the lives of the major characters.

ALCOHOL

While the observation of alcohol's recurring presence was only a small part of one student's analysis of the cover art, the dual nature of alcohol as both a destructive force and a cultural touchstone within the Kirkman family and the Appalachian culture around them is an interesting topic by itself. Abuse of alcohol is among the assumed causes behind a sudden trip by Jess's mother to help her brother Luden in California in the introductory unnumbered chapter, "The Overspill." Uncle Luden Sorrells, the only living sibling of Jess's mother, has three failed marriages and an unsuccessful relationship with Alcoholics Anonymous behind him when, early in the book, he drives cross-country from California for an extended family visit. The admiration Jess has for his freewheeling uncle, who at age sixteen fled the repetitive toil and social isolation of a mountain farm on a patched-up motorcycle, is mixed with pity by the time Luden clears the empty wine and liquor bottles from his room and heads back to the West, the victim of a practical joke devised by Jess's father, who has had his fill of the antics of the "prodigal son" and breathy phone calls from his numerous lady friends. In the first numbered chapter in the book, "The Good Time," readers meet Johnson Gibbs, an eighteen-year-old hired hand/foster child who was taken from alcoholic parents and raised in an orphanage. Storekeeper Virgil Campbell, a good friend of Joe Robert Kirkman, is so well known as a drinking man that local church members regularly stop in to exhort and harangue.

Alcohol appears in a more positive light as part of a bonding ritual during a family picnic planned and led by Uncle Luden, who insists, "Everybody has got to have some of this California wine. Comes from up in Sonoma" (*I Am One*, 40). Narrator Jess, who chooses this moment to remind readers that he is a middle-aged man inside whom ten-year-old Jess is himself only a memory, recalls that "it was the first wine of any sort I'd sipped and it has lingered always in my mind. Wine still tastes for me of the mountaintop of piny woods with a warm spring dawn coming on, and that Spanishy word, *Sonoma*, is an exotic flavor all to itself" (40). Jess is offered wine by an adult a second time on a fishing trip with his father, who cautions, "You can have some of this if you don't tell your mama" (155). But when Joe Robert is offered moonshine whiskey by the man who rents them a boat and is himself an alcoholic with no home or family, boundaries are reset and taboos reinstated as Joe Robert explains, "You can't have any of this. Your mother wouldn't leave me an inch of hide" (160). Though many students refer to one or more of these scenes in writing about rites of initiation and ways of achieving belonging, few choose the role of alcohol as their primary topic, since it requires the piecing together of scattered clues, and perhaps because they are in the process of setting their own boundaries with alcohol, now that rules established by their own fathers and mothers are no longer enforceable.

Reader Expectations and the Suspension of Disbelief

One of the most interesting class discussions of *I Am One of You Forever* invariably occurs after students have completed the first reading assignment, through the end of chapter 3, "The Beard." In this chapter the Kirkmans are visited by Uncle Gurton, a man whose past and family connections are apparently well known to Jess's maternal grandmother, with whom the Kirkmans live, but remain a mystery to Jess and his father, partly because Gurton answers all questions by shaking his head or nodding and smiling. The lone exception to this method of communication is a single absurd and unvarying sentence spoken at the conclusion of each meal. After Joe Robert and Jess give their guest buttermilk laced with horse tranquilizers in order to examine and measure the legendary beard tucked inside the bib of Gurton's overalls, the beard begins to grow, eventually filling the house and pouring out the windows and chimney. Before the two escape by sliding down the banister, they see in or atop the mass of flowing beard a variety of fantastic things, including a mermaid, two Indians paddling a canoe, and a white whale.

The range and intensity of reactions to the final scene in this chapter have always set the stage for a class discussion that at least begins to establish important precedents for subsequent discussions of the book: (1) It's fine to express confusion or dislike of some part of the book; (2) others probably share those feelings; and (3) visceral responses to creative work may have rational causes that can be isolated, discussed, and perhaps even resolved, at least to the extent that a viewer/listener/reader may be able to appreciate at least some aspect(s) of the work. The discussion of this scene and of readers' responses to it has never led directly to the formulation of suitable paper topics, but the strangeness of this scene, whether it delights, puzzles, or shocks, invites students to consider two essential components that the supposedly passive reader brings to the experience of reading, the one being prior experience, and the other expectation based upon that experience.

A faceless, nameless narrator is the one figure in story, film, or print we've been taught to trust absolutely from our first hearing of the phrase "Once upon a time, . . ." When a reader is suddenly caused to question the reliability of the narrator, reactions range from momentary disorientation to irritation to anger at having been personally betrayed by the breaking of an ancient and unspoken agreement. Since most college students are well acquainted with fantasy and science fiction, the fact that the story of the beard could not really have happened is not what troubles them. The problem is that something this fantastic shouldn't have happened almost a third of the way into book in which nothing beyond the realm of ordinary possibility has so far occurred. Examples of popular movies can be found to illustrate the fact that the limits on the reality of a story's setting, however tame or outrageous they might be, must be established early in the story and then strictly adhered to if the writer or filmmaker wishes to invoke the principle Coleridge described as the "willing suspension of disbelief," upon which students have a firm practical grasp, whether or not they can name or explain it.

This could be a place for teachers with sufficient understanding of magical realism, in which unrealistic events occur without the requisite warning in seemingly realistic settings, to introduce it into the discussion. Since I lack the background to pursue it with any authority, and since Chappell himself denies that as his intention (Lang 2000, 208), I do no more than mention it as a possibility. Some students with prior interest in magical realism have pursued this line of thinking on their own, but not always successfully, since this and other fantastic scenes in the book have other plausible explanations. I have found it more profitable instead to ask the class to reconsider their contention that nothing unrealistic has happened prior to the episode of the beard. It doesn't take long, with a few hints, for the last paragraph in the very first chapter, "The Overspill," to be recognized as equally fantastic, but for some reason so readily acceptable as to pass by completely unnoticed. In this scene, described later in more detail, a tear on Jess's mother's cheek expands until it absorbs both Jess's parents, and then Jess himself, who then swims through the tear toward his waiting parents.

Why does a shark-infested beard stop many readers short, when a floating tear the size of a backyard swimming pool is accepted without a murmur? The difference, someone will explain, is that the tear is a symbol and not a real tear at all. Because a tear represents love, sadness, pity, and joy, all of which are appropriate to a scene in which a young mother is reunited with her husband and son, the scene is plainly not meant to be interpreted as having actually happened. Rather than wrestle with the unsettling implications of a literal interpretation, most readers move on without a second thought.

Beards, on the other hand, may evoke strong associations, both personal and popular, for the average reader, but the variety of these associations, and the opposing natures of some, disqualify a beard as a universally recognized symbol of any single or group of closely related qualities or emotions. This conclusion is illustrated by soliciting examples of individuals or types of people associated with beards. Santa Claus and Abraham Lincoln suggest security, dignity, and wisdom; but Charles Manson and Osama bin Laden and other similarly notorious bearded figures suggest something else entirely. Since an unconscious comparison yields no single unambiguous match with a familiar symbol, readers may be compelled to conclude that the beard and its contents have to be taken as real, and the events concerning it must be happening as described. Since what is described is impossible, within the ordinary realm of possibility established by the apparent absence of fantastic elements in the first one-third of the book, either the narrator we trusted is unreliable, or characters who have appeared to us as people who think and feel much as we do despite their different circumstances, are in truth radically and perhaps dangerously different from us. Or the world they live in, which appeared at first to be only an earlier and more rural version of our own, may not be the same world at all. In any case, everything we thought we knew about this place and the people who live there is suddenly not so certain. Hence, a set of widely shared expectations, based on, first, the universal, implicit trust in a narrator; second, a shared intuitive understanding of the boundaries of the willing suspension of disbelief; and, third, a common storehouse of basic symbols, may account for the fact that most readers accept without hesitation a giant tear, but reject out of hand a magical beard.

Exactly how "The Beard" *can* be explained is left open-ended. Some writers suggest that Jess is simply describing a dream, induced by years of speculation about Uncle Gurton's legendary beard and compounded by Joe Robert's fascination with the same subject. Others propose that Jess's imagination, overheated by this lamp-lit, nighttime escapade, simply runs away with him and turns an old man's silvery, flowing beard into a magical body of water inhabited by people and animals transplanted from the books he reads. Still others, who may have some background in the folktale tradition of Appalachia, suggest that this is a deliberate tall tale, inserted by the grown-up Jess to tease the reader. So far none have taken this to the next level and considered that it is neither young Jess nor the adult Jess, but Chappell himself who is in control, but this would be an interesting line of inquiry for students with the time or inclination to study Chappell's poetry and/or his other works of fiction.

Novel or Collection of Short Stories?

A popular and comparatively risk-free group of related paper topics arises from another controversy that comes up in class discussions of the book's second half, in which students inevitably and very reasonably ask how Johnson Gibbs, a central character who is killed near the middle of the book, can reappear as a living character in subsequent chapters. As was just seen, aspects of the book that initially irritate students tend to generate good class discussions and can lead, albeit indirectly, to sound topics for analysis.

In taking up the question of chronology, students can always name at least one recent film or book in which events are presented out of chronological order, and can usually explain a director's or author's apparent purpose in doing this. Among students who maintain that events must be presented in the order of their actual occurrence, some are merely skeptical of any aesthetic benefit that would make the initial confusion worthwhile. A few feel betrayed (again) by a narrator already under suspicion because of the beard episode. But by this time they will have read the second italicized, unnumbered chapter, "The Telegram," in which an unopened telegram from the army is destroyed or hidden away separately by Jess and each of his parents, yet reappears each time on the kitchen table. Finally, faced with Jess's resolve to accept its message of Johnson's death, the telegram turned into a yellow rose, whimpered, and "tumbled down a hole in the darkness" (*I Am One*, 95). Having perhaps consciously considered the symbolic possibilities of telegrams, roses, and even the color yellow, they may now be more at ease with the blurring of lines between what really happened, how it was perceived by a young boy with a powerful imagination, and how it is remembered and told decades later. (As reluctant as some students are to engage in such abstract speculations, I am always grateful that they at least refrain from dampening the discussion by pointing out that *none* of it really happened.)

Some perspective on this second violation of literary convention, the narration of events out of order, can be gained by asking students to jot down memorable events in their own childhoods. This usually shows that principles other than strict chronology, such as associations with people, places, and other events, can influence the order in which we might narrate the events of our own preteen lives, even though this involves the relatively recent past for most college students.

Though, as noted before, few students are interested in exploring the complex relationship between narrator and reader, many do go on to develop a topic stemming directly from the discussion of chronology, once it has been pointed out that conventions of time order, as applied to most novels, do not apply to short story collections. Part of the appeal stems from the extension of literary concepts, such as plot and character development, typically explored in high school literature courses. Students of a decisive and perhaps linear nature quickly latch on to either of two theses, the first being most popular: (1) Despite the statement on the cover of the book that *I Am One of You Forever* is "A Novel," it is actually a collection of related short stories. (2) Although *I*

Am One of You Forever has many features characteristic of a collection of short stories, it is accurately described as a novel.

For students interested in this debate, but not wedded to a mutually exclusive interpretation, I suggest a defense of the notion that it is both a novel and a collection of short stories, since there is compelling evidence on both sides. Students who settle immediately on an either/or interpretation may be encouraged to attempt something more complex by pointing out that developing a persuasive defense of both ideas will fill up more of the paper's specified minimum length.

Three points for consideration in all three of these arguments (it's a collection of short stories; it's a novel; it's both a novel and a collection of short stories), beginning with the forthright cover statement that the book is "A Novel," can be discerned without actually reading a single page. This could tempt weaker students to write the paper without reading carefully, but we've read more than half the book by the time this topic emerges. Announced quizzes on the first and second halves of the novel, each covering about ninety pages, also help students complete the book before committing to a specific topic. But the fact that these same three bits of evidence are so concrete, almost like physical clues, no doubt encourages some students to choose and follow a path of development that appears, at least at first, to be clearly laid out and easily followed.

Clues within the front matter of the book include the acknowledgment that "parts of this book first appeared—often in radically different form—in . . ." ten separate publications. Since there are only thirteen chapters in all, including three without numbers, this is significant. It would take more research than could be expected of underclassmen to establish an exact portion, but it seems safe for them to assume that at least half the chapters have appeared separately as complete short stories. (In fact, John Lang, in *Understanding Fred Chappell*, says that "at least eight of the ten [numbered] chapters of *I Am One of You Forever* appeared as short stories in various literary journals" [2000, 201]). The table of contents also invites speculation about relationships between chapters as they were modified for and arranged within *I Am One*. As has been mentioned, there are three chapters with titles but no numbers. One is placed at the beginning, one in the exact middle, and the third at the end of ten chapters that have both names and numbers. Further, the text of the three unnumbered chapters is italicized, which breaks up the uniform appearance of the book, though it doesn't necessarily lend itself to either side of the novel vs. collection of short stories debate.

Once the book is actually open, the chronology issue is quite reasonably trotted out as a point against the validity of the novel label. We also consider in class discussion the defining presence of an overarching, continuous plot in conventional novels, whose separate chapters must advance that plot but need not resolve the questions or complications they introduce or further develop. Each short story in a collection, on the other hand, must include not only exposition, but also complication and resolution.

At this point the argument that the book truly is a novel begins at last to gain traction, since most students agree that the whole is greater than the sum of the parts in that at least two overarching and closely related themes, the search for belonging and the process of maturation, are advanced perceptibly in each successive chapter. While *I Am One* lacks an easily identified climax or single point of crisis, the resolutions of individual chapters can be seen to accumulate into a single collective revelation affirmed by the book's title. It might also be argued that any one of several key points does mark a turning point for the entire book. Among these are the death of Johnson Gibbs, the storytelling competition between Joe Robert and Uncle Zeno, and the final paragraph of the book, in which Jess is asked by Johnson Gibbs, "Are you one of us or not?" (*I Am One*, 184) at the close of a dreamlike hunting trip with Johnson, Joe Robert, and Uncle Luden.

The number of characters and the frequency with which each appears can also favor either or both interpretations. Jess and Joe Robert appear in every chapter, and Johnson Gibbs appears or is mentioned in seven of the thirteen chapters, both before and after the family learns halfway through the book of his death in a basic-training accident. Yet three "uncles" and an "aunt," all relatives of the maternal grandmother with whom Jess and his parents are living, each appear in only one chapter and are not mentioned again, before or after. Uncle Luden, the one uncle whose exact relationship to the Kirkman family is known, figures prominently in only one chapter, but is mentioned in at least three others.

Ambiguities notwithstanding, theses supporting the notion that *I Am One* is really a collection of short stories remain the easiest to develop and the most frequently chosen because of the concrete supporting evidence. But supporting the idea that the book also functions as a novel, despite having several identifying qualities of a short story collection, requires the most complex thinking. And choosing the notion of both over either is more consistent with the spirit of the book, which is filled with the sort of ambiguity that leads not to frustration, but rather to an awareness of greater depths of meaning with each subsequent reading or reconsideration. Appreciating new layers of mean-ing in *I Am One of You Forever*, happily, does not necessarily require rejecting or discarding the old ones.

Analyzing Structural Peculiarities

In exploring other topics having to do with the structure of the book, advanced readers and writers have attempted to explain the absence of chap-ter numbers and the use of italic font in only three chapters. These are "The Overspill," which precedes chapter 1; "The Telegram," which appears between chapters 5 and 6; and "Helen," which appears at the end of the book, following chapter 10. Some students have supposed that all three italicized chapters rep-resent dream states or flights of imagination, thus setting them apart from the ten numbered chapters. Although "The Beard" and other scenes disprove the implied assumption that strange things happen only in these three chapters, this notion is valid in that in "The Overspill" a tear on Jess's mother's cheek expands until it encompasses Cora and Joe Robert and then Jess himself, who recalls that "as soon as I got used to the strange light inside the tear, I began to swim clumsily toward my parents" (*I Am One*, 6). In "The Telegram," as already explained, a telegram described as unopened, although its contents have been shared with the reader, magically reappears and changes in size and shape. "Helen," the final chapter, begins with the enigmatic sentence: "It seemed that there were four of us in a hunting cabin high on a mountain near the Tennes-see border" (180). All four males, including Jess, appear to glimpse or dream of a phantom woman identified only as "Helen." Papers attempting this expla-nation are fleshed out with a discussion of the role of the imagination in the novel, as manifested in the possible exaggerations of young Jess, the imperfect memory of the middle-aged narrator, Jess, and the deliberate confusions em-bedded by author Chappell in the shared narrative of Jess the child and Jess the man.

Other explanations advanced for these distinctions include the assertion that "The Overspill" establishes Jess's identity at the beginning of a novel as a child, still bound to his mother but on the verge of shifting his allegiance and identity to the male world of his father. While Jess's mother visits her wayward brother in California, Jess and Joe Robert share the bonding experience of clearing and planting a garden and building an ornamental bridge to reach it as surprise gifts to Jess's mother, only to see it all ruined when an upstream paper mill illegally releases water from a holding pond. Dealing with Johnson

Gibbs's death in "The Telegram" introduces Jess to realities of life that even a close and loving family can neither prevent nor explain. And in "Helen," he is invited at last into the adolescent world through which he'll be led to awareness if not understanding of manhood by the figures who traditionally fill that role: father, older friend, (foster) brother, and uncle.

Belonging and Maturation

At first glance, the processes of achieving belonging and maturing emotionally may seem too similar to treat separately. They do often run on parallel tracks, and the same events can be significant to both. But belonging may be gained or conferred without personal growth, and emotional maturity can be achieved or at least advanced without gaining acceptance in specific groups. Incidentally, the fact that both these processes can be traced through the entire book, especially as they relate to Jess, is among the stronger points in a defense of the idea that *I Am One* functions as a novel.

Although he appears in only a few chapters, the concept of belonging and how it is achieved has regularly been explored as it applies to Johnson Gibbs, the hired hand/foster child liberated from a local orphanage by Jess's grandmother. Following a mock-serious fight the day after their first meeting, Johnson and Joe Robert become fast friends. Johnson is soon at the center of the pranks Joe Robert plays on his mother-in-law, his brother-in-law, and virtually everyone who spends more than a day or two in the Kirkman's home. Johnson Gibbs tells outrageous and mostly transparent lies to Jess and Joe Robert, enlists in the army (before realizing that the Kirkmans will accept him as a member of their family), and contemplates going AWOL to marry a girl he barely knows, all in an effort, conscious or not, to find the family he has never had.

Joe Robert also has issues with belonging, since he feels somewhat like a visitor himself, living with his mother-in-law, working on her farm, and enduring visits by a string of her relatives, while his schoolteacher wife brings in a cash income. His outsider status prods him to indulge in less than grown-up behavior. Although he is the oldest of three males in his household, his level of maturity is repeatedly called into question by his outrageous practical jokes, all seemingly schoolboyish attempts to win the applause of Johnson Gibbs and Jess, who are in effect playmates, although ten and nearly twenty years younger.

On the other hand, Joe Robert's practical jokes also precipitate the departures both of Uncle Luden, whose drinking and womanizing are setting a poor example for Jess and Johnson; and of Uncle Runkin, who brings along and sleeps in his own handmade coffin, and whose creepy presence infuses a funereal atmosphere into the Kirkman household. Joe Robert also uses laxative-laced chewing gum to dissuade Johnson Gibbs, over whom he has no parental authority, from running away from the army to marry a giggly neighbor girl, who is herself seeking escape from an unhappy home life. It can be argued, then, that this man who seems to be immature is actually fulfilling his fatherly duties and entertaining himself, Johnson, and Jess at the same time.

The character most often featured in either of these approaches is Jess, since he has an active part in every chapter, and his thoughts as well as his words and actions are known to us. That Jess is conscious early in the book of his lack of both physical and emotional maturity, and of the belonging the achievement of both states will one day confer upon him, is made plain when a peep-show gift brought to him by Uncle Luden is kept from him by Joe Robert and Johnson:

> That was going to be my whole destiny always, I thought. When I was as old as Ember Mountain they would still be keeping the important things from me. When I was ninety-nine years old and sitting on the porch in a rocking chair combing my long white beard, some towhead youngun would come up and ask, "What's it mean, grampaw, what is the world all about?" And I would lean over and dribble tobacco spit into a rusty can and say, "I don't know, little boy. The sons of bitches would never tell me." (*I Am One*, 33)

The book's title is of course presented as the clincher in a discussion of Jess's desire to fit in, although students seeking something more challenging have made the intriguing argument that it is actually Johnson, or the enduring spirit of Johnson, who speaks this line as a follow-up to his own question, a question that Jess himself has yet to answer.

Between these natural opening and concluding points, in the second (numbered) and final chapters, students cite Jess's longing to participate as coconspirator in Joe Robert's pranks as proof of his desire to belong. The fact that the final prank, planned by Jess and Johnson Gibbs together, is actually on Jess rather than a strange seeming neighbor is offered as proof of his acceptance as an equal. Jess also accepts with enthusiasm his first tastes of coffee and wine, though he cares for neither, in order to fit in. Perceptive students also note subtle evidences of jealousy when Johnson supplants Jess as Joe Robert's playmate, when Johnson is given a fishing rod far better than Jess's own, and when Joe Robert concludes their daylong father-son fishing trip with an emotional expression of his wish that Johnson Gibbs had not been killed.

The same points may be employed in an argument that one or more insights gained from each visitor somehow contribute to Jess's emotional growth. His overcoming of his initial jealousy of Johnson, and then of the girl who steals his adopted big brother away from him, is evidence of his growing maturity, as are his coming to terms with Johnson's death and the conclusions he draws about religion based on his grandmother's quiet, fervent belief, and Joe Robert's encounter with a local fanatic. Overheard and teasingly offered hints about sexuality also fit neatly into discussions of this topic.

In the same way that the role or presence of alcohol is both a useful subtopic and a topic all its own, aspects such as death and religion treated singly offer more challenging topics for students looking for something not so neatly laid out. A few have also looked specifically at the roles of women, and one or two have written memorable defenses of the assertion that Fred Chappell makes frequent and effective use of figurative language and vivid images and other tools of a poet within *I Am One*. A topic that is to me inviting, but as yet untried by my students, would delve into the multiple roles, identities, and functions of the storyteller in a novel whose characters are themselves storytellers, telling stories about stories.

I Am One of You Forever *as an Alternative Picture of Mid-Twentieth-Century Appalachia*

I Am One of You Forever illustrates as well as any contemporary Appalachian fiction what Danny Miller and his coauthors have described as "the willingness, particularly among writers native to the region, to incorporate local and regional beliefs and values into their work [, which] has resulted in a literature that offers insight into the distinguishing values of a particular place and time, even as it exposes the common threads linking lives lived in all places at all times" (2006, 199). Although Chappell has deliberately left undeveloped the characters of three visiting uncles, he avoids both relying upon and perpetuating stereotypes by creating central characters who are clearly of the region yet are universal in their complexity and appeal. At the same time, *I Am One* defies the stereotype of Appalachian homogeneity by reminding readers that Appalachia comprises several subregions. Although these are linked by similar preindustrial histories and numerous shared folk traditions, including music, storytelling, speech, religious practices, and foodways, there are important distinctions to be made between places and people who are no less Appalachian for those differences. Some of these differences, such as economic history, characterize entire subregions, while others may depend upon the personal choices and inclinations of a single family or even of an individual.

Differences in the Impact of Industrialization

The extent to which most inhabitants of a particular part of rural Appalachia were still living relatively self-sufficient, farm-centered lives by the 1940s, and the prospects of those same people for economic success in the post–World War II Appalachia, often hinged upon the presence or absence of commercially exploitable quantities of a single resource, coal. The acreage of a farm and the slope and fertility of its fields would also be factors. This geologic roll of the dice accounts for many differences between the economically stable lives of the Kirkmans in North Carolina and the unsettled existences of the Baldridges in the coalfields of Kentucky and of the Nevels family, first in Kentucky and ultimately in a wartime housing project in Detroit. In much of the Blue Ridge regions of Appalachian Virginia and North Carolina, on the eastern edge of the Appalachians, the change from an agrarian to an industrial lifestyle was neither so sudden nor complete, and the long-term impacts on the economy, environment, and culture were seldom so clearly and irreversibly destructive to all three. Farming remained a viable way of living through the 1940s, as wartime prices improved farm markets and incomes; and well into the last quarter of the century, when part-time farming was frequently combined with full-time work in local industry. Textile and furniture manufacturers, and various light industries fleeing Northern unions, continued to attract rural people, but unlike the coal industry, these industries typically brought raw materials in by truck or rail, or could purchase from local suppliers. High-quality logs for furniture makers, for example, could be supplied by anyone with a saw and a truck, whereas profitable extraction of coal in an increasingly competitive postwar market required expensive, extensive infrastructure and large landholdings adjacent to the processing facility. Industrial-scale timbering was at one time important in parts of Western North Carolina, and while lasting damage was done to huge tracts of land, the short-lived nature of timbering ensured that it would cycle through a sparsely settled region before it had time to permanently mold a place and people into a mirror image of itself. Although timber camps might operate for several years, they were understood to be impermanent. When they relocated, workers would have either to find other employment or to move along with the logging and milling operations.

As improvements in regional highways attracted diversified light industries into mountain towns outside the coalfields, secondary roads and automobiles improved as well, allowing farm families to cling to traditions by retaining family land and farming part-time, while one or more members of the family drew a steady if modest cash wage. And though most of these nonextractive industries have abandoned the Mountain South to exploit even cheaper labor markets, the landscape has been left more or less intact. The mountains of Fred Chappell's 1940s Appalachia may by now have become the sites of the summer retreats of wealthy urbanites, but while these are emblematic of the widening socioeconomic divisions of the twenty-first century and the decline of sustainable mountain communities, this is far better than having all to one's self mountains with the tops flattened and barren.

The single industry actually mentioned in *I Am One of You Forever*, the Champion Paper Mill, is environmentally threatening, since its indiscriminate demand for wood fiber encourages clear-cut timbering. But it appears to be more a nuisance than a direct threat to the Kirkmans. The plant's unannounced opening of a reservoir floodgate destroys a decorative bridge and floods a newly planted vegetable garden, but at least in this instance, no one is injured and no homes are damaged. And Joe Robert's angry observation that this release is illegal has far better and bigger teeth in it than would a similar outcry against a coal operation, for the simple reason that a steady supply of paper, while important, is not perceived to be as important to national interests.

The hundred-acre Sorrells farm Joe Robert works for his mother-in-law, Annie Barbara Sorrells, is not huge in comparison to farms in steeper parts of Appalachia, but the suitability of the climate for tobacco and the presences of large bottomland fields would make farming more profitable in the horse-drawn age, and more viable as mountain farms shifted to tractor power after World War II. Jess notes that "three huge fields stretched in the bottomland along both sides of Trivett Creek. . . . Even standing above . . . you couldn't see the ends of these fields" (*I Am One*, 7).

Differences in Personal Choices and Opportunities

While the vividly drawn characters of the Baldridge and Nevels families have distinct personalities, talents, and ambitions, as families they are typical of the times and places they represent, and would be difficult to distinguish from many of their neighbors in a demographic profile created by a census taker's report. Although they, too, are deeply rooted in mountain culture, Jess's immediate family and his father in particular display attitudes that distinguish them from families more typical of their own place and time, families more truly the counterparts of the Baldridges and the Nevels in family size, educational attainment and aspirations, and attitudes about gender roles and religion. In short, whereas many characters in Appalachian fiction are forced by circumstances to choose between mutually exclusive alternatives—stay/go, agrarian/industrial, rural/urban, traditional/modern—the Kirkmans have had both the luxury and the foresight to make more-deliberate, less-wrenching choices. In this context, ambiguity as it refers to the potential not only to see but also to possess more than a single possibility, continues to be a defining characteristic of this novel.

The Advantage of Education

While the entire community is safely distant from the coal camps of Central Appalachia and the river-dependent textile towns of the Carolina Piedmont, the Kirkmans in particular are insulated from the need to abandon the farm for wages in a garment factory or furniture factory by the qualifications of both parents to teach school. We learn in the second book, *Brighten the Corner Where You Are* (Chappell 1989), that Joe Robert Kirkman and Cora Sorrells met while both were teaching high school, a career that Joe Robert temporarily leaves to run the farm for his widowed mother-in-law. He has returned to teaching by the time *Brighten the Corner Where You Are* begins, several years after *I Am One of You Forever* ends. Along with medical professionals and state and county officials, teachers were among the few people with steady albeit modest cash incomes before World War II in areas that had not yet industrialized. With a favorably situated farm to produce most of what they ate and the cash supplement of a tobacco crop and surplus livestock, the Kirkmans would have been better off than most of their neighbors, as evidenced by their ownership of a Pontiac car, a necessity for Cora's daily commute to the high school, but also a luxury for weekend trips like the family picnic planned by Uncle Luden.

There is little doubt that Jess will also have the relatively wide array of career choices that formal education provided even in a rural community. Unlike the Baldridge children, whose school terms are broken up by their movements between coal camps and their mountain farm; and the Nevels children, who are either tormented for clinging to their rural identities and dialect, or willingly divested of them by the Detroit schools, Jess, as the only child of college-educated parents, reads well beyond his grade level and makes no mention of difficulties at school. Strangely, he seldom mentions school at all, and names not a single classmate or teacher, but it is nonetheless a foregone conclusion that Jess, who is given access to books and the leisure to read them after chores are done, will finish high school and attend college to become, in the words of his aunt Samantha, a scholar "of high renown" (*I Am One*, 173). Neither his grandmother's farm nor the Champion Papermill, which approximate the two choices available to most children in Appalachian fiction set in that era, figures in the getting of his living, except as material for his stories. In this sense, the title of the third book in the Kirkman tetralogy, *Farewell I'm Bound to Leave You* (1996), might have served as well for *I Am One of You Forever*.

Although this is unknown to readers of *I Am One*, Joe Robert's iconoclastic philosophy of education is a central theme in *Brighten the Corner Where You Are*. An excellent if somewhat eccentric teacher, he resigns rather than face a hearing with a school board he assumes (wrongly) to be on the verge of firing him. He is no friend to traditions he sees as outmoded or inconsistent with enlightenment and human progress and is described by John Lang, in his explication of *Brighten the Corner*, as "the enemy of custom" (2000, 231). It is ironic that while he is apparently a fine lecturer, Joe Robert is an abject failure at impromptu storytelling, the folk tradition he most admires.

Shifting Social Norms: Family Size

The setting of *I Am One* of predates by only a few years the beginning of the baby boom in the United States, but the 1940s marked the beginning of a decline in the number of very large families in much of rural Appalachia. As farm incomes were replaced or became supplemental to "public work," large families became economic liabilities rather than the assets they had been when success at farming depended upon the availability of inexpensive, home-grown labor. Jess will eventually have a sister, but the spacing and the number of children put the Kirkmans more in line with the average family of the late rather than the middle twentieth century. Joe Robert even mentions birth control, expressing his hope to Cora, in front of a mystified Jess, that Johnson Gibbs make a stop in "Rubber Junction" on his way "up the Primrose Path to Sweet Perdition" (*I Am One*, 81–82).

Patriarchy

While there are no debates over significant family decisions in *I Am One*, it seems clear that Cora would have more say in such cases than do Alpha Baldridge and Gertie Nevels. This is due partly to the fact that the Kirkmans appear to have compatible natures whereas both Gertie and Clovis Nevels and Brack and Alpha Baldridge are poorly matched, at least in terms of their preferences of where and how to make a living. But the fact that Cora has real economic resources and options, apart from the fact that the family is living on her mother's farm, has a part in this as well. An experienced high school teacher, with a single child who is already enrolled in school, her chances of succeeding on her own in a cash-based economy are far better than those of Alpha or Gertie. Ironically, with the help of like-minded children and extended family, both Alpha and Gertie demonstrate that they *could* survive on their own, at least at a subsistence level. But neither could think of separating from her husband, since the imagined social consequences seemed worse than the real physical and mental misery, for themselves and their children, that result from submitting to their husbands' decisions about where and how they should live.

This is not to say that Joe Robert is totally at ease with his situation. He lives in his mother-in-law's house more or less by her rules, and works her farm under her direction. Even the income that results directly from his farmwork is not exactly his, since the milk and calves they sell, along with tobacco, all belong to Jess's grandmother. Joe Robert delights in testing his mother-in-law's patience, as well as his wife's, with occasional off-color jokes and light-duty swearing, but there is an edge to his humor that goes beyond his innate teasing nature. He refers to his wife's dissolute brother Luden as "the prodigal son" (*I Am One*, 26), and while he is amused by the string of eccentric uncles who drop in for extended visits, he is also annoyed that they contribute nothing to the maintenance of the farm or the family. In addition to less obvious and more noble purposes, the pranks and practical jokes aimed at these nomadic uncles, at Luden, and even at the grandmother herself, offer him a means of asserting his independence and expressing his resentment.

Fred Chappell's novel *I Am One of You Forever* (if it is a novel) is a versatile teaching tool, whether as a rich subject for literary analysis or as a resource for appreciating diverse conditions and individual attitudes within a region whose past, like its people, is often viewed as homogeneous. But to assume, in the first application, that a work so fraught with ambiguity can't speak confidently to a wide variety of readers would be to underestimate a writer of immense talent. And to conclude, in the second application, that Jess and his family are not really typical Appalachians after all, may simply be to concede that they are not *stereotypical* Appalachians. They are people, like people everywhere, whose lives are shaped by the places they call home, but also by the individual wants, needs, and values that distinguish people, one from another, in all places and all times.

Notes

1. Hereafter cited in text parenthetically as *I Am One.*

References

Arnow, Harriette. 1954 (2009). *The Dollmaker.* Reprint, New York: Simon and Schuster.

Chappell, Fred. 1985. *I Am One of You Forever.* Baton Rouge: Louisiana State University Press.

———. 1989. *Brighten the Corner Where You Are.* New York: St. Martin's.

———. 1996. *Farewell, I'm Bound to Leave You.* New York: St. Martin's.

Jones, Loyal. (1975) 1996. "Appalachian Values." In *Voices from the Hills: Selected Readings of Southern Appalachia,* edited by Robert J. Higgs and Ambrose N. Manning, 507–17. 2nd ed. Dubuque, IA: Kendall Hunt.

Lang, John. 2000. *Understanding Fred Chappell.* Columbia: University of South Carolina Press.

Miller, Danny, Sandra Ballard, Roberta Herrin, Stephen D. Mooney, Susan Underwood, and Jack Wright. 2006. "Appalachian Literature." In *A Handbook to Appalachia: An Introduction to the Region,* edited by Grace Toney Edwards, JoAnn Aust Asbury, and Ricky L. Cox, 199–216. Knoxville: University of Tennessee Press.

Still, James. (1940) 1996. *River of Earth.* Reprint, Lexington: University Press of Kentucky.

TEN

Startling Morals: Teaching Ecofiction with Barbara Kingsolver's *Prodigal Summer*

FELICIA MITCHELL

> Our whole life is startlingly moral. There is never an instant's truce between virtue and vice. Goodness is the only investment that never fails. In the music of the harp which trembles round the world it is the insisting on this which thrills us.
>
> —Henry David Thoreau, *Walden*

> A thing is right when it tends to preserve the integrity, stability and beauty of the biotic community. It is wrong when it tends otherwise.
>
> —Aldo Leopold, *A Sand County Almanac*

TO LEARN WHAT IS WRONG with our environment, and why one ought to think about saving the world, a reader need only turn to a number of treatises, case studies, congressional hearings, and scientific measures giving alarming readings. The Environmental Protection Agency, along with "watchdog" agencies such as Environmental Defense, is more than happy to provide details about the air we breathe, toxins in our streams, and miscellaneous risks humans face if they do not modify certain behaviors. If scientific treatises are difficult to interpret, other environmental nonfiction abounds. Barbara Kingsolver's own *Small Wonder* (2002b) is a popular choice in college courses. Also widely read since its publication is her foreword to *The Essential Agrarian Reader* (2003), edited by Norman Wirzba, an essay that explains how Kingsolver's commitment to the land is exhibited through not only her imaginative writing but also her life's choices, most recently the choice to farm, a choice discussed in, among other writings, *Animal, Vegetable, Miracle: A Year of Food Life* (2007), written with Steven L. Hopp and Camille Kingsolver. Why, then, read Kingsolver's fiction—or any fiction—to learn about ecology? Donna Seaman offers a good rationale:

> Fiction . . . is all about flaws, errors, weakness, and confusion. Stories and novels make room for everyone; and while fiction exposes our faults and failings, it also expresses compassion and finds nobility in our struggles and strengths. Stories can be funny and irreverent. Fiction is more tolerant of ambiguity and contradiction. It asks questions without forcing answers. Fiction is about feelings, not statistics. (2002, 14)

In addition to showing how cooperation with the environment can be beneficial, fiction addressing ecological issues helps readers to strike a balance between emotional reactions to and scientific dimensions of nature.

Ecofiction integrates the goals of the writer with the goals of the ecologist in order to invite a reader to enter an imaginative dimension that not only points out problems with the environment but also entertains the reader, both literally and figuratively, with alternatives. Appalachian fiction traditionally includes references to ecological concerns. The lush landscape of the region can provide a striking backdrop to human interactions, and it can cultivate symbolism to illustrate concerns about the relationship of its inhabitants to the environment. In the Appalachian classic *River of Earth* ([1940] 1989), James Still illustrated conflicts between farming and mining, or pastoral values and change, that have continued to influence Appalachian literature. More recent, Denise Giardina's *Storming Heaven* (1987) provides a provocative examination of the ravages of coal mining on the land and its inhabitants as it shows how women can be empowered by the assertion of alternative choices. One character in Sharyn McCrumb's *The Hangman's Beautiful Daughter* (1992) suffers the consequences of a chemical spill in a river, while another character in *The Rosewood Casket* (1996) is a naturalist whose values educate the reader. According to Elizabeth Harrison (1990), Southern women writers especially have illustrated ways a sense of community can help characters develop relationships with the land that honor cooperation.

These writers with what have come to be called ecofeminist concerns more aggressively assert, according to critic Barbara T. Gates, "the interconnectedness of all living things" as they explore opportunities for social change that will benefit a more inclusive perspective (1998, 20–21). Well before the publication of *Prodigal Summer* (2000),[1] which is situated within her familiar territory of Appalachia, Kingsolver had established a reputation as a literary activist with her fiction as well as her prose. *Animal Dreams* (1990), with multilayered themes addressing Native Americans, US politics, human relationships, and women's strengths, invited its readers to look at complicated relationships we have with the land. When a small farming town addresses the threat of water pollution, the community learns, along with the novel's readers, to be wary of easy solutions. With *The Poisonwood Bible* (1998), Kingsolver took her readers to the Belgian Congo, a country where both the landscape and the hearts of its inhabitants were being exploited by imperialists. The symbolic failure of seeds brought in from Kentucky to thrive in Africa epitomizes the interrelation of politics and nature. *Prodigal Summer* shows that it is possible find equilibrium based on a different paradigm of power struggles, a paradigm based on an ecological sense of community. Building on a perspective that rejects the notion that nature exists solely to serve humans, Kingsolver's fiction invites readers to reflect deeply on alternatives to established practices, especially practices that are harmful to our natural environment and, by extension, human ecology.

With the composition of *Prodigal Summer*, and its choice of setting, Kingsolver was turning her attention to the natural environment of her childhood and the landscape to which she was returning after a period of years spent residing in the Southwest. Her love of the land is exposed with every nuanced detail. "The natural history and culture of southern Appalachia were the most appealing and defining moments of my childhood," Kingsolver has said (Ballard and Hudson 2003, 330). Educated as a scientist with an emphasis on ecology, the writer influenced by her childhood culture would naturally include ecological concerns in her fiction, as well as her nonfiction. "I was trained as a biologist," Kingsolver noted in an interview with Lisa See after the publication of *Animal Dreams*, "so I know intellectually that human beings are one of a number in the animal and plant family. We are only as healthy as our food chain and the environment" (See 1990, 47). Scholar Patti Capel Swartz recognizes this assertion: "Kingsolver's *Prodigal Summer* is concerned with ... destruction, the destruction that has too often been a part of improving agricultural yields or the supposed protection of farm animals from wild predators, and it is very critical of animal and habitat destruction that rises from those areas" (2003). Kingsolver was not being unpatriotic when she commented in *Audubon* shortly after September 11, 2001, that she wished "our national anthem were not the one about bombs bursting in air but the one about purple mountain majesties and amber waves of grains" (Kingsolver 2002a, 41–42). As some use songs to elicit patriotic fervor, she would like her fiction to help others to respect the land that is compromised by the crop dust that burns the nose of a coyote and pesticides that create more problems with pests.

As a writer with ecological and feminist concerns, Kingsolver tends to construct theme-driven novels imaginatively illustrating the moral and ethical directives addressed in her nonfiction. Themes addressed throughout Kingsolver's fiction include, as classified by Sandra L. Ballard and Patricia L. Hudson, "the tension between individualism and one's need for community, the search for justice in an unjust world, and the need for reconciliation between humans and the natural world" (2003, 330). In *Prodigal Summer*, the writer integrates these themes on the first page as the narrator describes forest ranger Deanna Wolfe: "Her body moved with the frankness that comes from solitary habits. But solitude is only a human presumption. Every quiet step is thunder to beetle life underfoot; every choice is a world made new for the chosen. All secrets are witnessed" (*Prodigal*, 1). The moral lesson embedded in a character description introduces readers to a novel that asserts the ecocentric idea that humans are only part of a larger picture. In a review of moral literature, Nancy Pearl affirms Kingsolver's choice to assert such a moral: "A wildlife biologist living alone, an urban entomologist turned farmer's widow, and a feuding pair of elderly neighbors all find themselves connecting to each other and to the natural world they inhabit in a fine ecological balance that must be revered" (2001, 164).

While "ecology" generally signifies "nature," *Prodigal Summer* reminds us that the word more specifically embraces that delicate balance among plants, animals (including humans), and minerals. In her discussion of the book on its website maintained by HarperCollins, in fact, she reminds readers to be wary of the more general term:

> There is no main character. My agenda is to lure you into thinking about whole systems, not just individual parts. The story asks for a broader grasp of connections and interdependencies than is usual in our culture. If you have a biologist in your book club, ask for a definition of the scientific field

of Ecology; otherwise, look it up. (Hint: it has nothing to do with saving the earth or recycling.) Think about why the story's three main narrators are obsessed with what they call ghosts: extinct animals, dispossessed relatives, the American chestnut. In the networks of life described in this story, notice how the absence of a thing is as important as its presence. Notice the sentence that begins and ends the book: "Solitude is only a human presumption." (2012)

Kingsolver's guidance is useful since the novel, a complicated one, is challenging with its narrative structure and interlocking ecological themes.

With no single main character, a narrative strategy to reinforce the interdependence, the novel interrelates three plots with the subtitles that help to ground the reader: "Moth Love," "Predators," and "Old Chestnuts." In addition, as Priscilla Leder reminds us in "Contingency, Cultivation, and Choice: The Garden Ethic in *Prodigal Summer*," the stories invite readers to speculate about a myriad of possibilities, which is a way to reinforce the notion that no one action happens in isolation. Leder writes, "By inviting readers to speculate, Kingsolver reminds us of the delicate, nuanced negotiations—with each other, between biology and consciousness, and between ourselves and our environment—that makes for responsible action, making new worlds for chosen and chooser alike" (2010, 249). Imaginative literature invites readers to reclaim the possibility of hope as it illustrates clearly a web of relationships that links all that is living, from human to tree.

Since its publication in 2000, *Prodigal Summer* has come to serve a number of courses at the college and high school levels, including courses in biology, English, philosophy, environmental studies, sociology, women's studies, and religion (see appendix at the end of this chapter). Its ecological themes serve diverse audiences. At Western Carolina University, Laura E. DeWald, who teaches environmental science courses, has used the novel in an introductory course "to motivate students to read their textbook and think critically about natural resource management issues" (2012). English courses include those in Appalachian Studies, environmental fiction, and survey courses. A course description from Jo Ann Dadisman of West Virginia University for English 252, Appalachian Fiction, exemplifies the spirit of survey courses devoted to Appalachian literature:

This course is designed as an introduction to Appalachian fiction, with an emphasis on critical reading and thinking about the literature of the region.

> The course will attempt to increase understanding of this regional literature by reading what outsiders and insiders have to say about the region, its people and its rich literary heritage; by reading some stories which generally take the oral tradition and both short and long forms of fiction by Appalachian poets, short story writers, and novelists. (2003)

Students end this course, which includes works by Denise Giardina and Robert Morgan, with *Prodigal Summer*. A course in "Literature of the Environment" taught by Renny Christopher of California State University-Channel Islands includes the novel alongside Edward Abbey's *Desert Solitaire* ([1968] 1973) and Ana Castillo's *So Far from God* (1993). At the high school level, the text is seen in college prep and advanced-placement reading lists in both English and biology. The novel's wide appeal suggests that its place in the canon of ecofiction, and Appalachian fiction, is secure.

Ecocriticism: Connecting Ecology and Ecofiction

Teachers can help their students approach *Prodigal Summer* by introducing the tools of ecocriticism to help them make connections between ecology and ecofiction. Ecocriticism, like feminism, includes not one theory but a collection of theories that share a regard for certain literary and environmental ideals. Inspired by the environmentalist movement given momentum by Rachel Carson's *Silent Spring* (1962) and called "literary ecology" initially, "ecocriticism" emerged in the 1970s as a way to connect a growing awareness with the environment with the study of literary texts. In his landmark essay "Literature and Ecology: An Experiment in Ecocriticism," William Rueckert asserted that literary critics should use ecological principles to probe texts. His point was that "ecology (as a science, as a discipline, as the basis for a human vision) has the greatest relevance to the present and future of the world we all live in" (1978, 73). Chris Cokinos has since defined ecocriticism within the field of literary studies as "the critical and pedagogical broadening of literary studies to include texts that deal with the nonhuman world and our relationship to it" (1994). Novels such as *Prodigal Summer*, ecocriticism would assert, play a role in helping humans to understand the balance of relationships as they remind readers to cherish a natural world that is essential for them to continue their own relationships with one another, an assertion particularly important in Appalachia, with its tradition of struggle between humans and the environment.

Ideas illustrated in *Prodigal Summer* are based in a branch of environmental ethics known as "deep" ecology, a perspective that grew out of response to what came to be seen by some environmentalists as "shallow" ecology (Næss). Shallow ecology purportedly focuses on environmental issues as they affect the livelihood and health of people within an ecosystem, with the result being that neither short-term nor long-term solutions may take into account the sustainment of the ecosystem. Ecofiction based in the philosophy of deep ecology counters shallow concerns as it addresses a more egalitarian view of the individual's relationship with nature. General questions raised in *Prodigal Summer* illustrate some basic concerns of deep ecology that can inform a critical approach in the classroom:

- Do all living things, including animal predators and blights to trees, have intrinsic value apart from their relationship to the needs of humans?

- What can humans do to preserve the integrity of ecosystems as they interact with the environment to meet their needs?

- What consequences to the environment do we find when humans assert that it exists solely for their sustenance?

The first question, based in the notion of ecocentrism, is related to the second, which is grounded in the notion of sustainability, while the third reacts to an anthropomorphic perspective. Just as all three competing perspectives abound in theoretical, practical, and literary discussions of the environment, a conscious reader will be engaged at once with centuries-old debates about the relationship between humans and their environment.

All living things, according to *Prodigal Summer*, have intrinsic value apart from their relationships with humans. To reinforce that point, the novel is told with lush references to the physical world that make nature more like another character than a setting or a backdrop to human interactions, in much the same way Wendell Berry has used nature in his fiction (see, for example, *That Distant Land: The Collected Stories of Wendell Berry* [2004]). This natural world, cited by readers and critics as equal to the characterization, is found in a fictional community called Zebulon County in Southern Appalachia that is not unlike Southwest Virginia. In contrast with Appalachian novelist Lee Smith, whose nature imagery often connects readers to the spiritual values of her characters, Kingsolver uses nature to help her reader feel more grounded with the earth and yet connected with something larger than the self at the same time. The mystical power Conrad Ostwalt (1998) attributes to Smith's female characters in their relationships with nature appears as a different kind of power in *Prodigal Summer*. In the mountainous Zebulon National Forest, Deanna Wolfe finds an opulence that she reveres but one that keeps her humble through experience, including the time she captures a moth in her cabin to liberate it, only to find a phoebe swooping down to eat it as she sets it free (*Prodigal*, 184). In the valley, Garnett Walker meets a weed that has escaped his ire one day and admires "its big, slick leaves and bunches of green berries—all that growth accomplished in just four months" (367). Nannie Rawley cuts back blackberry vines to protect her orchard but admires them nonetheless. "You can love them or hate them, either one, but there's no stopping them," she tells Garnett (370). One day when Lusa Maluf Landowski picks cherries, a neighbor stops by to comment that he is surprised that the trees had fruit left on them since he had not "shot all the birds out of there for Cole" (108). When Lusa says, "Miracles happen" (108), she is talking about the miracle of nature.

Just as they need to recognize the miracles of nature, humans must learn to interact with the environment in ways that will help them to meet their needs and the needs of ecosystems, the novel asserts. To that end, hope for the environment must grow from the willingness of humans to become less self-centered and more responsible to the web of life. Thus *Prodigal Summer* symbolically does not have a main character, a feature that reinforces Kingsolver's desire to emphasize the interrelationships embodied in and symbolized by nature—and her assertion that humans share the earth. The characters that invite readers to contemplate ecology are presented in three interlocking narratives from the perspectives of two women and a man who communicate about various subjects with others in the community. These sections weave in and out of one another, with common threads that ultimately connect. Each chapter save the last is marked by subtitles to indicate perspectives. "Predators" focuses on Deanna Wolfe, a reclusive wildlife biologist who works for the National Forest Service and establishes an ethereal relationship with the coyotes in the region, as well as a fleeting relationship with a man who serves as her mate. "Moth Love" presents Lusa Maluf Landowski, an entomologist who moves to a rural community to be with Cole Widener, but then who must make peace with her inheritance of the land and her sense of family when Cole dies. "Old Chestnuts" gives us Garnett Walker, an eighty-year-old farmer whose agrarian values are based on a different value system than those of his neighbor, Nannie Rawley. Just as important as the web of stories is a last chapter that does not have a subtitle, a chapter that takes us back to the scene of the first chapter through the senses of a coyote and that represents the coyotes that have ended up in this part of the world, both predators and prey.

Prodigal Summer suggests that one way to be more conscious of ecosystems is to recognize how theories of natural order operate or can be disturbed. One such theory illustrated in the novel is the Lotka-Volterra model, a theory correlated to an environmental predator-prey theory (Wang, Wang, Chen, and Zhu 2002). This theory helps us to understand how coyotes end up in Appalachia and trees there become extinct. For example, an article in *Audubon* discusses how coyotes, once inhabitants of the West, now live in forty-nine states and are flourishing, despite government-sponsored killing contests of the sort that brings Eddie Bondo from Montana to Zebulon County and into Deanna Wolfe's life. Bob Crabtree, a real-life researcher who studies coyotes with Jennifer Sheldon in Yellowstone, notes, "The more coyotes are attacked by humans, the more they become entrenched. It is easy to view nature as strictly linear—coyotes kill sheep, so we kill coyotes—but the truth is that nature is extraordinarily dynamic. If we stopped killing coyotes, it might actually reduce the coyote population and decrease the kills of sheep" (Finkel 1999). Crabtree and Sheldon think that more coyote pups are surviving to adulthood because the killing of the adults gives them more food. Given their rightful place in the ecosystem, coyotes would function as nature intended them to. Deanna Wolfe believes that, and Kingsolver does too.

Kingsolver interweaves references to coyotes throughout the novel to show different perspectives about them and to assert how they are integral to the damaged landscape of the novel. In its last chapter of the novel, she abandons an anthropocentric narrative voice to help readers address ecological concerns from the point of view of a coyote:

> She had reached the place where the trail descended into a field of wild apple trees, and she hesitated there. She wouldn't have minded nosing through the hummocks of tall grass and briars for a few sweet, sun-softened apples. That whole field and the orchard below it had a welcoming scent, a noticeable absence of chemical burn in the air, that always made it attractive to birds and field mice, just as surely as it was drawing her right now. (*Prodigal*, 442)

As the coyote moves by a "steep, rocky bank that was fetid with damp moss," she ends up in a "nutty-scented clearing where years of acorns and hickory nuts had been left buried under the soil by the squirrels that particularly favored this place, for reasons she couldn't fathom" (*Prodigal*, 442). With the creation of an omniscient third-person narrator that is not human but that offers the insights of a human, Kingsolver reinforces her opening moral and shifts from the three narrative perspectives. Reviewer Marion W. Copeland comments that "through its function in the novel, Kingsolver makes clear that this voice is what has been missing in mainstream literature (though certainly not in a variety of so-called popular genres)" (2001). The pristine setting of the scene described by the coyote is challenged by nearby farms, with the noise and scent of domestic animals, and roads; with the dust of herbicides; and with gasoline fumes that waft up from the road.

When humans assert that the environment exists for them, damage is done. One way Kingsolver illustrates this damage is through references to pesticides and herbicides in the novel. For example, when farmer Garnett goes to the store one day, he sets out to purchase "weed killer, one gallon concentrate!!" along with "malathion (for Japanese beetles!!)" (*Prodigal*, 133). Garnett mourns the extinction of the grand American chestnut tree that once flourished in Appalachia, providing lumber and food and an economic boon until the blight began in 1904. "If he lived long enough," he thinks, "he would produce a tree with all the genetic properties of the original American chestnut, except one: it would retain from its Chinese parentage the ability to stand tall before the blight" (130). Unfortunately, the Japanese beetle—which is not a pest in its native country, where natural predators keep it in check—offers a new challenge to the hybrid chestnut. To illustrate the persistence of nature, there are two old chestnuts growing on the edge of Nannie's land, chestnuts that her father would not allow to be cut down when people panicked over the blight and essentially annihilated much of the stock that could have evolved to adapt to the threat of the blight, which was introduced into the United States by horticulturalists who wanted to breed the American chestnut with its Asian counterparts in the nineteenth century (Exum 1992).

A foil to Garnett Walker's herbicide-fixated character, organic farmer Nannie Rawley has, according to her neighbor Garnett, "not only declared war on the county's Two-Four-D but also on the Sevin dust and other insecticides Garnett was bound and obligated to put on his own seedling trees to keep them from being swallowed whole by the army of Japanese beetles camped out on Nannie Rawley's unsprayed pastures" (*Prodigal*, 86). Garnett may want to bring back the American chestnut in a genetically modified version resistant to blight, but he could learn a few lessons about how to do that from Nannie, who is committed to organic farming. The ongoing discussions of these two characters help to illustrate the possibility of dialogue and hope for the environment. While the debates Nanny and Garnett engage in may offer what Gary MacEoin has called "comic relief" (2001, 20), they also lead the reader into deeper issues. As Garnett and Nanny debate their different approaches to agriculture, the reader learns more about each and learns how compromise is possible. When Garnett learns to temper his antipathy toward Nanny, he finds that she can offer him the best gift of all: a chestnut that has grown in the back of her organic apple orchard, one that has been fertilized by bees the old-fashioned way.

Damage may be done, but hope is an option if the right balance is struck and if humans exercise reason. While the environment suffers when humans assert an anthropocentric perspective, ironically only humans can exercise a sense of moral responsibility to make changes to the environment that will make it compatible with every element involved. With the character of Lusa, Kingsolver illustrates this moral responsibility as she shows how Lusa must cultivate or use her farm in a moral way to make a living after her husband's death—a living that rejects problematic values implicit in her husband's choices and in the choices of good-natured relatives and friends who show up to give advice after he dies. Reading Darwin one evening the way some women read pop psychology for self-help, Lusa finds affirmation for her decision to raise goats instead of tobacco and for her assertion that she will care for the yard as hired helpers tend the farm. When Lusa recalls how she "ripped out every climbing vine from the row of old lilacs so they could bloom again," alongside a memory of how she has asked her helpers to use spades instead of Roundup to clear brush, we see clearly how Kingsolver acknowledges the complicated relationship a person must have with the land (*Prodigal*, 440). Lusa, who mourned the honeysuckle her husband would pull from the barn, begins to take the Darwinian perspective she has used as a scientist and apply it to her practical approach to farming. To live on the land, one must take a few cues from it.

For generations, Southern Appalachia has inspired writers to celebrate both its beauty and the conflicts that have arisen as humans have tried to cultivate the land. *Prodigal Summer* offers a rich resource for discussions of both the beauty and the conflict. Other questions that can guide ecocritical discussions of the novel, and of other novels, include these:

- How does this story illustrate ethical and moral ideals?

- What literary techniques serve the ecological ideals?

- What themes emerge to help guide the reader?

- In what symbolic ways is the environment described?

- How does the writer help the reader to make sense of the relationships humans have with the physical world?

- How does this book add to our understanding of the natural world?

- What sort of ecological perspective (deep vs. superficial) emerges from the text?

While each question inspires an array of related questions, the broad categories can help a discussion remain faithful to the goals of ecocriticism.

The Challenge of Ecofiction

Given the goals of ecofiction and the ideas addressed in *Prodigal Summer*, should ecocritical discussions lead students to believe what Kingsolver believes? There is not an easy answer to that question. Dominic Head acknowledges that ecological concerns can be a challenge to contemporary literary critics and, by extension, students in the classroom. Head suggests that we not lose sight of Lawrence Buell's (1995) sense of the term "ecocriticism" as inquisitive, not prescriptive. The imaginative nature of fiction especially demands that a reader become inquisitive, not necessarily convinced. Barbara Currier Bell also urges caution and asserts that pluralism is essential to courses in environmental literature. She reminds teachers that "consciousness raising" is not the primary goal of such courses (1985, 63). While Bell's concern is a valid one, and it is appropriate to address competing theories, the nature of ecocriticism is such that a reader must entertain value judgments at some point. Patrick D. Murphy reminds us that "the study of literary works with special attention to the representation of relationships among human beings and the rest of the 'more-than-human' world has always been concerned with the agency of human beings and the need for rethinking social behaviors and actions" (2002, 75). "Rethinking" is the key word here.

Writers of ecofiction would suggest that they want students, at the very least, to leave with a clearer understanding of the implications of certain environmental choices—if not a certain sense of enlightenment. In the case of *Prodigal Summer*, "enlightenment" could mean simply that a student comes to care about the characters and their issues, the land and its inhabitants, and the lack of connection often found between humans and nature. It could mean that the student develops a fuller appreciation of Appalachia. "Enlightenment" could also mean that a student decides to learn more about the issues raised, turning from fiction to reports by the Environmental Protection Agency and the like. Rick Van Noy, a professor at Radford University, says, "The most important purpose of environmental literature is to make us think more cogently about our ethical responsibilities regarding environmental issues, to teach us that it is important for people to develop an understanding of the earth and its life forms" (2003, 75). Lizbeth J. Phillips wrote in an essay on Kingsolver's novel for an English course at Virginia Highlands Community College, "We must be critical of the wallpaper that festoons our homes and go out into the world to experience nature. Once we get a real taste for life, we will use our instincts and resources to protect it, not just for ourselves, but for nature as a whole" (2001). Ultimately, *Prodigal Summer* so clearly reveals that every choice has repercussions that its central message—that humans are but one piece of the universal landscape—is not so radical.

Even so, within any classroom, a teacher will find students with diverse ethical principles, some of which will conflict with the ones espoused in *Prodigal Summer* or other novels selected to represent ecological fiction. There will be students who assert that they are different from the moth, the salamander, and the coyote. There will be students who reject the predator-prey theory, especially students engaged with conflicting theories that suggest humans should transcend animal origins and avoid killing even for food. Reading ecofiction, as with any other type of fiction, these students need to feel free to explore ideas rather than to parrot what they sense is a teacher's dogma—or a novelist's—to grow into the conscious thinkers writers such as Kingsolver value. Bell observes, "Ethically, what the pluralistic environmental literature course has to offer students is a fresh chance to debate their criteria for debating right and wrong" (1985, 67). She would assert that a pluralistic model counters bias by eliciting a range of responses to a text such as *Prodigal Summer* during class discussion. Another way to address diversity would be to present a range of texts that address different theories. Companion texts for *Prodigal Summer* in a general literature course might well include Yann Martel's *Life of Pi* (2002), a novel that implicitly confronts certain notions of the predator-prey theory. Within a course devoted solely to Appalachian literature, a companion text could include Robert Morgan's *Gap Creek* (1999), a novel set in an earlier time that could give a sense of context to some of the changing attitudes toward nature in Appalachia with its descriptions of the struggles between humans and the natural world.

"I have to believe that, don't I?" Barbara Kingsolver said once when asked if she felt her writing could make a difference. "What keeps me going is the hope that I might be able to leave the world a little more reasonable and just. I grew up in the '60s when convictions were fashionable. We believed we could end the war just by raising a ruckus. I've been raising a ruckus ever since" (See 1990). The words of reviewer Gwen Glazer may be relevant if criticisms of the value-laden fiction she writes to raise a ruckus arise in the classroom: "Critics who look down on Kingsolver for not being subtle admittedly have a point, but they are also missing the mark by condemning her for it. Just as it's unfair to dismiss a story as fluff because it's entertaining, it's unfair to dismiss a story as preachy or schoolmarmish because it has an obvious message" (2000). In addition, Seaman notes, "Kingsolver's tightrope act reminds the critic that novelists driven to write by strong moral convictions have to walk a thin line between proselytizing and telling a convincing story, between burdening characters and ideas and allowing them to emerge as complex, fully dimensional personalities the reader will care about" (2002, 19). A successful "tightrope act," *Prodigal Summer* deftly illustrates the idea that the best way to save the world we live in is to open our eyes to its lessons, its beauty, and its wonder. What better setting than Appalachia, a region symbolizing both pristine nature and compromised landscape, for a reader to be drawn into that lesson? It is a lesson that Kingsolver continues in her most recent novel, *Flight Behavior* (2012), and one that readers internationally need to address.

Note

1. Hereafter cited parenthetically in text as *Prodigal*.

References

Abbey, Edward. (1968) 1973. *Desert Solitaire*. Reprint, New York: Ballantine.

Bakopoulos, Dean. 2000. Review of *Prodigal Summer*. *Progressive* 64 (December): 41–43.

Ballard, Sandra L., and Patricia L. Hudson, eds. 2003. "Barbara Kingsolver." In *Listen Here: Women Writing in Appalachia*, 330–37. Lexington: University Press of Kentucky.

Bell, Barbara Currier. 1985. "Environmental Literature: An Approach Emphasizing Pluralism." In *Teaching Environmental Literature: Materials, Methods, Resources*, edited by Frederick O. Waage, 63–72. New York: MLA.

Berry, Wendell. 2004. *That Distant Land: The Collected Stories of Wendell Berry*. Washington, DC: Shoemaker and Hoard.

Buell, Lawrence. 1995. *The Environmental Imagination: Thoreau, Nature Writing, and the Formation of American Culture*. Cambridge, MA: Harvard University Press.

Carson, Rachel. 1962. *Silent Spring.* New York: Houghton Mifflin.

Castillo, Ana. 1993. *So Far from God.* New York: Norton.

Cokinos, Christopher. 1994. "What Is Ecocriticism?" Western Literature Association Conference, Salt Lake City, Utah. 6 October.

Copeland, Marion W. 2001. "Review of Barbara Kingsolver, *Prodigal Summer*: A Novel." H-Nilas, H-Net Reviews. February. http://www.h-net.msu.edu/reviews/.

Dadisman, Jo Ann. 2003. English 252 course description. http://www.clc.wvu.edu/r/download/44245.

DeWald, Laura E. 2012. "Getting Students to Read and Think: Using Popular Literature in an Introductory Natural Resources Course." 2012 Biennial Conference on University Education in Natural Resources. Colorado State University, Fort Collins, 23 March.

Exum, Ellen Mason. 1992. "Tree in a Coma." *American Forests* 98 (November–December): 20–31.

Finkel, Mike. 1999. "The Ultimate Survivor." *Audubon* 101, no. 3 (May–June). http://archive.audubonmagazine.org/coyote/index.html.

Gates, Barbara T. 1998. "A Root of Ecofeminism: *Ecoféminisme.*" In *Ecofeminist Literary Criticism: Theory, Interpretation, Pedagogy,* edited by Greta Gaard and Patrick D. Murphy, 15–22. Urbana: University of Illinois.

Giardina, Denise. 1987. *Storming Heaven.* New York: Norton.

Glazer, Gwen. 2000. Review of *Prodigal Summer,* by Barbara Kingsolver. *Flakmagazine* 15 (December). http://www.flakmag.com. Site discontinued.

Harrison, Elizabeth Jane. 1990. *Female Pastoral: Women Writers Re-Visioning the American South.* Knoxville: University of Tennessee Press.

Head, Dominic. 1998. "The (Im)Possibility of Ecocriticism." In *Writing the Environment: Ecocriticism and Literature,* edited by Richard Kerridge and Neil Sammells, 27–39. London: Zed Books.

Kingsolver, Barbara. 1990. *Animal Dreams.* New York: HarperCollins.

———. 1998. *The Poisonwood Bible.* New York: HarperCollins.

———. 2000. *Prodigal Summer.* New York: HarperCollins.

———. 2002a. "Saying Grace." *Audubon.* (January–February): 40-42.

———. 2002b. *Small Wonder: Essays.* New York: HarperCollins.

———. 2003. Foreword to *The Essential Agrarian Reader: The Future of Culture, Community, and the Land,* edited by Norman Wirzba, ix–xvii. Lexington: University Press of Kentucky.

———. 2012. "FAQ." Barbara Kingsolver. Accessed 18 July. harpercollins.com

———. 2012. *Flight Behavior.* New York: HarperCollins.

Kingsolver, Barbara, with Steven L. Hopp and Camille Kingsolver. 2007. *Animal, Vegetable, Miracle: A Year of Food Life.* New York: HarperCollins.

Leder, Priscilla. 2010. "Contingency, Cultivation, and Choice: The Garden Ethic in *Prodigal Summer.*" In *Seeds of Change: Critical Essays on Barbara Kingsolver,* edited by Priscilla Leder, 233–49. Knoxville: University of Tennessee Press.

Leopold, Aldo. 1949. *A Sand County Almanac: And Sketches Here and There.* Oxford: Oxford University Press.

MacEoin, Gary. 2001. "Nature Triumphs in Novel Buzzing with Life." Review of *Prodigal Summer*, by Barbara Kingsolver. *National Catholic Reporter* (November): 19–20.

Martel, Yann. 2002. *Life of Pi*. New York: Harcourt.

McCrumb, Sharyn. 1992. *The Hangman's Beautiful Daughter*. New York: Scribner's.

———. 1996. *The Rosewood Casket*. New York: Dutton.

Morgan, Robert. 1999. *Gap Creek*. Chapel Hill, NC: Algonquin Books.

Murphy, Patrick D. 2002. "The Four Elements and the Recovery of Referentiality: Ecocriticism as Pivotal Localist Theory." *Studies in the Humanities* 29 (1): 70–82.

Naess, Arne. (1973). "The Shallow and the Deep, Long-range Ecology Movement: A Summary." *Inquiry* 16:95–100.

Ostwalt, Conrad. 1998. "Witches and Jesus: Lee Smith's Appalachian Religion." *Southern Literary Journal* 31 (1): 98–110.

Pearl, Nancy. 2001. "The Moral of the Story: Fiction of Conscience." Review of *Prodigal Summer*, by Barbara Kingsolver. *Library Journal* 15 (April): 164.

Phillips, Lizbeth J. 2001. "The Truth about Wallpaper: The Illustration Revolution in *Prodigal Summer*." Class essay, Virginia Highlands Community College, 1 March.

Rueckert, William. 1978. "Literature and Ecology: An Experiment in Ecocriticism." *Iowa Review* 9, no. 1 (Winter): 71–86.

Seaman, Donna. 2002. "Many Shades of Green, or Ecofiction Is in the Eye of the Reader." *TriQuarterly* (Summer): 9–28.

See, Lisa. 1990. "Barbara Kingsolver: Her Fiction Features Ordinary People Heroically Committed to Political Issues." *Publishers Weekly* (31 August): 46–47.

Still, James. (1940) 1989. *River of Earth*. Lexington: University Press of Kentucky.

Swartz, Patti Capel. 2003. "Expanding the Tradition: Resistance in Denise Giardina's *Storming Heaven* and *The Unquiet Earth* and Barbara Kingsolver's *Prodigal Summer*." Appalachia Wired: Webs of Diversity Conference, Marshall, West Virginia, 6–8 March.

Thoreau, Henry David. (1854) 1906. *Walden; Or, Life in the Woods*. Boston: Houghton.

Van Noy, Rick. 2003. "Teaching American Environmental Literature Abroad." *Academic Exchange Quarterly* 7, no. 4 (Winter): 72–75.

Wang, Zong-Ling, Fei-Zhi Wang, Shang Chen, and Ming-Yuan Zhu. 2002. "Competition and Coexistence in Regional Habitats." *American Naturalist* 159 (5): 498–508.

Wilson, Jennifer. 2000. Review of *Prodigal Summer*. *Literal Mind*. http://literalmind.com/0080.html. Site discontinued.

Appendix: Sample Courses Requiring *Prodigal Summer*

English 1B: Composition and Reading. Berkeley City College. Peralta Community College. Berkeley, CA: Terri Tricomi, Instructor.

English 386/586: The Rhetoric of Literature, The Effects of Story. University of Wisconsin, Oshkosh. Oshkosh, WI: Marguerite Helmers, Instructor.

English 399W: English Honors Seminar. Representing the Environment: Literature and Ecocriticism. Queens College. Flushing, NY: Frederick Buell, Instructor.

English 475: Southern Environmental Writing. University of Mississippi: Jay Watson, Instructor.

English 3534: Literature and Ecology. Virginia Tech University. Blacksburg, VA: Marie C. Paretti, Instructor.

English/Women's Studies 4950: Women in Popular Culture. Georgia College. Milledgeville, GA: Mary Magoulek, Instructor.

First-year Experience Seminar. Can Literature Save the Environment? Skidmore College. Saratoga Springs, NY: Michael Marx, Instructor.

First-year Experience (Engaging the Liberal Arts): The Human Animal in Literature. Emory & Henry College. Emory, VA: Jim Harrison, Instructor.

Literature 499-5: Ecocriticism. College of New Jersey. Ewing, NJ: Larry McCauley, Instructor.

Philosophy 122: Environmental Ethics. Bellevue College. Bellevue, WA: Erick Haakenson, Instructor.

Rhetoric 8520: The Rhetoric of Biodiversity (Ethics, Aesthetics, Ecosystems). University of Minnesota (Twin Cities). Minneapolis, MN: Dan Philippon, Instructor.

Theology, Ethics, and Spirituality 4: The Christian Tradition. Santa Clara University. Santa Clara, CA: Sally Vance-Trembath, Instructor.

Women's Studies 582: Junior Seminar (Women, Plants, and Politics). Allegheny College. Meadville, PA: Catharina Coenen and Judith Rose, Instructors.

Women's Studies/English 4950: Women in Popular Culture. Georgia College. Milledgeville, GA: Mary Magoulek, Instructor.

PART FOUR

Appalachian Poetry and Prose

ELEVEN

Appalachian Poetry: A Field Guide for Teachers

R. PARKS LANIER JR.

WHERE ARE THE APPALACHIAN POETS? A glance at a map of the Appalachian region as defined by the Appalachian Regional Commission (ARC) will provide one answer. The Appalachian poets are, or have been, where the mountains in the eastern United States are. That is an incomplete answer, however, for even an ARC map may not show all the mountains or even the entire length of the Appalachian Trail northward into Maine. Not all the mountain counties of Virginia, for example, are included within the ARC's domain.

Not all poets fit neatly within the ARC's boundaries. Fred Chappell has spent most of his career at UNC-Greensboro, off the map. Jim Wayne Miller wrote a great deal while professor of German at Western Kentucky University, off the map. David Huddle is at the University of Vermont, off the map. Marilou Awiakta has lived for many years in Memphis, Tennessee, off the map. Jeanne Shannon is way, way off the map in Albuquerque, New Mexico. But no one can challenge their credentials as "Appalachian poets," though they, unlike Jesse Stuart of Kentucky, who lived, wrote, and died in W-Hollow, are "off the map." All these poets named were born within the ARC's domain, but there are many others who were born "off the map" but migrated into the mountains and identified with more than mere geography. The author of this article is one of them.

Where Does One Read the Work of Appalachian Poets and Find Commentary about Them?

There are quite a few anthologies that feature their work, and now a growing number of critical volumes aid in their appreciation. For many years, the Higgs and Manning *Voices from the Hills* (1975) was a classroom fixture. In 1995, Higgs, Manning, and Miller prepared its two-volume sequel, *Appalachia Inside Out*.

Also useful are Edwards, Asbury, and Cox's *A Handbook to Appalachia* (2006); Miller, Hatfield, and Norman's *An American Vein: Critical Readings in Appalachian Literature* (2005); Ballard and Hudson's *Listen Here: Women Writing in Appalachia* (2003); Mitchell's *Her Words: Diverse Voices in Contemporary Appalachian Women's Poetry* (2002); Smith and Judd's *Wild Sweet Notes: Fifty Years of West Virginia Poetry* (2000); Dyer's *Bloodroot: Reflections on Place by Appalachian Women Writers* (1998); Williamson and Arnold's *Interviewing Appalachia: The "Appalachian Journal" Interviews* (1994); Baber, Lyon, and Norman's *Old Wounds, New Words: Poems from the Appalachian Poetry Project* (1994); Lyon, Miller, and Norman's *A Gathering at the Forks: Fifteen Years of Hindman Settlement School Writing* (1993); Lanier's *Poetics of Appalachian Space* (1991); Quillen's *Looking for Native Ground: Contemporary Appalachian Poetry* (1989); Thomas's *The Uneven Ground: An Anthology of Appalachian Materials* (1985); and Askins and Morris's *New Ground* (1977).

All teachers of Appalachian literature should consider subscriptions to *Appalachian Journal* (Appalachian State University) and *Appalachian Heritage* (Berea College). From the latter, back issues dedicated to specific poets are available. Both journals feature contemporary poetry, critical reviews, and critical analyses.

Annual celebrations of individual Appalachian writers at Emory & Henry College have resulted in the annual *Iron Mountain Review* (edited by John Lang), featuring such poets as Maggie Anderson, Kathryn Stripling Byer, Fred Chappell, David Huddle, George Ella Lyon, Jeff Daniel Marion, Michael Martin, Michael McFee, Jim Wayne Miller, Robert Morgan, Ron Rash, George Scarbrough, James Still, and Charles Wright. See also Lang's *Appalachia and Beyond: Conversations with Writers from the Mountain South* (2005), as well as his *Six Poets from the Mountain South* (2010).

What Are Some Distinguishing Characteristics of Appalachian Poetry?

Some superficial and uninformed readers might think that Appalachian poets are just Southern poets, and let it go at that, not realizing that

Appalachia has both southern and northern extensions (the Appalachian Trail extends from Georgia to Maine). As one looks closely at Appalachian poetry, however, especially that which is represented in anthologies, three clear areas of concern emerge: the *political*, the *pastoral*, and the *personal*. Teachers and students will delight in identifying "pure" examples of each kind and then, as their acquaintance with Appalachian poetry grows, they will delight in identifying the metaphorical mingling of these elements. The way these three elements are blended in the crucible of Appalachian experience and history is what distinguishes Appalachian poetry from other regional poetry.

If the poet takes a *political* stance, he or she puts art at the service of a cause, often ecological (anti–strip-mining, for example). Poems by Don West and Bob Henry Baber are fine examples, and also the "Brier poems" of Jim Wayne Miller. Poets who take a *pastoral* stance are intensely lyrical in celebrating the mountains and mountain people. The risk here is too much nostalgia and sentimentality. Some of the best work of Jeff Daniel Marion, Fred Chappell, Louise McNeill, and also Jim Wayne Miller are to be found here. Poets who take a *personal* stance write about their own feelings, personal history, psychological history, sexual history, or religious history in an Appalachian context. James Still's "Heritage," which says "I shall not leave these prisoning hills," is an archetypal example for thousands more.

The tone of a *political* poem is often belligerent, hostile, or aggressive—argumentative in the best sense. Bob Henry Baber's *A Picture from Life's Other Side* (1994) offers excellent examples. The *pastoral* poem is usually mildly "conversational" in tone, often tinged with melancholy. There is a great range of tone among *personal* poems, but usually they are intimate and confessional.

Mountain dialect, if it is used in a *political* poem, suggests an antiestablishment attitude, a rejection of language related to exploitation. In a *pastoral* poem, mountain dialect may suggest the superiority of primitivism or suggest a holdover from the Old Country, invoking the myth of mountain dialect as Chaucerian or Elizabethan English or tying it to the ballad tradition. In a *personal* poem, dialect may be something the poet has worked to overcome, something that held parents or grandparents back. The reprinting of Ann Cobb's *Kinfolks and Other Selected Poems* ([1922] 2003), edited and introduced by Jeff Daniel Marion, gives readers an opportunity to consider dialect poems from an earlier era.

Characters in *political* poems may appear as victims of an oppressive economic system. Miners with black lung, mothers on welfare, injured military veterans, or displaced farmers interest the poet. Characters in *pastoral* poems may appear to be quaint old-timers who play dulcimers, sew quilts, or make gardens. They work hard and die with dignity. Chappell's "My Mother's Hard Row to Hoe" comes to mind. In *personal* poems, male poets may present themselves as atavistic good ol' boys. Women may recall the blessed or baleful influence of grandmother, mother, or aunt on their upbringing and character. Poets may also use relatives (cousins are very convenient) as "masks" for themselves, or as emblems of their hidden second-selves.

Home or the homeplace is a powerful consideration. For the *political* poet, if there is a cabin in the laurel, it is usually threatened by a bulldozer, by gigantic power lines, or by faceless mass-produced plastic bric-a-brac. The homeplace of a *pastoral* poet may be falling down, but memories keep the boards in place better than nails. Jim Wayne Miller's elegiac "Small Farms Disappearing in Tennessee" (Higgs and Manning 1975, 350–51) is characteristic. The *personal* poet often echoes the sad paradox of Thomas Wolfe's "You can't go home again."

Nature—the mountain forests, plants, streams, and animals—serves the *political* poet as contrast and counterpoint to disruptive industrialization. Nature accuses the despoilers. *Pastoral* poets enjoy nature for its own sake. There is an interest in exact description and accurate naming of animals and plants. The task here is not to be cliché about babbling brooks. For the *personal* poets, outer nature mirrors or contrasts inner feelings. A storm on the mountain means inner turmoil as well.

Time is an important topic. For the *political* poet, today without the menacing bulldozer is better than tomorrow with it. For the *pastoral* poet, yesterday is likely to be better than today. For the *personal* poet, there may seem to be no tomorrow; yesterday may well be a pain in the brain.

Religion may be of little interest to the *political* poet unless it serves political or social ends. Jim Wayne Miller's "The Brier Sermon" (1997) is a famous example of Appalachian polemic couched in the style of religious oratory. *Pastoral* poets relish old-time religion—hymn singing, deep-water baptizing, Bible reading by lamplight. For the *personal* poet, religion may be an index of doubt or questioning rather than deeply held faith.

To summarize, *political* poetry at its best is calm and reasoned argument. At its worst, it is shrill and illogical. *Pastoral* poetry at its best is sensitive and thoughtful. At its worst, it is sentimental and full of stereotypes. *Personal* poetry at its best is full of insight into what it means to be human. At its worst, it is purely a gut-spilling ego trip for the author. As these three strands are shaped in the shadow of the mountains, intertwining like the laurel and the rhododendron in the hollows, poetry with a unique voice emerges.

Where Might Teachers Focus Their Attention?

Appalachia is a nest of singing birds. Every month seems to bring new songsters. In the recently published *Encyclopedia of Appalachia* (1,832 pages; Abramson and Haskell 2006), however, only seventy-two pages are devoted to literature. Among those pages, fewer than two dozen poets receive full (half a page or less) treatment. These are likely the poets whom you will study because students can easily find supplemental material about them on the Internet. In alphabetical order they are:

Marilou Awiakta, who combines Native American Cherokee topics and concerns with contemporary issues of technology and environment. "An Indian Walks in Me," her signature poem, says, "Long before I learned the / universal turn of atoms, I heard / the Spirit's song that binds us / all as one" ([1978] 2006, 14). Her books *Abiding Appalachia: Where Mountain and Atom Meet* ([1978] 2006); and *Selu: Seeking the Corn-Mother's Wisdom* (1993) offer profound poems in the pastoral and personal traditions as lovely and as inspiring as her native east Tennessee (See Grace Toney Edwards's chapter in this collection, "Teaching the Poetry and Prose of Marilou Awiakta".)

Kathryn Stripling Byer, who served as poet laureate of North Carolina from 2005 to 2009, is famous for her Alma poems, first in *Alma* (1983), then in *Wildwood Flower* (1992), which tell the story of a mountain woman's survival. Byer's is a strong and sensitive voice in the personal and pastoral traditions. In her *Black Shawl* (1998), the poem "Mountain Time" declares, "Up here in the mountains / we know what extinct means" (ix). And "New Hat" recalls how "its ribbons knot under my chin / like the goiter my grandmother / hid under lace collars / when there was company" (10).

Fred Chappell, who also served as poet laureate of North Carolina, has won many major national honors for his poetry. He collected four volumes into *Midquest* (1981), which contains his famous Mother, Father, Grandmother, and Grandfather poems. One is the hilariously exaggerated "My Father's Hurricane," about a "right smart blow" named Bad Egg that "blew the lid off a jar of pickles we'd / Been trying to unscrew for years" (116–20). Chappell perfected the personas of "Ol' Fred" and Virgil Campbell as quintessential Appalachian voices. A prolific writer, he masterfully blends pastoral and personal traditions, sometimes with a satirical twist in which readers delight, as in *C* (1993), one hundred epigrams suggesting Chappell is a mountain Martial.

Doris Diosa Davenport, who is an Affrilachian poet with north Georgia roots (see Theresa L. Burriss's chapter on Affrilachian writers, "From Harlem

Home to Affrilachia: Teaching the Literary Journey," in this collection), writes in the personal and the political traditions, celebrating the beauty of her native region and power of its working people.

Nikki Giovanni, who emerged in the 1960s and 1970s as a voice of African American activism, finds now in Virginia much that is attractive in the pastoral traditions of her native Tennessee region, but that interest has not diluted either her strong personal presence in her poetry, or its political significance. She likes but has not adopted the term "Affrilachian."

George Ella Lyon, who began with a chapbook, *Mountain* (1983), is a prolific Kentucky writer in the pastoral and personal tradition (*Catalpa* [1993]), a singer of songs, a lover of language, a teller of stories whose "My Grandfather in Search of Moonshine" (1993, 11–12) is a lesson in how a great Appalachian poem need not indulge in stereotypes.

Jeff Daniel Marion, who began with *Out in the Country, Back Home* (1976), is esteemed for poems in the pastoral and personal tradition that capture the essence of east Tennessee rural life, especially those collected in *Ebbing and Flowing Springs: New and Selected Poems and Prose, 1976–2001* (2002). His collection *Letters Home* (2001) is a collection of tender, sometimes sad but sometimes humorous, poems about the World War II period.

Marion's earlier volume *The Chinese Poet Awakens* (1999) shares with Larry Smith and Mei Hui Huang's *Chinese Zen Poems: What Hold Has This Mountain?* (1998), Edwina Pendarvis and Harry Grieg's *Like the Mountains of China* (2003), and George Scarbrough's collection of poems in memory of Han-Shan and his friend Shi-te, *Under the Lemon Tree* (2011) a witty fascination with China and the ancient Chinese as subject and persona. (See also Charles Wright below.)

Michael McFee, who published *The Napkin Manuscripts* in 2006, essays on his work as a poet, and on the work of fellow North Carolinians Chappell, Byer, and Morgan, has five collections of poetry to his credit. Students admire *Sad Girl Sitting on a Running Board* (1991) for its expansion of the personal tradition into profound meditations on the transcendent.

Emma Bell Miles (1879–1919), who is numbered now among the earliest significant Appalachian voices, had one collection of poetry, and that posthumous, *Strains from a Dulcimore* ([1930] 2001). Feminist studies honor her struggle against poverty, neglect, abuse, and ill health in the Tennessee mountains to create a lasting body of work.

Jim Wayne Miller (1936–1996), who was a professor of German outside the region, nevertheless captured its essence from memories of his North Carolina mountain upbringing in such collections as *Copperhead Cane* ([1964]

1995) and *Dialogue with a Dead Man* ([1974] 1978); *The Mountains Have Come Closer* (1980); and *Brier, His Book* (1988). With the Brier, Miller created a persona whose political savvy combined with pastoral lyricism is unsurpassed in Appalachian poetry for its edgy sensibility and elegiac tonalities. The great "Brier Sermon:'You Must be Born Again'" declares, "You don't have to live in the past. / You can't, even if you try. / You don't have to talk old-fashioned, / dress old-fashioned. / You don't have to live the way your foreparents lived.... You don't have to think ridge-to-ridge, / the way they did. / You can think ocean to ocean" (1997, 63).

Robert Morgan, whom Oprah discovered as a novelist, has long turned to his native Western North Carolina for poetic inspiration, from *Zirconia Poems* (1969) to *The Strange Attractor: New and Selected Poems* (2004), fifteen collections in all. His poems, largely in the pastoral and personal traditions, celebrate mountain stories ("Mountain Bride"), family and folk lore ("Death Crown"), mountain history ("The Hollow"), and religion ("Bricking the Church") in an exciting array of poetic forms. His fame as a novelist may eclipse his renown as a poet, but it is as a poet that he has most eloquently defined his native region. (See Robert West's chapter in this collection, "Toward 'Crystal-Tight Arrays': Teaching the Evolving Art of Robert Morgan's Poetry.")

Ron Rash, who draws inspiration from the hills of his native South Carolina and nearby North Carolina, collected poems in *Eureka Mill* (1998) to chronicle a family's move from the mountains of North Carolina to a mill town in South Carolina. The one who speaks these poems, as son and as grandson, translates personal yearnings for a lost pastoral landscape into a subtle parable of the American Dream. Like Thoreau, he warns of "improved means to unimproved ends." (See Erica Abrams Locklear's chapter on Rash in this collection, "Building Bridges with Ron Rash's *The World Made Straight*: Results from One University and High School Partnership.")

Byron Herbert Reece (1917–1958), from north Georgia, was a poet in the meditative pastoral and personal traditions whose first volume was *Ballad of the Bones and Other Poems* ([1945] 1985). Students aware of his suffering from tuberculosis and ultimate suicide are likely to read his poems as premonitions of an unhappy end. The Byron Herbert Reece Society has produced *The Bitter Berry* (1992a), a thoughtful media commentary on his life and work that does much to dispel the melancholy.

Timothy Russell, who often sets his poetry among the industrial mill towns along the Ohio River (he was born in Ohio), collected poems in *Adversaria* (1993). Before that, however, he shared *A Red Shadow of Steel Mills: Photos* *and Poems* (1991) with fellow Ohioans Richard Hague, Kip Knott, and David Adams. Russell's twenty-six poems have Latin titles, such as "In Adversa" and "In Novus Ordo." The latter mentions a family called the Mulkeys to whom Rick Mulkey, author of *Bluefield Breakdown* (2005), belongs. "For now, though, there is hope / sprouting between the bricks / in the Mulkeys' paved playyard / and certainty springing from the hand / of every Mulkey child," Russell prophesied. In 1999, Timothy Russell traveled to Japan as the winner of an Internet haiku contest.

Bennie Lee Sinclair (1939–2000), who was poet laureate of South Carolina at the time of her death, published *Little Chicago Suite* ([1971] 1978), *The Arrowhead Scholar* (1978), *Lord of Springs* (1990), and *The Endangered* (1992). In *Bloodroot: Reflections on Place by Appalachian Women Writers* (Dyer 1998), Sinclair speaks eloquently of her own life and work in Appalachia. Hers is an intensely lyrical personal tradition, as in "Going Blind," which meditates on her diminishing sight. What never diminished, however, was her courageous spirit and steadfast love of the mountains she called home, her beloved Wildernesse in South Carolina.

James Still (1906–2001), who was in the class of 1929 with Jesse Stuart and Don West at Lincoln Memorial University in Tennessee, survived them both. With theirs, his poetry also survives, honored for both its pastoral sincerity— but never simplicity, for his work has much intellectual complexity—and its personal honesty. "I cannot leave these prisoning hills," he declared in "Heritage" (1937), his signature poem. From the foothills of Alabama, he made his way to Hindman in Knott County, Kentucky. In 1937 he published *Hounds on the Mountain*. Novels and collections of fiction followed, but in 1986 *The Wolfpen Poems* and in 2001 *From the Mountain From the Valley: New and Collected Poems* appeared. Mr. Still's preference for "the speech of the folk" informs all his masterful work;

Jesse Stuart (1906–1984), who with James Still and Don West defined a generation of Appalachian poets, was always closely associated with his beloved W-Hollow, Greenup County, in Kentucky. He was nationally famous, however, not only for his short stories, but also for *Man with a Bull-Tongue Plow* (1934), a collection of 703 sonnets (later abridged to 622). Although the book shows a marked fondness for the Shakespearean sonnet, Stuart often introduces variations. Just as he was fond of putting fictional characters up a tree and never getting them down, he sometimes introduces end-words for which he provides no rhyme. A few times, but not often, dialect pronunciation ("windows/cinders") accounts for rhyme. The poems are strongly pastoral, strongly indicative of a love of place, but sometimes there is a personal note, as in "I put away madness like an old shoe. / I said that I would never fight again" (1934, 190). A score of poems, some written as epitaphs, some as voices of the dead themselves, bear characters' names, some male, some female. The narrative impulse was never far away from Stuart, even in poetry.

Frank X Walker, who coined the term "Affrilachia" and who titled his first poetry collection *Affrilachia* (2000), celebrates his African American and Appalachian heritage with other writers, such as Doris Diosa Davenport and Crystal Wilkinson (see Burriss's chapter in this collection). There is no period after the X in his name, symbolizing as it does the silenced names of African slaves. Out of that silence there issues now his clear voice, impassioned but not impatient, a voice speaking eloquently of family and friends, of those whom another poet in another time called "mute inglorious Miltons" who have inspired him to be their voice. Students who read "Death by Basketball," for example, might profitably compare it to "We Real Cool" by Gwendolyn Brooks and "Ex-Basketball Player" by John Updike. All the poems in *Affrilachia* are personal, deeply personal, and therein lies their success.

Don West (1906–1992), who was the college classmate of Still and Stuart, is one to whom the label "political poet" proudly applies. As George Brosi, coeditor of a Don West collection, says of him, "[West] was burned out, shot at, subpoenaed by the House Un-American Activities Committee, chased down mountain highways, and jailed" because he was courageously politically active.[1] Brosi says the publication of West's fourth book of poetry, *Clods of Southern Earth* (1946), earned West the accolade "a Walt Whitman in overalls" from a newspaper reviewer (Hite 1946), but it did not prevent the same newspaper from later attacking him. Sheryl James, another newspaper reporter, said West "sold the most copies of any book of poetry since Walt Whitman's *Leaves of Grass*" (1989); but Chris Green (2005), who reviewed *No Lonesome Road: A Don West Reader* (2004), edited by Brosi and Jeff Biggers, suggests such statistics may have been manipulated by West himself. To Biggers, who also authored *The United States of Appalachia* (2006), West said, "You cannot understand America until you understand Appalachia." Appalachia, it seems, is still trying to understand Don West.

Charles Wright, whose roots are in Tennessee, won the Pulitzer Prize for *Black Zodiac* (1997). It was followed by *Appalachia* (1998) and preceded by *Chickamauga* (1995), the three volumes composing the trilogy *Negative Blue: Selected Later Poems* (2000). Influenced by both Ezra Pound and Emily Dickinson, Wright also shares an affinity for things Chinese with Marion,

Scarbrough, Pendarvis, and Smith (see Marion above). His poem "Waiting for Tu Fu" alludes to an eighth-century Confucian poet. "A Journal of the Year of the Ox" (1986) concerns a visit to Dickinson's Amherst home. "I liked the boxwood and evergreens / And the wren-like, sherry-eyed figure / I kept thinking I saw there," the visitor says. Wright has written that "language, landscape, and the idea of God" are his perennial subjects. In "All Landscape Is Abstract and Tends to Repeat Itself," Wright says, "All forms of landscape are autobiographical," an interesting opinion from one who acknowledges the Appalachian landscape as his own (1997).

Where Else Might a Teacher and Student Look for Interesting Appalachian Poetry?

In a summary called "Post–World War II Poets," *Encyclopedia of Appalachia* (Abramson and Haskell 2006) devotes one paragraph each to nineteen poets who have more than a passing claim to fame. They include:

M. Ray Allen from Virginia, author of *Between the Thorns: Windcarver Songs of Appalachia* (1991) and *Beyond Star Bottom and Other Poems* (2000), poems rich in the personal tradition. The title poem of the latter declares, "I realize / that my old wounds / are still driving me / toward my own blind leap of faith."

Bill Brown from Tennessee, with five collections of poetry, including the latest, *Yesterday's Hay* (2006), who writes in the pastoral tradition and spins memorable stories in an elegant vernacular style. The title poem of *Yesterday's Hay* says, "On the porch hummingbirds / weather the weather. I smell / wet dirt, hear the earth yawn, / feel some mystery underfoot / exhale from a place I've known."

Mark DeFoe from West Virginia, for a decade editor of *Laurel* Review, who has work in six books, including his latest, *Greatest Hits, 1977–2003* (2004). Students will admire "Late Winter Snow: Driving South of Morgantown, WV" at www.wvwc.edu/lib/wv_authors/authors/a_defoe.htm.

Richard Hague from Ohio, who finds unexpected beauty in the gritty urban and industrial world. *Alive in Hard Country* (2003) contains his masterful "Picture of a Steel Mill as a Nativity Scene," with steelworkers "huddled near the great white heated center" of the steel mill like shepherds or magi at the manger "smelting in His first swift hour's heat."

Pauletta Hansel, a Kentucky native and author of *What I Did There*, who, as an original member, named the famous Soupbean Poets centered in West Virginia from 1975 on. Urban Appalachia has a vital place in her poetry. Her website (www.wovenword.com/diviningauthor.htm) says, "Her professional work is now mostly divided between the Urban Appalachian Council, and advocacy, service, and cultural organization serving the descendants of Cincinnati's Appalachian migrants, and Women Writing for (a) Change, a feminist creative writing center that provides time, space, and a supportive community to encourage women and girls in their writing."

David Huddle, from Ivanhoe, Wythe County, Virginia, who taught at the University of Vermont but grounds his poetry in his Appalachian memories. Students strongly identify with the recollections in *Paper Boy* (1979), some of which appear in *Summer Lake: New and Selected Poems* (1999). The recent *Grayscale* (2004) takes its title from a photographer's term, and a photograph inspires its opening poem, "Three Generations of Blue Ridge Mountain Women Speak Across Time." They say, "Our faces must tell you our lives / aren't easy—but difficulty lives / in every heart." But the delightful "Penguin Sonatas" are also part of the same volume.

Louise McNeill (1911–1993), poet laureate of West Virginia and author of *Gauley Mountain* (1939), *Paradox Hill: From Appalachia to Lunar Shore* (1972), and *Elderberry Flood* (1979), who is amply represented by *Hill Daughter: New & Selected Poems* ([1991] 2008). The hill daughter speaks in the title poem, declaring, "Land of my fathers and blood, oh my fathers, whatever / Is left of your hearts in the dust, / I have brought you a son." She did have a son, Douglas, born into a world with an uncertain future. That uncertainty is reflected in the poem's tone. With Marilou Awiakta (see above), McNeill shared a concern about potential nuclear holocaust and baleful technological transformations.

Rita Sims Quillen, from Virginia, who is the author of *Looking for Native Ground* (1989) and two poetry collections, *October Dusk* (1987), and *Counting the Sums* (1995). The title poem of the latter begins, "I must tell them someday / when they are old enough for memory / about the family of twelve / huddled in a creaking cabin."

Bettie Sellers, retired from Young Harris College in north Georgia, who promotes the work of Byron Herbert Reece (see above). Among her many collections of poems, *Morning of the Red-Tailed Hawk* (1981) is exemplary. The title poem is among the "practicing religion" poems in *Listen Here: Women Writing in Appalachia* (Ballard and Hudson 2003). (And see www.bpj.org/index/S.html#Sellers%20Bettie%20M for the *Beloit Poetry Journal* printing.)

R. T. Smith, who currently resides in Virginia and edits the Washington and Lee University review *Shenandoah*. He has many affinities with Ireland, where *Split the Lark: Selected Poems* was published (1999). Emily Dickinson's line "Split the lark, and you'll find the music" introduces the title poem, which continues, "Savage as a raven's beak, / you will find the bliss / that engined into song." *Brightwood: Poems* (2004) is his twelfth book of poetry.

What Poets Emerged after Publication of the Encyclopedia of Appalachia, *or Were Overlooked by Its Compilers?*

Most notably, **George Scarbrough**, of Oak Ridge, Tennessee, was inadvertently omitted. The *Iron Mountain Review* celebrated his work in a spring 2000 "George Scarbrough Issue," so he is not without honor in his region. Students delight in the poetry of *Tellico Blue* ([1949] 1999), and are amazed to learn that Scarbrough was born in 1915. The recent release of *Under the Lemon Tree* (2011), his poems in memory of Chinese Han-Shan and his friend Shi-te, was an exciting literary event.

Jeff Mann's *Loving Mountains, Loving Men: Poems and Essays* (2005) clears new ground for discussion. A half-page *Encyclopedia of Appalachia* (Abramson and Haskell 2006, (1062) literary entry titled "Gays and Lesbians" suggests that though something has been said, much more needs to be said. Mann's eloquent poetry and lucid prose are a good start. West Virginia and Virginia will be proud to claim him.

Diane Gilliam Fisher's *Kettle Bottom* (2004) is inspiring readers in and beyond the region. It is the Ohio poet's third volume. A class reading Giardina's (1987) novel *Storming Heaven* would find Fisher's collection of fifty poems about the 1920–1921 West Virginia mine wars a thoughtful complement. Together, with many voices of many characters (male and female), the poems read like a novel. The title refers to "the petrified tree trunk / buried in the mountain, two, three hundred / pounds. *Drops through the mine roof / . . . Kills a man / just like that.*" It is a metaphor for all of life's uncertainties waiting to fall, perhaps even to kill.

Amy Tipton Gray's chapbook *The Hillbilly Vampire* (1989) has a reputation far larger than its slender forty pages. The wit and the satire of the poems leave readers marveling, laughing, or tearing their hair. As North Carolina novelist Amy Cortner, the poet has recently risen from the grave of academia to delight readers yet again.

Tennessean **Jane Hicks** is another poet whose fame and reputation have outraced her publication. Her poem "How We Became Cosmic Possums (Suburban Appalachian Baby Boomers)" instantly created a new term for the Appalachian lexicon. Sharyn McCrumb also popularized the Cosmic Possum concept in her novel *The Songcatcher* (2001). Now readers can enjoy Hicks's *Blood and Bone Remember: Poems from Appalachia* (2005), a Weatherford Award nominee, which takes a long and satisfying look at being a Cosmic Possum.

Darnell Arnoult of Tennessee won the Weatherford Award for *What Travels with Us* (2005), forty-one poems about the people of Fieldale, a community of textile workers, largely Appalachian mountain folk. With Ron Rash's *Eureka Mill* (1998), a collection of forty-two poems that depict Appalachians transplanted to life in a South Carolina mill and mill village, and Michael Chitwood's *The Weave Room* (1998), forty-five poems about life in and around a Virginia textile mill, Arnoult's book forges a compelling trilogy of experience.

Lying on my table are more marvelous books by distinguished poets Cathryn Hankla, Dana Wildsmith, Lee Pennington, Elizabeth Howard, Betsy Sholl, Rita Riddle, Ed Davis, Lee Howard, Jeanne Shannon, Jim Clark, Harry Brown, John Thomas York, Isabel Zuber, Steve and Barbara Eberly, Rudy Thomas, Harry Dean, Patricia Shirley, Garry Barker, Don Johnson, Francis Pledger Hulme, and Albert Stewart. There are hundreds more I never bought, and hundreds more I want to buy. In the spring 1979 issue of *Appalachian Journal*, heralding the emerging Appalachian literary renaissance, Frank Steele wrote, "It's still too soon to try to say anything definitive about the energy rolling through Appalachian writing at the moment. The likelihood that it will continue to produce good poems—and perhaps even better ones—is something to affirm and celebrate for all readers who keep their ears to the ground, waiting to hear that 'clean break with the world'" (238). More than twenty-five years later, we are still trying to say—and teach—something definitive. It is delightfully impossible because the poets' creativity ever outdistances us.

Note

1. Quotation confirmed by George Brosi in personal e-mail to Theresa L. Burriss, 12/18/12.

References / Teaching Resource List

Abramson, Rudy, and Jean Haskell, eds. 2006. *Encyclopedia of Appalachia*. Knoxville: University of Tennessee Press.

Agee, James. 1968. *The Collected Poems of James Agee*. Edited by Robert Fitzgerald. Boston: Houghton Mifflin.

Allen, Gilbert, and William E. Rogers, eds. 2005. *A Millennial Sampler of South Carolina Poetry*. Greenville, SC: Ninety-Six Press.

Allen, M. Ray. 1991. *Between the Thorns: Windcarver Songs of Appalachia*. Edited by Joseph D. Adams. Fairfax Station, VA: Road Publishers.

———. 2000. *Beyond Star Bottom and Other Poems*. Clifton Forge, VA: Mountain Empire.

Anderson, Maggie. 1979. *The Great Horned Owl*. Riderwood, MD: Icarus Press.

———. 1980. *Years That Answer*. New York: Harper and Row.

———. 1986. *Cold Comfort*. Pittsburgh: University of Pittsburgh Press.

———. 1992. *A Space Filled with Moving*. Pittsburgh: University of Pittsburgh Press.

———. 2000. *Windfall: New and Selected Poems*. Pittsburgh: University of Pittsburgh Press.

Appalshop Radio. 1995. *Tell It On the Mountain: Appalachian Women Writers* audio series. WMMT, Whitesburg, KY.

Arnoult, Darnell. 2005. *What Travels with Us*. Baton Rouge: Louisiana State University Press.

Askins, Donald, and David Morris, eds. 1977. *New Ground*. Jenkins, KY: Southern Appalachian Writers' Co-operative.

Awiakta, Marilou. (1978) 2006. *Abiding Appalachia: Where Mountain and Atom Meet*. Blacksburg, VA: Pocahontas Press.

———. 1993. *Selu: Seeking the Corn Mother's Wisdom*. Golden, CO: Fulcrum.

Baber, Bob Henry. 1994. *A Picture from Life's Other Side: Appalachian Poems*. Richwood, WV: B. H. Baber.

Baber, Bob Henry, George Ella Lyon, and Gurney Norman, eds. 1994. *Old Wounds, New Words: Poems from the Appalachian Poetry Project*. Ashland, KY: Jesse Stuart Foundation.

Ballard, Sandra L., and Patricia L Hudson, eds. 2003. *Listen Here: Women Writing in Appalachia*. Lexington: University Press of Kentucky.

Barker, Garry. 1989. *Bitter Creek Breakdown: Poems*. Berea, KY: Hollytree Press.

Bathanti, Joseph. 1986. *Communion Partners*. Davidson, NC: Briarpatch Press.

———. 1989. *Anson County: Poems*. Greenville, NC: Williams and Simpson.

———. 1994. *The Feast of All Saints*. Troy, ME: Nightshade Press.

———. 1996. *This Metal*. Laurinburg, NC: St. Andrews College Press.

———. 2009. *Land of Amnesia*. Winston-Salem, NC: Press 53.

Bentley, Laura Treacy. 2006. *Lake Effect*. Huron, OH: Bird Dog Publishing.

Berry, Wendell. 2010. *Leavings: Poems*. Berkeley, CA: Counterpoint.

Biggers, Jeff. 2006. *The United States of Appalachia: How Southern Mountaineers Brought Independence, Culture, and Enlightenment to America*. Emoryville, CA: Avalon.

Boggess, Ace, ed. 2004. *Wild Sweet Notes II: More Great Poetry from West Virginia*. Huntington, WV: Publishers Place.

Bottoms, David. 1998. *We Almost Disappear*. Port Townsend, WA: Copper Canyon.

Bowers, Cathy Smith. 2010. *Like Shining from Shook Foil*. Winston-Salem, NC: Press 53.

Brown, Bill. 2006. *Yesterday's Hay*. Columbus, OH: Pudding House.

Brown, Harry. 2005. *Felt Along the Blood: New and Selected Poems*. Nicholasville, KY: WindPublications.

Bryner, Jeanne. 1999. *Blind Horse: Poems*. Huron, OH: Bird Dog.

———. 2010. *No Matter How Many Windows*. Nicholasville, KY: Wind Publications.

Byer, Kathryn Stripling. 1983. *Alma.* Waynesville, NC: Phoenix.

———. 1986. *The Girl in the Midst of the Harvest.* Lubbock: Texas Tech University Press.

———. 1992. *Wildwood Flower.* Baton Rouge: Louisiana State University Press.

———. 1998. *Black Shawl.* Baton Rouge: Louisiana State University Press.

———. 2002. *Catching Light.* Baton Rouge: Louisiana State University Press.

———. 2006. *Coming to Rest.* Baton Rouge: Louisiana State University Press.

Casteen, John. 2011. *For the Mountain Laurel.* Athens: University of Georgia Press.

Chappell, Fred. 1981. *Midquest.* Baton Rouge: Louisiana State University Press.

———. 1993. *C.* Baton Rouge: Louisiana State University Press.

———. 2000. *Family Gathering: Poems.* Baton Rouge: Louisiana State University Press.

———, ed. 2003. *Locales: Poems from the Fellowship of Southern Writers.* Baton Rouge: Louisiana State University Press.

———. 2004. *Backsass: Poems.* Baton Rouge: Louisiana State University Press.

———. 2009. *Shadowbox: Poems.* Baton Rouge: Louisiana State University Press.

Chitwood, Michael. 1992. *Salt Works.* Athens: Ohio Review Books.

———. 1995. *Whet.* Athens: Ohio Review Books.

———. 1998. *The Weave Room.* Chicago: University of Chicago Press.

———. 2002. *Gospel Road Going.* Chapel Hill, NC: Tryon.

———. 2007a. *From Whence.* Baton Rouge: Louisiana State University Press.

———. 2007b. *Spill.* Dorset, VT: Tupelo Press.

———. 2010. *Poor-Mouth Jubilee.* North Adams, MA: Tupelo Press.

Clark, Billy C. 1999. *To Leave My Heart at Catlettsburg.* Ashland, KY: Jesse Stuart Foundation.

———. 2002. *Creeping from Winter.* Farmville, VA: Persimmon Hill.

———. 2007. *To Catch an Autumn.* Nicholasville, KY: Wind Publications.

Clark, Jim. (1983) 1997. *Dancing on Canaan's Ruins.* Memphis, TN: Ars Gratiis Publishing; rpt. Wilson, NC: Eternal Delight Productions.

———. 1999. *Handiwork: Poems by Jim Clark.* Laurinburg, NC: St. Andrews College Press.

———. 2007. *Notions: A Jim Clark Miscellany.* Mount Olive, NC: Rank Stranger Press.

———. 2010. *The Service of Song: Jim Clark's Musical Settings of the Poems of Byron Herbert Reece.* CD. Eternal Delight Productions, Wilson, NC.

Cobb, Ann. (1922) 2003. *Kinfolks and Other Selected Poems.* Edited by Jeff Daniel Marion. Hindman, KY: Hindman Settlement School.

Connolly, Geraldine. 1988. *The Red Room.* Meadville, PA: Heatherstone Press.

———. 1990. *Food for the Winter.* West Lafayette, IN: Purdue University Press.

———. 1998. *Province of Fire.* Oak Ridge, TN: Iris Press.

———. 2009. *Hand of the Wind.* Oak Ridge, TN: Iris Press.

Crowe, Thomas Rain. 2011. *Crack Light.* Nicholasville, KY: Wind Publications.

Crutchfield, John. 2002. *Still.* Self-published. www.johncrutchfield.com.

———. 2004. *What Space Is For.* Self-published. www.johncrutchfield.com.

———. 2005. *Yearbook.* Self-published. www.johncrutchfield.com.

———. 2006. *The Art of Poetry.* Self-published. www.johncrutchfield.com.

———. 2007. *Arrivals.* Self-published. www.johncrutchfield.com.

Davenport, Doris Diosa. 1995. *Soque Street Poems.* Sautee-Nacoochee, GA: Sautee-Nacoochee Community Association.

Davidson, Shae. 2010. *Appalachian Buddha*. Georgetown, KY: Finishing Line Press.

Davis, Ed. 1987. *Haskell*. Big Timber, Montana: Seven Buffaloes Press.

Dean, Harry. 2004. *Local: Poems and Songs*. Blacksburg, VA: Rowan Mountain Press.

DeFoe, Mark. 2004. *Greatest Hits, 1977–2003*. Columbus, OH: Pudding House.

Depta, Victor. 2007. *An Afterthought of Light*. Ashland, KY: Blair Mountain Press.

Downer, Hilda. 1979. *Bandana Creek: Poems*. Charlotte, NC: Red Clay Books.

Doyle, Donna. 2009. *Heading Home*. Georgetown, KY: Finishing Line Press.

Dyer, Joyce, ed. 1998. *Bloodroot: Reflections on Place by Appalachian Women Writers*. Lexington: University Press of Kentucky.

Ebel, Julia Taylor 2011. *Mama's Wreaths*. Vilas, NC: Canterbury House Publishing.

Edwards, Grace Toney, JoAnn Aust Asbury, and Ricky L. Cox, eds. 2006. *A Handbook to Appalachia: An Introduction to the Region*. Knoxville: University of Tennessee Press.

Fedukovich, Casie, and Steve Sparks, eds. 2006. *Low Explosions: Writings on the Body*. Knoxville, TN: Knoxville Writers' Guild.

Fisher, Diane Gilliam. 1999. *Recipe for Blackberry Cake*. Kent, OH: Kent State University Press.

———. 2003. *One of Everything*. Cleveland, OH: Cleveland State University Poetry Center.

———. 2004. *Kettle Bottom*. Florence, MA: Perugia Press.

Garin, Marita, ed. 2008. *Southern Appalachian Poetry: An Anthology of Works by 37 Poets*. Jefferson, NC: McFarland.

Giardina, Denise. 1987. *Storming Heaven*. New York: Norton.

Giovanni, Nikki. 1996. *The Selected Poems of Nikki Giovanni*. New York: William Morrow.

Graves, Jesse, Paul Ruffin, and William Wright, eds. 2010. *The Southern Poetry Anthology*. Vol. 3, *Contemporary Appalachia*. Huntsville, TX: Texas Review Press.

Gray, Amy Tipton. 1989. *The Hillbilly Vampire*. Blacksburg, VA: Rowan Mountain Press.

Green, Chris. 2005. "Don West's 'No Lonesome Road: Selected Prose and Poems.'" *Appalachian Heritage* 33, no. 3 (Summer): 93–98.

Green, Chris, and Edwina Pendarvis, eds. 2006. *Coal: A Poetry Anthology*. Ashland, KY: Blair Mountain Press.

———. 2009. *Rushlight: Poems*. Huron, OH: Bottom Dog Press.

Green, Connie Jordan. 2007. *Slow Children Playing*. Georgetown, KY: Finishing Line Press.

———. 2011. *Regret Comes to Tea*. Georgetown, KY: Finishing Line Press.

Hague, Richard. 2003. *Alive in Hard Country*. Huron, OH: Bottom Dog Press.

Hague, Richard, Kip Knott, David Adams, and Timothy Russell. 1991. *A Red Shadow of Steel Mills: Photos and Poems*. Edited by David Shevin and Larry Smith. Huron, OH: Bottom Dog Press.

Hampton, David Wayne. 2010. *What Makes It Taste Better*. Morganton, NC: Maul and Froe Press.

Hankla, Cathryn. 2000. *Texas School Book Depository: Prose Poems*. Baton Rouge: Louisiana State University Press.

———. 2002. *Poems for the Pardoned*. Baton Rouge: Louisiana State University Press.

———. 2004. *Last Exposures: A Sequence of Poems*. Baton Rouge: Louisiana State University Press.

Hansel, Pauletta. 2011. *What I Did There*. Loveland, OH: Dos Madres Press.

Harshman, Marc. 2004. *Local Journeys*. Georgetown, KY: Finishing Line Press.

Haughton, Matthew. 2011. *Bee-Coursing Box*. Lexington, KY: Accents.

Hicks, Jane. 2005. *Blood and Bone Remember: Poems from Appalachia*. Ashland, KY: Jesse Stuart Foundation.

Higgs, Robert J., and Ambrose N. Manning, eds. 1975. *Voices from the Hills: Selected Readings of Southern Appalachia*. New York: Ungar.

Higgs, Robert J., Ambrose N. Manning, and Jim Wayne Miller, eds. 1995. *Appalachia Inside Out: A Sequel to "Voices from the Hills."* Knoxville: University of Tennessee Press.

Hite, Alex. 1946. "Poetry Books Are Written by Georgians." *Atlanta Constitution*, 4 August.

Holden, Laurence. 2010. *Take Me to the River: Poems and Paintings for Coming Home*. Self-published.

———. "A River of Words and Images." Accessed 17 December 2012. http://theartists path1.blogspot.com/.

hooks, bell. 1978. *When Angels Speak of Love: Poems*. New York: Simon and Schuster.

Horne, Jennifer, ed. 2003. *Working the Dirt: An Anthology of Southern Poets*. Montgomery, AL: NewSouth Books.

Houchin, Ron. 2004. *Among Wordless Things*. Nicholasville, KY: Wind Publications.

———. 2008. *Birds in the Tops of Winter Trees*. Nicholasville, KY: Wind Publications.

———. 2009. *Museum Crows*. Knockeven, Ireland: Salmon Publishing.

Howard, Lee. 2010. *Harvest of Fire: New and Collected Works*. Edited by George Ella Lyon. Louisville, KY: MotesBooks.

Huddle, David. 1979. *Paper Boy*. Pittsburgh: University of Pittsburgh Press.

———. 1988. *Stopping by Home*. Salt Lake City: Peregrine Smith Books.

———. 1992. *The Nature of Yearning: Poems*. Salt Lake City: Peregrine Smith Books.

———. 1999. *Summer Lake: New and Selected Poems*. Baton Rouge: Louisiana State University Press.

———. 2004. *Grayscale: Poems*. Baton Rouge: Louisiana State University Press.

———. 2008. *Glory River: Poems*. Baton Rouge: Louisiana State University Press.

Hughes, Charlie G. 2010. *Body and Blood*. Nicholasville, KY: Wind Publications.

Hulme, Francis Pledger. 1975. *Mountain Measure: Southern Appalachia Verse Notebook*. Boone, NC: Appalachian Consortium Press.

Ivie, Doris, and Leslie M. LaChance, eds. 2001. *Breathing the Same Air: An East Tennessee Anthology*. Knoxville, TN: Celtic Cat.

James, Sheryl. 1989. "A Radical of Long Standing." *St. Petersburg Times*, March. http://www .aldha.org/donwest.htm.

Janeshek, Jessie. 2010. *Invisible Mink*. Oak Ridge, TN: Iris Press.

Jennings, Rachel. 2010. *Knoxville Girl: The Walk to the River*. Georgetown, KY: Finishing Line Press.

Johnson, Don. 1984. *The Importance of Visible Scars*. Green Harbor, MA: Wampeter Press.

———. 1990. *Watauga Drawdown*. Johnson City, TN: Overmountain Press.

———. 2009. *Here and Gone: New and Selected Poems*. Hammond, LA: Louisiana Literature Press.

Jordan, Judy. 2000. *Carolina Ghost Woods*. Baton Rouge: Louisiana State University Press.

———. 2005. *60 Cent Coffee and a Quarter to Dance*. Baton Rouge: Louisiana State University Press.

————. Forthcoming. *Hunger*. Baton Rouge: Louisiana State University Press.

Kallet, Marilyn. 2009. *Packing Light: New and Selected Poems*. Boston, MA: Black Widow Press.

Kendrick, Leatha. 2008. *Second Opinion*. Cincinnati, OH: David Robert Books.

Kinder, Chuck. 1973. *Snakehunter*. New York: Knopf.

————. 2004. *The Last Mountain Dancer*. New York: Carroll and Graf.

Kirkpatrick, Kathryn. 2011. *Unaccountable Weather*. Winston-Salem, NC: Press 53.

Lang, John, ed. 2000. *Understanding Fred Chappell*. Columbia: University of South Carolina Press.

————. 2005. *Appalachia and Beyond: Conversations with Writers from the Mountain South*. Knoxville: University of Tennessee Press.

————. 2010. *Six Poets from the Mountain South*. Baton Rouge: Louisiana State University Press.

Lanier, Parks, Jr., ed. 1991. *Poetics of Appalachian Space*. Knoxville: University of Tennessee Press.

Larsen, Jeanne. 1980. *James Cook in Search of Terra Incognita*. Charlottesville: University of Virginia Press.

————, trans. 1987. *Brocade River Poems: Selected Works of the Tang Dynasty Courtesan Xue Tai*. Princeton: Princeton University Press.

————, trans. 2005. *Willow, Wine, Mirror, Moon: Women's Poems from Tang China*. Rochester, NY: BOA Editions.

————. 2010. *Why We Make Gardens*. Woodstock, NY: Mayapple Press.

Laska, P. J. 2010. *Night and Day: New and Selected Poems*. Bloomington, IN: Xlibris.

Ledford, Brenda Kay. 2006. *Shew Bird Mountain*. Georgetown, KY: Finishing Line Press.

Lee, Ernest. 2002. *Being of These Hills: Readings from Appalachian Writers*. Boston: Pearson.

Loest, Judy. 2007. *After Appalachia*. Georgetown, KY: Finishing Line Press.

Loest, Judy, and Jack Renfro, eds. 2004. *Knoxville Bound: A Collection of Literary Works Inspired by Knoxville*. Knoxville, TN: MetroPulse.

Lofaro, Michael, ed. 2012. *Agee at 100: Centennial Essays on the Works of James Agee*. Knoxville: University of Tennessee Press.

Lyon, George Ella. 1983. *Mountain*. Hartford, CT: Andrew Mountain Press.

————. 1993. *Catalpa*. Lexington, KY: Wind Publications.

————. 2010. *Back*. Nicholasville, KY: Wind Publications.

————. 2012. *She Let Herself Go*. Baton Rouge: Louisiana State University Press.

Lyon, George Ella, Jim Wayne Miller, and Gurney Norman, eds. 1993. *A Gathering at the Forks: Fifteen Years of Hindman Settlement School Writing*. Wise, VA: Vision Books.

Mackin, Randy. 2011. *George Scarbrough, Appalachian Poet: A Biographical and Literary Study with Unpublished Writings*. Jefferson, NC: McFarland.

Mann, Jeff. 2003. *Bones Washed with Wine*. Arlington, VA: Gival Press.

————. 2005. *Loving Mountains, Loving Men: Poems and Essays*. Athens: Ohio University Press.

————. 2006. *On the Tongue*. Arlington, VA: Gival Press.

————. 2011. *Ash: Poems from Norse Mythology*. Bar Harbor, ME: Rebel Satori Press.

Manning, Maurice. 2001. *Lawrence Booth's Book of Visions*. New Haven, CT: Yale University Press.

———. 2010. *The Common Man.* Boston: Houghton Mifflin.

Marion, Jeff Daniel. 1976. *Out in the Country, Back Home.* Winston-Salem, NC: Jackpine Press.

———. 1981. *Tight Lines.* Emory, VA: Iron Mountain Press.

———. 1994. *Lost & Found.* Abingdon, VA: Sow's Ear Press.

———. 1999. *The Chinese Poet Awakens.* Lexington, KY: Wind Publications.

———. 2001. *Letters Home.* Abingdon, VA: Sow's Ear Press.

———. 2002. *Ebbing and Flowing Springs: New and Selected Poems and Prose, 1976–2001.* Knoxville, TN: Celtic Cat.

Marion, Linda Parsons. 1997. *Home Fires: Poems.* Abingdon, VA: Sow's Ear Press.

———. 2008. *Mother Land.* Oak Ridge, TN: Iris Press.

———. 2011. *Bound.* Nicholasville, KY: Wind Publications.

Martin, Brent, Barbara R. Duncan, and Thomas Rain Crowe, eds. 2011. *Every Breath Sings Mountains.* Taos, NM: Center for the Study of Place.

McFee, Michael. 1991. *Sad Girl Sitting on a Running Board.* Frankfort, KY: Gnomon Press.

———. 2006a. *The Napkin Manuscripts: Selected Essays and an Interview.* Knoxville: University of Tennessee Press.

———. 2006b. *Shinemaster.* Pittsburgh: Carnegie Mellon University Press.

———. 2007. *The Smallest Talk: One-Line Poems.* Durham, NC: Bull City Press.

———. 2012. *That Was Oasis.* Pittsburgh: Carnegie Mellon University Press.

McKernan, Llewellyn. 2005. *Greatest Hits, 1979–2004.* Columbus, OH: Pudding House.

———. 2010. *Pencil Memory.* Georgetown, KY: Finishing Line Press.

McKinney, Denise R., ed. 2004. *Poetry As Prayer: Appalachian Women Speak.* Nicholasville, KY: Wind Publications.

McNeil, Nellie, and Joyce Squibb. 1989. *A Southern Appalachian Reader.* Boone, NC: Appalachian Consortium Press.

McNeill, Louise. 1939. *Gauley Mountain.* New York: Harcourt, Brace.

———. 1972. *Paradox Hill: From Appalachia to Lunar Shore.* Morgantown: West Virginia University Library.

———. 1979. *Elderberry Flood.* Charleston, WV: Elderberry Books.

———. (1991) 2008. *Hill Daughter: New and Selected Poems.* Edited by Maggie Anderson. Pittsburgh, OH: University of Pittsburgh Press.

Miles, Emma Bell. (1930) 2001. *Strains from a Dulcimore.* Atlanta, GA: E. Hartsock. Reprint, Signal Mountain, TN: Mountain Press.

Miller, Danny L., Sharon Hatfield, and Gurney Norman, eds. 2005. *An American Vein: Critical Readings in Appalachian Literature.* Athens: Ohio University Press.

Miller, Jim Wayne. (1964) 1995. *Copperhead Cane: Poems.* Nashville, TN: Allen. Reprint, Louisville, KY: Green River Writers/Grex Press.

———. (1974). 1978. *Dialogue With a Dead Man.* Reprint, University Center, MI: Green River Press.

———. 1980. *The Mountains Have Come Closer.* Boone, NC: Appalachian Consortium Press.

———. 1988. *Brier, His Book.* Frankfort, KY: Gnomon Press.

———. 1997. *The Brier Poems.* Frankfort, KY: Gnomon Press.

Minick, Jim. 2008a. *Burning Heaven*. Nicholasville, KY: Wind Publications.

———. 2008b. *Her Secret Song*. Louisville, KY: MotesBooks.

Mitchell, Felicia, ed. 2002. *Her Words: Diverse Voices in Contemporary Appalachian Women's Poetry*. Knoxville: University of Tennessee Press.

Moeckel, Thorpe. 2002. *Odd Botany*. Eugene, OR: Silverfish Review Press.

———. 2008. *Making a Map of the River*. Oak Ridge, TN: Iris Press.

———. 2010. *Venison*. Wilkes-Barre, PA: Etruscan Press.

Moore, Janice Townley. 2005. *Teaching the Robins*. Georgetown, KY: Finishing Line Press.

Morgan, Robert. 1969. *Zirconia Poems*. Northwood Narrows, NH: Lillabulero Press.

———. 1972. *Red Owl*. New York: Norton.

———. 1976. *Land Diving*. Baton Rouge: Louisiana State University Press.

———. 2000. *Topsoil Road: Poems*. Baton Rouge: Louisiana State University Press.

———. 2004. *The Strange Attractor: New and Selected Poems*. Baton Rouge: Louisiana State University Press.

———. 2009. *October Crossing*. Frankfort, KY: BroadStone Books.

———. 2011. *Terroir*. New York: Penguin.

Mulkey, Rick. 1998. *Before the Age of Reason*. San Antonio, TX: Pecan Grove Press.

———. 2005. *Bluefield Breakdown*. Georgetown, KY: Finishing Line Press.

———. 2007. *Toward Any Darkness*. Cincinnati, OH: Word Press.

Nantahala. 2007. Summer/Fall. Features seventeen Appalachian poets.

Nazario y Colón, Ricardo. 2010. *Of Jibaros and Hillbillies*. Austin, TX: Plain View Press.

Neufeld, Rob. 2012. *27 Views of Asheville: A Southern Mountain Town in Prose and Poetry*. Hillsborough, NC: Eno Publishers.

Now & Then: The Appalachian Magazine. 1998. (Summer): 1–40. Special issue: Appalachian Poetry: Articles, Essays, Poetry, and Reviews. East Tennessee State University.

Olson, Ted. 2006. *Breathing in Darkness: Poems*. Nicholasville, KY: Wind Publications.

Olson, Ted, and Kathy H Olson, eds. 2007. *James Still: Critical Essays*. Jefferson, NC: McFarland.

Parker, Lisa J. 2010. *This Gone Place*. Louisville, KY: MotesBooks.

Pauley, Michael Joseph. 1986. "Songs of the Hills: Poetry in West Virginia." *Wonderful West Virginia: A Special Issue of West Virginia Poetry*. www.mountainlit.com/essays.

Pendarvis, Edwina, and Harry Grieg. 2003. *Like the Mountains of China*. Ashland, KY: Blair Mountain Press.

———. 2005. *Duets: Poems*. Lavelette, WV: Shoestring Publications.

Pennington, Lee. 1993. *Thigmotropism*. Louisville, KY: Green River Writers/Grex Press.

Powell, Lynn. 1995. *Old and New Testaments*. University of Wisconsin Press.

———. 2003. *The Zones of Paradise*. Akron, OH: University of Akron Press.

Presnell, Barbara. 2007. *Piece Work*. Cleveland, OH: Cleveland State University Poetry Center.

Quillen, Rita Sims, ed. 1987. *October Dusk*. Big Timber, MT: Seven Buffaloes Press.

———. 1989. *Looking for Native Ground: Contemporary Appalachian Poetry*. Boone, NC: Appalachian Consortium Press.

———. 1995. *Counting the Sums*. Abingdon, VA: Sow's Ear Press.

———. 2007. *Her Secret Dream*. Nicholasville, KY: Wind Publications.

Range, Melissa. 2010. *Horse and Rider*. Lubbock: Texas Tech University Press.

Rash, Ron. 1998. *Eureka Mill*. Corvallis, OR: Bench Press.

———. 2000. *Among the Believers*. Oak Ridge, TN: Iris Press.

———. 2002. *Raising the Dead*. Oak Ridge, TN: Iris Press.

———. 2011. *Waking*. Spartanburg, SC: Hub City Press.

Reece, Byron Herbert. (1945) 1985. *Ballad of the Bones and Other Poems*. New York: Dutton. Reprint, Atlanta, GA: Cherokee Publishing.

———. (1950) 1985. *Bow Down in Jericho*. New York: Dutton. Reprint, Atlanta, GA: Cherokee Publishing.

———. (1955) 1994. *The Hawk and the Sun*. Reprint, Athens: University of Georgia Press.

———. 1992a. *The Bitter Berry*. Edited by Bettie Sellers. Atlanta: Georgia Humanities Council.

———. 1992b. *The Bitter Berry: The Life of Byron Herbert Reece*. Northbrook, IL: Film Ideas.

———. 2002. *Fable in the Blood: The Selected Poems of Byron Herbert Reece*. Edited by Jim Clark. Athens: University of Georgia Press.

Riddle, Rita. 2008. *All There Is to Keep*. Edited by Jim Minick. Oak Ridge: Iris Press.

Russell, Timothy. 1993. *Adversaria*. Evanston, IL: Northwestern University Press.

Sasser, Jane. 2008. *Recollecting the Snow*. Greensboro, NC: March Street Press.

———. 2009. *Itinerant*. Georgetown, KY: Finishing Line Press.

Savage, Elizabeth. 2011. *Jane & Paige or Sister Goose*. Baltimore, MD: Furniture Press Books.

Scafidi, Steve. 2006. *For Love of Common Words*. Baton Rouge: Louisiana State University Press.

Scarbrough, George. (1949) 1999. *Tellico Blue*. New York: Dutton. Reprint, Oak Ridge, TN: Iris Press, 1999.

———. 1951. *The Course is Upward*. New York: Dutton.

———. 1956. *Summer So-Called*. New York: Dutton.

———. 1997. *Ice Storm and Other Poems Read by the Author*. Oak Ridge, TN: Iris Press audio.

———. 1977. *New and Selected Poems*. Oak Ridge, TN: Iris Press.

———. 1989. *Invitation to Kim*. Oak Ridge, TN: Iris Press.

———. 2011. *Under the Lemon Tree*. Edited by Robert B. Cumming and Rebecca P. Mobbs. Oak Ridge, TN: Iris Press.

Sellers, Bettie M. 1981. *Morning of the Red-Tailed Hawk*. University Center, MI: Green River Press.

———. 1986. *Spring Onions and Cornbread*. Athens, GA: Agee Publishers.

———. (1989) 2006. *Wild Ginger*. Kennesaw, GA: Kennesaw State University Press.

Shannon, Jeanne. 2002. *Meditations for the Earth*. Johnstown, OH: Pudding House.

Shelby, Anne. 2006. *Appalachian Studies: Poems*. Nicholasville, KY: Wind Publications.

Shenandoah: The Washington and Lee University Review. 2005. (1): 5–63. A portfolio of thirty-four Appalachian poets.

Shipley, Vivian. 2005. *Hardboot: Poems New and Old*. Hammond, LA: Louisiana Literature.

———. 2010a. *All of Your Messages Have Been Erased*. Hammond, LA: Southeastern Louisiana University Press.

———. 2010b. *Greatest Hits 1974–2010*. Youngstown, OH: Pudding House.

Shirley, Patricia. 1986. *Pearl*. Big Timber, MT: Seven Buffaloes Press.

———. 1990. *Mary Pearl Kline*. Big Timber, MT: Seven Buffaloes Press.

Simpson, Nancy, ed. 2010. *Echoes Across the Blue Ridge: Stories, Essays, and Poems*. Winding Path.

Simpson, Nancy, and Shirley Uphouse, eds. 2003. *Lights in the Mountains: Stories, Essays and Poems by Writers Living in and Inspired by the Southern Appalachian Mountains*. Hayesville, NC: Winding Path.

Sinclair, Bennie Lee. [1971] 1978. *Little Chicago Suite*. 2nd ed. Cleveland, SC: Wildernesse Books.

———. 1978. *The Arrowhead Scholar*. Cleveland, SC: Wildernesse Books.

———. 1990. *Lord of Springs*. Blacksburg, VA: Rowan Mountain Press.

———. 1992. *The Endangered: New and Selected Poems*. Greenville, SC: Ninety-Six Press.

Sizemore, Judy. 2007. *Asymmetry*. Louisville, KY: MotesBooks.

Smith, Arthur. 1985. *Elegy on Independence Day*. Pittsburgh: University of Pittsburgh Press.

———. 1996. *Orders of Affection*. Pittsburgh: Carnegie Mellon University Press.

———. 2002. *The Late World*. Pittsburgh: Carnegie Mellon University Press.

Smith, Barbara. 2006. *Demonstrative Pronouns*. Shinnston, WV: Mountainechoes.com Books.

Smith, Barbara, and Kirk Judd, eds. 2000. *Wild Sweet Notes: Fifty Years of West Virginia Poetry, 1950–1999*. Huntington, WV: Publishers Place.

Smith, Daniel, Edwina Pendarvis, and Philip St. Clair. 1997. *Human Landscapes: Three Books of Poems*. Huron, OH: Bottom Dog Press.

Smith, Larry, and Mei Hui Huang. 1998. *Chinese Zen Poems: What Hold Has This Mountain?* Huron, OH: Bottom Dog Press.

———. 2006. *A River Remains*. Cincinnati, OH: WordTech Communications.

Smith, Noel. 2008. *The Well String*. Louisville, KY: MotesBooks.

Smith, R. T. 1996. *Trespasser*. Baton Rouge: Louisiana State University Press.

———. 1999. *Split the Lark: Selected Poems*. Cliffs of Moher, Co. Clare, Ireland: Salmon.

———. 2003. *The Hollow Log Lounge: Poems*. Urbana: Illinois University Press.

———. 2004. *Brightwood: Poems*. Baton Rouge: Louisiana State University Press.

———. 2007. *Outlaw Style: Poems*. Fayetteville: University of Arkansas Press.

Snyder, Bob. 1977l. *We'll See Who's a Peasant Now: Poems of Love and Family*. Huntington, WV: Appalachian Press.

Soniat, Katherine. 1993. *A Shared Life: Poems*. Iowa City: University of Iowa Press.

Sparks, Betty J. 2004. *Poets Laureate of Kentucky, 1921–2003*. Nicholasville, KY: Wind Publications.

Spriggs, Bianca. 2010. *Kaffir Lily*. Nicholasville, KY: Wind Publications.

———. 2011. *How Swallowtails Become Dragons*. Lexington, KY: Accents Publishing.

Staudt, David. 2001. *The Gifts and the Thefts*. Omaha, NE: Backwater Press.

Steele, Frank. 1979. "Two Kinds of Commitment: Some Directions in Current Appalachian Poetry." *Appalachian Journal* 6, no. 3 (Spring): 228–38.

Stewart, Albert. 1987. *The Untoward Hills*. Morehead, KY: Morehead State College Press.

———. 1993. *The Holy Season: Poems Sacred and Profane*. Berea, KY: Berea College Press.

Stewart, D. Antwan. 2006. *The Terribly Beautiful*. Editor's Choice Chapbook series. Charlotte, NC: Main Street Rag.

———. 2008. *Sotto Voce*. Editor's Choice Chapbook series. Charlotte, NC: Main Street Rag.

Stewart, Ida. 2011. *Gloss*. Florence, MA: Perugia Press.

Still, James. 1937. *Hounds on the Mountain*. New York: Viking Press.

———. 1986. *The Wolfpen Poems*. Berea, KY: Berea College Press.

———. 2001. *From the Mountain, From the Valley: New and Collected Poems*. Edited by Ted Olson. Lexington: University Press of Kentucky.

Stryk, Dan. 1984. *The Artist and the Crow*. Lafayette, IN: Purdue University Press.

———. 2002. *Taping Images to Walls: A Medley of Informal Sonnets*. San Antonio, TX: Pecan Grove Press.

———. 2007. *Solace of the Aging Mare*. Warrensburg, MO: Mid-America Press.

———. 2008. *Dimming Radiance*. Nicholasville, KY: Wind Publications.

Stuart, Jesse. 1934. *Man with a Bull-Tongue Plow*. New York: Dutton.

Swanson, Charles A. 2009a. *After the Garden: Selected Responses to the Psalms*. Louisville, KY: MotesBooks.

———. 2009b. *Farm Life and Legend*. Georgetown, KY: Finishing Line Press.

Taylor, Nancy Dew. 2008. *Stepping On Air*. Greenville, SC: Emrys Press.

Tener, Robert L. 2006. *Depression Days on an Appalachian Farm*. Huron, OH: Bottom Dog Press.

Thacker, Larry D. 2011. *Voice Hunting*. Georgetown, KY: Finishing Line Press.

Thomas, Rudy, ed. 1985. *The Uneven Ground: An Anthology of Appalachian Materials*. Berea, KY: Kentucke Imprints.

Trethewey, Eric. 2004a. *Heart's Hornbook*. Monterey, KY: Larkspur Press.

———. 2004b. *Songs and Lamentations*. Cincinnati, OH: Word Press.

Underwood, Susan O'Dell. 2010. *From*. Georgetown, KY: Finishing Line Press.

Walker, Frank X. 2000. *Affrilachia*. Lexington, KY: Old Cove Press.

———. 2003. *Buffalo Dance: The Journey of York*. Lexington, KY: University Press of Kentucky.

———. 2005. *Black Box*. Lexington, KY: Old Cove Press.

———. 2008. *When Winter Come: The Ascension of York*. Lexington: University Press of Kentucky.

———. 2010. *Isaac Murphy: I Dedicate This Ride*. Lexington, KY: Old Cove Press.

———. N.d. *Coal Black Voices: The History of Affrilachian Poets*. Web-based study guide. http://coalblackvoices.com.

Walsh, William. 1993. *The Ordinary Life of a Sculptor*. N.p.: Sandstone Publishers.

———. 2005. *The Conscience of My Other Being*. Atlanta, GA: Cherokee Publishers.

West, Don. 1946. *Clods of Southern Earth*. New York: Boni and Gaer.

———. 1974. *O Mountaineers!: A Collection of Poems*. Huntington, WV: Appalachian Press.

———. 2004. *No Lonesome Road: A Don West Reader*. Edited by George Brosi and Jeff Biggers. Urbana: University of Illinois Press.

West, Robert. 2005. *Best Company*. Chapel Hill, NC: Blink Chapbooks.

———. 2007. *Out of Hand*. Louisville, KY: Scienter Press.

Wheeler, Jackson. 1993. *Swimming Past Iceland*. Mille Grazie Press.

———. 1999. *A Near Country: Poems of Loss*. Carpinteria, CA: Solo Press.

Wildsmith, Dana. 1995. *Alchemy*. Abingdon, VA: Sow's Ear Press.

———. 1999a. *Annie*. Aiken, SC: Palanquin Press.

———. 1999b. *Our Bodies Remember*. Abingdon, VA: Sow's Ear Press.

———. 2005. *One Good Hand*. Oak Ridge, TN: Iris Press.

Williamson, J. W., and Edwin T. Arnold. 1994. *Interviewing Appalachia: The "Appalachian Journal" Interviews*. Knoxville: University of Tennessee Press.

Worthington, Marianne. 2006. *Larger Bodies Than Mine*. Georgetown, KY: Finishing Line Press.

Wright, Amy. 2009. *There Are No New Ways to Kill a Man*. apostrophebooks.org.

———. 2010. *Farm*. Georgetown, KY: Finishing Line Press.

Wright, Charles. 1983. *Country Music: Selected Early Poems*. Middletown, CT: Wesleyan University Press.

———. 1986. "A Journal of the Year of the Ox." *New Yorker*, 4 August, 26–27.

———. 1995. *Chickamauga*. New York: Farrar, Straus and Giroux.

———. 1997a. "All Landscape Is Abstract and Tends to Repeat Itself." *Virginia Quarterly Review* (Winter): 74. http://www.vqronline.org/articles/1997/winter/wright-all-landscape/.

———. 1997b. *Black Zodiac*. New York: Farrar, Straus and Giroux.

———. 1998. *Appalachia*. New York: Farrar, Straus and Giroux.

———. 2000. *Negative Blue: Selected Later Poems*. New York: Farrar, Straus and Giroux.

———. 2007. *Scar Tissue*. New York: Farrar, Straus and Giroux.

———. 2011. *Bye-and-Bye: Selected Late Poems*. New York: Farrar, Straus and Giroux.

Wright, Sheri L. 2011. *The Slow Talk of Stones*. Georgetown, KY: Finishing Line Press.

York, Jake Adam. 2005. *Murder Ballads*. Denver, CO: Elixir Press.

———. 2008. *Murmuration of Starlings*. Carbondale: Southern Illinois University Press.

———. 2010. *Persons Unknown*. Carbondale: Southern Illinois University Press.

York, John Thomas. 1982. *Picking Out*. Wilmington, NC: Nebo Poetry Press.

———. 1994. *Johnny's Cosmology*. Winston-Salem, NC: Hummingbird Press.

———. 2010. *Naming the Constellations*. Sylva, NC: Spring Street Editions.

Zuber, Isabel. *Winter's Exile: Poems for My Father*. Whispering Pines, NC: Scots Plaid Press.

———. 2010. *Red Lily*. Winston-Salem, NC: Press 53.

TWELVE

From Harlem Home to Affrilachia: Teaching the Literary Journey

THERESA L. BURRISS

MOST READERS OF APPALACHIAN LITERATURE would not expect to find riffs of 1920s Harlem jazz wafting through this mountain writing. Nor would they anticipate an encounter with the politics of the 1960s Black Arts Movement (BAM). But these unexpected discoveries and more are what readers will find in the poetry and short stories of Affrilachians Frank X Walker, Nikky Finney, and Crystal Wilkinson. The writers meld the aesthetics and social agendas of the Harlem Renaissance with the Black Arts Movement to inspire writing chiseled from their Appalachian homeplace. In the process they have forged a new movement, a continuation of these African American literary precursors but infused with Appalachian characteristics, and called it Affrilachian.

When asked to define the Affrilachian aesthetic, Walker explains, "I would define [it] as a collective commitment to make the invisible visible, to redefine the literary landscape of the region as one that is more diverse than mass media portrays it as."[1] Nell Irvin Painter, in the foreword to *Blacks in Appalachia* (Turner and Cabbell 1985), discusses the problem of invisibility when she explains, "Black Appalachians, whose experiences have not conformed to stereotypes of black life, are . . . an invisible people" (xi). In the same work, Edward J. Cabbell demonstrates the result of this problem, for "black invisibility provides strong support to the myth that the number of black people in the mountains is inconsequential" (3).

Because Appalachian literature has traditionally excluded blacks, both in its content and from its canon, the Affrilachians formed to give voice to African Americans and other people of color in the mountains, to demonstrate that they are indeed a people of consequence in the region. Walker continues:

> This [Affrilachian] aesthetic serves to encourage its members to produce original work that acknowledges a regional consciousness and seeks to validate our own individual stories, defining our selves, our families and our communities rather than conforming to the definitions of others. . . . I feel it is inspired by our relationship to and love of literature and our sense of responsibility to document our families' stories and cultural traditions.[2]

In this naming of themselves, Affrilachians obtain control over both their cultural histories and their destinies. And Affrilachia becomes more than just a movement, as the very word "Affrilachia" provides a specific identity and calls attention to an entire group of historically neglected people.

I can testify to such a need to call attention to Appalachians of color regardless of whether I'm teaching at the graduate or the undergraduate level. When I introduce the Affrilachians and have students read their poetry and prose, almost all have never heard of the term "Affrilachian," and the vast majority never realized that Appalachians of color have inhabited the region for hundreds of years. I teach at a medium-sized public comprehensive institution in Southwest Virginia, with about a third of my students coming from Northern Virginia, another third from the Tidewater/Richmond area, and the final third split between Southside and Southwest Virginia. Only a few hail from outside the Commonwealth. Even many of those students born and raised in the region discover this relatively new term. And while a few may know that black Appalachians have lived in the region for decades, the students are not aware that slavery existed in the mountains. Thus, I've found it important to draw attention to Wilma Dunaway's primary research and publications and to refer students to her work for more in-depth scholarship on the issue.

Through their poetry and prose, the Affrilachians contribute to both historical and contemporary documentation of black Appalachians by sharing family stories, responding to past and current events, and providing insight into different Affrilachian experiences. They also respond to Jim Wayne Miller's claim that "[a] mirror for Appalachia is needed" ([1975] 1996, 448). And Miller quotes Loyal Jones to clarify the use of this mirror, "which will help Appalachians to become 'aware of who we are and why, and be at ease with this knowledge'" (448). Miller goes on to explain, "The record of the past suggests that Appalachians cannot expect others to provide that mirror. It must be a mirror of our own making" (448). Residents, writers, and educators from the region, who intimately understand and live the culture, are the most adept at creating a mirror that accurately reflects Appalachian experiences. Because mountaineers have been subjected to an educational system that "has not been an expression of [their] own culture, but has been imposed from the outside," residents oftentimes do not find the knowledge useful (449).

The Affrilachian writers address this problem. They have crafted their own mirror to reflect experiences that defy the hegemonic thinking of most outsiders and even many insiders of the region. Affrilachian writing demonstrates the long-standing diversity of Appalachia. It testifies to the presence and contributions of people of color in an area stereotypically portrayed as homogeneously white. And as black writers, the Affrilachians additionally draw inspiration from their African American literary ancestors of the Harlem Renaissance and Black Arts Movement. Walker clarifies his understanding of the Affrilachian movement, its evolution, as a result of historical cultural movements. Walker reflects on the traditions that inspire him and others:

> The Affrilachian Writers were started by a group of writers, mostly English Majors, who have read and are familiar with both the Harlem Renaissance and the Black Arts movement of the '60s. Our/my influential literary role models are out of these traditions. We can't help but be shaped and influenced and acknowledge a connection to the continuum of literature that preceded us.[3]

Walker recognizes the "genres of poetry and fiction as vehicles to carry [the aesthetic] forward" through self-definition.[4]

The overt political maneuvering inherent in such naming and documenting is reminiscent of both the Harlem Renaissance and the Black Arts Movement. W. E. B. DuBois, a key figure of the Harlem Renaissance, rankled many of the literati when he proclaimed in his essay "Criteria of Negro Art," "All art is propaganda and ever must be, despite the wailing of purists. . . . I do not care a damn for any art that is not used for propaganda. But I do care when propaganda is confined to one side while the other is stripped and silent" ([1926] 1994, 103). Testifying to the pervasive power of oppressive institutions, DuBois reveals the doublespeak of the oppressors who claim that Eurocentric art contains no agenda, no political motivations. Yet, this white Eurocentric aesthetic has been issued as the norm, unchallengeable, and any artistic endeavor that diverges from it is seen as aesthetically inferior, even primitive.

While some of my students have a superficial familiarity with the Harlem Renaissance, most have no exposure to the Black Arts Movement. Thus, I have found it vital to provide students foundational knowledge of both these historical African American arts and political movements to fully appreciate how the Affrilachians draw from them. Harlem Renaissance writer Claude McKay's seminal novel *Home to Harlem* ([1928] 1987) obviously inspired the very title of this essay. When I include Frank X Walker's first poetry collection, *Affrilachia* (2000), in undergraduate American literature classes, I place the text at the end of the semester. Because I use an American literature anthology for all other readings and teach the material chronologically, students have read the anthology editors' introductions to not only the Harlem Renaissance and the Black Arts Movement, along with a sampling of the movements' writers, but they also have read various slave narratives before learning about the Affrilachians. Therefore, students witness the evolution of black literature from the 1700s to the present and how each period builds upon and/or reacts to the previous ones.

For students enrolled in other courses who need more contextual information, David Levering Lewis's edited collection, *The Portable Harlem Renaissance Reader* (1994), provides a fine introduction to the movement's artists, writers, and social critics. Larry Neal's essay "The Black Arts Movement," found in Angelyn Mitchell's *Within the Circle: An Anthology of African American Literary Criticism from the Harlem Renaissance to the Present* (1994), gives students insight into the politics of this charged era of the 1960s and '70s. This anthology also supplements Lewis's as it spans the decades between the movements. Students then better understand both periods' influences on the Affrilachians. They specifically see how the writers incorporate the political, social, and artistic themes of the Harlem Renaissance and Black Arts Movement into their Appalachian writing as a way to speak out against limitations imposed by others.

Literary critic and scholar Joyce A. Joyce speaks directly to the need to counter white-European hegemony, proclaiming,

> If we are going to be successful at identifying a theory of African American poetry, we must look to the works of our own writers and develop the theory from within our tradition, from their works and not from the outside. We must not follow the established trend of black theoreticians who

have theorized about fiction by imposing alien terminology from outside the culture or who have cleverly taken an African folktale and imbued it with Eurocentric intellectual thought that has nothing to do with the culture from which the tale was taken. (1999, 100)

Joyce's edict echoes Jim Wayne Miller's claim that Appalachians must create their own mirror to accurately reflect the truth of their experiences. Joyce speaks directly to the co-optation of black intellectuals, those who succumb to white European aesthetic standards as the sole measure of quality. This move is made in sacrifice to their own aesthetic and involves a compromise of their cultural identity and roots.

While both African Americans and Appalachians have endured cultural oppression, though of different natures, the Affrilachians draw from both traditions to inform their works, counter dismissive stereotypes, and highlight the contributions of people of color to the region and nation. Editor Stephen L. Fisher's work *Fighting Back in Appalachia: Traditions of Resistance and Change* (1993); as well as Dwight Billings, Gurney Norman, and Katherine Ledford's edited text, *Confronting Appalachian Stereotypes: Back Talk from an American Region* (1999), showcase writers who speak out against popular myths that present Appalachians as lazy, inbred, moonshine-drinking vigilantes steadfast against progress and education. The Affrilachians carry on this important work in their poetry and prose and write to critique and highlight the multiple rich histories from which they come.

Yet another appeal when teaching the Affrilachians and their work lies in their transcendence of one discipline and one theory. In fact, their work demands a multidisciplinary, cross-theoretical reading. Disciplines such as history, political science, sociology, psychology, literature, and music all play a role in discerning meaning in the Affrilachians' work. Marxist, feminist, postcolonial, African American, and New Historicist literary theories aid readers as they interpret the poetry and prose of the Affrilachians, as they dissect the ideological and aesthetic structures of the pieces. Affrilachian works broaden notions of what Appalachia is and who Appalachians are. As a result, readers employ a broad knowledge base and intensify their understanding of not only Appalachian history and black Appalachians' place in it, but also of the greater African diaspora.

Frank X Walker's 2004 collection, *Buffalo Dance: The Journey of York*, demonstrates part of the Affrilachians' history. In this work Walker mirrors Harlem Renaissance writers' efforts to analyze and publicize the civic contributions, creativity, and intellectual talents of African Americans, who historically have been denigrated in America and viewed as inferior in all capacities by many whites. He follows the Black Arts Movement and Black Power Movement artists and participants as he employs a New Historicist maneuvering to re-write and retell what has been accepted as fact but has been proved to be half true or outright false. Through the poems, readers join the 1804 expedition of Meriwether Lewis and William Clark across the Louisiana Territory. Yet they come to understand the journey through the eyes of York, Clark's slave, who accompanied the two during the entire trip. Walker describes York as the very first Affrilachian, proclaiming, "On my best days, I think of myself and the people I love and respect as sons and daughters of York" (2004, preface). Though York served many vital roles on the trip, carrying more than any other man and protecting the expedition party from aggressive animals encountered out west, his story is absent from history. One Lewis and Clark website dem-onstrates this, for the authors proclaim, "These true American heroes faced unknown people, harsh conditions and unexplored lands to secure a place in history as two of the world's greatest explorers."[5] Frank X Walker corrects York's omission from the tales. After conducting extensive primary research on the life of York, Walker assumes York's voice through poetry and provides a New Historicist rendering of this infamous excursion.

Walker even titles one of the later poems in the collection "Revisionist History," thereby directly confronting York's purposeful exclusion. As with many of the other poems, Walker begins this one with an excerpt from Clark's actual journal, dated 23 September 1806, that documents the expedition par-ty's return to St. Louis. Because the residents believed the party had died along the journey due to their long absence, Walker explains through York, "When we set foot back in old Saint Louie / there was much celebration an putting on.... / We paraded through the streets firing our guns / an made a home in the nearest tavern. / No one seemed to tire a hearing us tell / our stories night after night" (2004, 61). As is likely to happen, however, the tales grew taller with time and alcohol. Instead of one grizzly bear, "herds a grizzlies" came upon them, along with "big talking fish an Indian women ten foot tall" (61).

At this point, readers gain insight into York's exclusion from the his-tory books. From York's perspective Walker recounts, "The truth seemed to stretch so / that by an by I seem to disappear from they tongues / as if I had never even been there / as if my blackness never saved they hides. / Them twist the tales an leave out my parts in it / so much so, that directly I become Massa Clark's boy, again / just along to cook / an carry" (2004, 61). Despite his substantial contributions to the success of the journey, York witnesses himself being written out of the story, even as he sits among the expedition party members. He is reduced to less than a man, a mere "boy," as that term connotes a long-standing pejorative meaning. Walker does not paint York as a flawless individual, however; in the telling, Walker portrays the complexity and short-comings of this real human being, even in the midst of York's growth over the course of the transcontinental journey.

After reading the York poems, many of my students feel deceived by their education for they begin to wonder what and who else has been absent from their learning. I take this opportunity to discuss with them the old adage "Winners typically write the history books." Or in the case of York and the Affrilachians, the oppressors or socially dominant dictate whose stories are passed on and whose are intentionally silenced. While it may be easier for students to identify absent voices in history and literature when they know groups of people existed at the time of the events, it is much more difficult to exhume individuals who are buried so deeply in vaults or of whose lives no records whatsoever exist. We talk about the efforts of even dedicated scholars who inevitably miss important figures, histories, and herstories due to record-ing practices of the past.

Frank X Walker's poetry collection *Affrilachia* (2000) also includes many themes reminiscent of the Black Arts Movement (BAM), as well as of the Harlem Renaissance. In "C P Time," Walker employs a twenty-first-century American urban street vernacular to confront and dismantle many of the ste-reotypes whites still utilize to oppress blacks today. In this poem Walker's "we" narrator, just as Langston Hughes's "I" narrator in many of his Harlem Renaissance poems, represents the collective black community. Walker's con-frontation parallels the battle fought by the Harlem Renaissance and BAM artists who strove through their craft to dispel the myriad myths of their own time. Walker begins his poetic political commentary:

> we be rapping
> about time
> about
> being on it
> and in it
> this colored people's clock thang
> an appendage
> more like

fried chicken
and watermelon
and less like inventing jazz
or building pyramids (2000, 29)

Because "colored people" don't adhere to white "western standards" that are "designed to ignore / cultural differences," because "colored people" honor instead their own time, they are on trial (Walker 2000, 29). Similar to the minstrel shows of the early twentieth century that parodied blacks through the use of blackface, Walker inserts reductive caricatures of African Americans with their fried chicken and watermelon, appropriating these images for his own purposes. He juxtaposes the caricatures with the real accomplishments of blacks throughout the world, whether "inventing jazz or building pyramids" (29).

Deeper into Walker's poem, readers discover sentiments reminiscent of W. E. B. DuBois. In "Criteria of Negro Art," DuBois claims black America has a "bounden duty . . . to begin this great work of the creation of beauty, . . . and we must use in this work all the methods that men have used before. And what have been the tools of the artist in times gone by? *First of all, he has used the truth—not for the sake of truth, . . . but as one upon whom truth eternally thrusts itself as the highest handmaid of imagination, as the one great vehicle of universal understanding*" ([1926] 1994, 102–3, emphasis added). Moreover, he boldly asserts, "white publishers catering to white folk . . . want Uncle Toms, Topsies, good 'darkies' and clowns" (102).

Almost a century later, Walker explains:

our internal clocks
dictate that to be
in truth
in sync
with the universe
we must do it
whatever our it is
when
and only when
it feels right
and not because assimilation
rang the bell (2000, 30)

Just like DuBois, Walker understands that living the truth of one's culture is crucial in the struggle for equality. And one does not live truth or become equal by selling out, by assimilating into mainstream white society. In fact, Walker becomes DuBois's "apostle of beauty [who] thus becomes the apostle of truth and right not by choice but by inner and outer compulsion" (DuBois [1926] 1994, 103). Walker becomes a modern-day griot, sharing stories of truth that reflect his Affrilachian community.

In the final stanza, Walker administers a warning to those who are tempted to acquiesce by evoking images of black political icon Marcus Garvey, who "painted all our / white flags / red black and green" (2000, 30). According to Mary White Ovington in her essay "On Marcus Garvey," "The colors of the new movement were Black, Red, and Green. 'Black for our race,' as His Excellency said, in his regal robes of colors, 'Red for our blood, and Green for our hope'" (1994, 32). Walker's position is clear, and the color white is significant in two ways. In wartime, white flags traditionally symbolize surrender. But Walker utilizes the white flag to admonish blacks not to surrender to the Eurocentric white way.

Despite the decades that separate DuBois and Walker, and despite the gains African Americans have made in America over the last eighty years, Walker reveals the persistent oppression of racism in the twenty-first century. He asserts at the close of his poem:

> So don't confuse our tardiness
> with laziness or irresponsibility
> we who are rebels
> by western standards
> will be
> who we are
> all the time
> and when
> our life cycles
> end
> and ancestral ones begin
> may the timekeeper note that
> though we may have always been late
> we were always
> right on
> time (2000, 31)

In tune with both African and Appalachian culture, Walker acknowledges the importance of the ancestral spirit and its persistence and presence beyond death. Moreover, Western standards cannot control people of color, will not dictate their rhythm, for they are in tune with the "cyclical rhythm / of the universe" and are consequently "always / right on / time" (2000, 31). In this poem, Walker harkens back to Larry Neal's proclamation in his essay "The Black Arts Movement": "A main tenet of Black Power is the necessity for Black people to define the world in their own terms" (1994, 184).

Walker's *Affrilachia* contains many poems that prompt students to think critically about who controls and dictates ways of being in our society, along with what is or is not accepted. Moreover, we discuss the power of paradigms, whether familial, religious, social, ethnic, or political, and how individuals are affected by popular mass media that promote certain ways of living while ignoring or discounting others. Indeed, Walker provides students an opportunity to engage in epistemological inquiry rooted in the particular of Affrilachia yet capable of being exploded to a more universal level of critique that is applicable the world over.

Affrilachian Nikky Finney, 2011 National Book Award winner, furthers the mission to present the realities of black American experiences as she documents 1990s racism in her poem "My Old Kentucky Home: Where the darkies are gay," which is found in her 2003 collection, *The World Is Round*. The title of this poem comes directly from the Kentucky state song, and she begins the poem with an epigraph that explains, "From the week of October 25, 1994, after the killing of 18-year-old Antonio Sullivan, shot in the head at close range by a policeman" (2003, 71). Though this poem shares certain thematic similarities with many of the other poems in the work, the structure is vastly different. Finney separates the poem into sections that begin in the present, shift to what she imagines, and then predict the future.

In the first section, "What I See: Shiloh Baptist Church," she reports the happenings of this young black male's funeral: "A domino of young men from every local / village, eyes bursting like tall hydrants, they / circle around his open casket, brown faces / shining" (Finney 2003, 71). We see how they "huddle, afraid of death staring up / at them but they are more terrified of leaving / him there, alone" (71). The living find it difficult to move away from the dead, so "they put private male things all around him. / Things we can't see from our seats. It is an old / Affrilachian mountain custom, to put things / in the pocket of the young dead, it is done / in grand hip-hop style" (72). Finney invokes both mountain tradition and urban pop culture to convey the death ritual of these young black males. At the conclusion of this section, we learn that "life will not wait for them to finish their mourning. / It will call them back to the land of the living-dead / before they are ready" (73). Moreover, in this last line, Finney calls attention to the social plight of so many young black men in the United States, namely a life without hope. This land of the living-dead is one without any real means of escape from dominant society's prescribed yet subtle dead ends, black male ego-busters that still serve as lingering remnants from the eras of sanctioned slavery and Jim Crow.

The second section, "What I Dream: The Lexington Cemetery," contains musings of what will happen when no more burial land exists, when "every set of bones over one hundred will be / moved to one mass grave site, set aside by the / Commonwealth" (Finney 2003, 74). Though on first thought this may seem disrespectful, Finney argues otherwise. She comments, "They will / think they are saving precious, irreplaceable / bluegrass farms, but they will be saving more" (74), for bones have no visible color differentiations as skins do. "They will just be the dead. / We will have to do this because we will no longer / have the space to be as thoughtful about the dead, / because we have been so thoughtless about the living" (74). Death, the great leveler, or as Finney describes it, "the common denominator," will usher in a new day, for "finally, white bones will fall and / snuggle up next to black bones and no one will care / or be able to tell who was ever who" (75). Finney closes what she "dreams" with a stanza that praises the finality of death and this mixing of bones "to create on / this earth what we were supposed to be all along" (76), namely, one human race.

In the final section, "What I Think: The Press Conference," we are catapulted into the year 2595 and "listen" to an archaeologist who attempts, without success, to explain why "the darker ones / of the species (not all but certainly far too many / for it to have been mere coincidence) and / primarily the young adult males, had these / strange holes searing some part of their craniums" (Finney 2003, 76). This social phenomenon of the late twentieth and early twenty-first centuries, where young black males die en masse from bullets, will stump a "brilliant scientific mind" six hundred years later. He will only be able to compare it to another strange finding,

> *which we had not seen evidence of since*
> *79 A.D., a continent away in the city of Pompeii,*
> *where the mummified bodies of the smaller*
> *children in the same housing structures as their*

> *older siblings were found crouching in corners,*
> *99% of whom seemed to have died with their mouths*
> *wide open as if in the middle of one long unbroken*
> *scream.* (77, emphasis in original)

Finney's choice in comparing violence against young black males to the natural disaster violence of Pompeii in actuality speaks to the contrasts of the two, for where one was indeed "natural" in the way we understand "caused by nature," the other was not. Bullet holes in the heads of young black males present a social phenomenon, not a natural one, and are preventable, not unstoppable. The glaring similarity, however, involves the "one long unbroken scream" of the younger siblings. Where the older ones perhaps resolve themselves to the tragedy unfolding, the younger ones do not. They refuse to give in to death, screaming to stop it, despite their futility. And hence the "one long unbroken scream" unites the young of Pompeii with the young of black America.

"My Old Kentucky Home: Where the darkies are gay" exemplifies the diversity of issues from which Finney crafts her poems. The setting is Affrilachia, with distinct mountain customs; yet Finney illustrates the universal in the particular throughout this poem because the issues transcend Appalachia. Many blacks throughout America deal with these same tragedies, battle the same hate-inspired crimes. Finney blends long-held Affrilachian traditions with urban street culture popularized by the media. She exposes the corrupt politics of her society as well as the pervasive institution of racism. When students research the incident that inspired Finney's poem, they discover that a twenty-two-year veteran police officer "accidentally" shot Sullivan as he emerged unarmed from a closet in his living room where he was hiding. Finney predicts the tragedy of our future if current events do not change. Implied in this last is Finney's message that *we* must make these changes. They will not automatically unfold. And in this way, Finney, like the rest of the Affrilachians, employs bell hooks's notion of unshackling imaginations from oppressors in order to envision and then create a different future. Readers witness myriad associations in her work that bring to life a richly crafted world that not only mirrors reality but also inspires creative visioning for a more promising, egalitarian future.

Native Kentuckian Crystal Wilkinson also draws from African American and Appalachian literary traditions in her short story collections. *Blackberries, Blackberries* (2000), her first published work, contains themes and characters that represent this blending of traditions, as well as their perfect union. She also creates characters that prompt readers to employ multiple theories to reveal the characters' psyches and understand their motives for certain life choices. In "Music for Meriah," Wilkinson allows her readers a brief but telling glimpse into the life of the title character, a Kentucky woman described as "plain. Twenty-eight years old. A recent escapee of her mama's possessive clutches" (2000, 4). Though she merely throws in this last descriptor with the rest, readers soon realize that Meriah's attempted escape from her mother is the crux of the story, while also understanding that she has not truly freed herself from her mother's suffocating grip. Wilkinson interlaces present-day happenings with flashbacks to Meriah's childhood before her father left and returned to New York.

The thread that weaves these fragments together is jazz, for Wilkinson explains that Meriah "had loved jazz since hearing her daddy's records when she was a little bitty girl" (2000, 4). Now, as an adult looking for escape from her mundane life and her mama's psychological guilt-tripping, Meriah turns to the music in Lexington nightclubs where she follows the smooth, mesmerizing performances of a jazz pianist, Osmond. Meriah possesses only a superficial knowledge of Osmond but hangs on to his music, gestures, and cryptic cocktail-lounge conversation as though they were a lifeline. Indeed they are a lifeline, for they not only feed her imagination when she departs alone from the nightclubs and returns to her lonely apartment; they serve as a vital link between Osmond and Meriah's lost father—again, with jazz binding the seam.

Although she specifically does not employ jazz as a literary idiom in her writing, Wilkinson does utilize it as a cultural connector, demonstrating the influence of jazz *on* her characters. As a historical black musical genre, jazz unites African Americans across most of the twentieth century. Gerald Early, writing in the *Antioch Review* (1999), explains the African American affinity for jazz that burgeoned during the 1960s Black Arts Movement and can be attributed primarily to Amiri Baraka's promotion of the music. Early notes, "Jazz musicians became heroes to a certain set of people who were, in their way, unhappy with the commercialism of the modern world. Black intellectuals were drawn to music, jazz particularly, as a kind of demanding, perfected orgasm of spontaneity" (379). According to Wilkinson's time reference in the story, Meriah's father would have been a young adult at the peak of the Black Arts Movement, hence the importance of jazz in his life. I recommend bringing jazz into the classroom while teaching this short story because, rather unfortunately, most twenty-first-century students are unfamiliar with such jazz greats as Miles Davis, John Coltrane, Charles Mingus, and Billie Holiday.

YouTube offers opportunities to not only hear but also see these jazz masters in action.

Wilkinson also employs a psychoanalytic rendering of Meriah as her character seems to suffer from the Jungian Electra complex, the female version of Freud's Oedipus complex, although at an older age than traditionally defined by Jung and Freud. Reflecting on the last time she saw her father when she was fifteen years old, Meriah "carried the smell of him with her even now. The smell of a freshly ironed shirt even through the sweater he wore. The slightly musty smell of a man" (2000, 9). Wilkinson goes on to demonstrate the burgeoning of Meriah's conflict in the silent confrontation with her mother:

> When he told her he would always love her, *no matter what*, she had cried into his arm. Her mama had stood at the door, her arms folded into herself, with fear in her eyes. When Meriah had hugged and kissed her daddy goodbye, she had seen her mama's mouth twist. In that instant, with the November wind at her back, a great loathing for her mama had blown in with her daddy's leaving. (2000, 9, emphasis in original)

And her loathing only increases over time. In a flashback, Wilkinson explains Meriah's determination to get to New York when she turns eighteen. She has even purchased a plane ticket to get there. Yet her mother's melodramatic theatrics break her resolve. Her mother screams hysterically, "'Your daddy left me and now you too. . . . If you are leaving, then you might as well shoot me. . . . Kill me dead right this minute because it will be the last of me'" (2000, 8). Wilkinson goes on to reveal how at that point, Meriah "placed every dream and hope of her own upon a shelf [and] had stayed behind to be swallowed up by her mama's misery" (8).

With a life such as hers, Meriah seems to have no other choice but to find fulfillment, no matter how ephemeral, in the sultry melodies Osmond evokes from his jazz piano. Meriah transfers her longing for her father onto Osmond, which ushers in the sexual element of the Electra complex. As Wilkinson describes Meriah's perception of Osmond, readers understand the intermingling of all these demons in Meriah because Osmond "always reminded her of the best of her former lovers. Every gentle touch, every soft kiss she had ever felt was offered back to her through some movement or expression that Osmond made" (2000, 6). Her intense loneliness and lament over so many lost opportunities envelop her whole being despite her efforts to feign a different persona. Wilkinson provides insight into the split lives of Meriah when she explains that she "never wore jewelry to work, but wore rings on her fingers and large bangles around her wrist when she frequented the nightclubs and bars where Osmond played. She fancied herself looking more experienced, more worldly, when she dressed this way" (5). To compensate for her lack of confidence and inability to live as she truly wishes, Meriah postures, portraying something, some woman, of whom she can only dream.

Wilkinson brings Meriah's many tensions to a head and sets the concluding tone as Meriah enters yet another nightclub searching for satiation in the elusive character of Osmond, an illusion that tragically mirrors her father's. "A hunger clicked into the Pearly Peacock on the heels of Meriah's shoes as she sauntered toward the table" (2000, 13). Readers can interpret her hunger as stemming from both the empty woman longing for relationship and the girl-child yearning for her father. Wilkinson notes, "Meriah focused her wonder on Osmond. His fingers gliding, the way the muscles in his back rode each note" (13). As the evening fades into early morning hours, Meriah reels from the wine and music she has consumed and then grows distracted by a familiar face in the crowd, an old boyfriend sitting with "a small, delicate woman the color of butterscotch pudding" (14). Readers come to know that Billy Martin left Meriah because she "had refused to quit sneaking behind her mama's back. To do things that normal couples did. Meriah was content to keep slipping through the shadows, picking up what bits of freedom she could muster there" (14). As Wilkinson demonstrates repeatedly throughout the story, Meriah has allowed her mother to control every aspect of her life. But her mother's psychological shackling is so strong and ever-present that Meriah is unable to break free, even now as a grown woman.

Meriah's evening turns emotionally tragic, though readers easily could conclude the inevitability of her fall. After all, the imaginary life Meriah has fabricated so elaborately becomes real to her. After Osmond's band wraps up the last session of the night and begins the stage breakdown, he walks to her table where she sits alone. "'You all right?' he said, bending down close to her and patting her shoulder. 'A little too much to drink?'" (2000, 15). Meriah assures him she is fine and Osmond walks away with a "'See you next time?'" (15). Instead of waiting until his next gig, however, Meriah waits in the parking lot for Osmond to leave the nightclub and follows him home, trailing just far enough behind so as to remain inconspicuous. With wine flowing through her body, her imagination in high gear, Meriah lingers in her car until Osmond enters his house and clicks on the lights. Only then does she approach the door to ring the bell. But her nerve to push it quickly dissolves. Wilkinson describes Meriah's antics: "She crept along the side of Osmond's house, happy to see that he had an abundance of flowerbeds. Meriah imagined herself gardening there in the spring. Osmond would call out to her, *Baby, I'm home,* and she would run into his arms" (16). Meriah's make-believe world suddenly is shattered by the appearance of another figure in the window, a woman who snuggles into Osmond's arms. And as all the times before, Meriah is left alone.

In the next scene of the following day, Wilkinson portrays Meriah as defeated, seeking refuge in the depths of her bed where she has remained the entire day. Typical of her character, Meriah flashes back to her childhood as she lies there, recalling when her mother and father hovered over her while she was sick in bed. In the process, Wilkinson enables readers to appreciate the melding of Meriah's past life with her present, jazz again coming to the fore, serving as tonic. "In their house there was always music. Always jazz. Monk, Miles Davis, Strayhorn, Coltrane" (2000, 17). The jazz masters follow Meriah the following day to her mother's as she finally relents to eat dinner with her. After fretting over her grown but only baby, after bread has been broken between the two, Meriah's mother wraps herself in the warm, familiar melodies of Meriah's daddy's records, remnants of a lost life. As if she could conjure the deceased musicians from the dead, and in the process bring her long-gone husband home, Meriah's "mama's fingers [moved] over the posed faces on the [album] covers" until she falls asleep (18). And Meriah finds an unexpected peace in sitting with her mother. Wilkinson explains, "She listened to the in and out of her mama's breath as it danced through her daddy's music and did not even think about leaving" (18). With this resolve Meriah seems to ease into the reality that is her life, no longer tempted to fabricate fantasies of her father or Osmond.

This stripping away of fantasies, of instead focusing on the sometimes joyful, sometimes hurtful truths of diverse human experiences, is found in the work of all three Affrilachians—Frank X Walker, Nikky Finney, and Crystal Wilkinson. The mirrors they flash before readers reflect the complexity of their fictitious characters who display traits evident in real-life individuals. The messages of their poems and short stories cut through superficial niceties counterproductive to social critique and true racial justice and equality. Through the crafting of their words, the authors explode limited views held by many outsiders and insiders of Appalachia to present a more accurate representation of the region and to abolish romanticized notions of the mountains and their residents.

It is apparent that the Affrilachians offer students many learning opportunities due to the multidisciplinary themes in their writing and the various theoretical lenses through which the writing can be critiqued. Indeed, the writers provide insight into multiple cultural traditions. Whether discerning the literary impact of the Harlem Renaissance and Black Arts Movement or identifying specific Appalachian cultural characteristics, students of the Affrilachians' poetry and prose will come away with a richer, fuller understanding of the importance of these writers not only to the region but to the entire nation.

Notes

1. Frank X Walker, e-mail message to author, 17 March 2003.
2. Ibid.
3. Ibid.
4. Ibid.
5. See http://www.lewisclark.net/index.html?vm=r.

References / Teaching Resource List

Baber, Bob Henry, George Ella Lyon, and Gurney Norman, eds. 1994. *Old Wounds, New Words: Poems from the Appalachia Poetry Project.* Ashland, KY: Jesse Stuart Foundation.

Baker, Houston A., Jr., and Patricia Redmond, eds. 1989. *Afro-American Literary Study in the 1990s.* Chicago: University of Chicago Press.

Ballard, Sandra L., and Patricia L. Hudson, eds. 2003. *Listen Here: Women Writing in Appalachia.* Lexington: University Press of Kentucky.

Berry, Faith. 1983. *Langston Hughes: Before and Beyond Harlem.* Westport, CT.: L. Hill.

Best, Bill, comp. 2000. *One Hundred Years of Appalachian Visions.* Berea, KY: Appalachian Imprints.

Billings, Dwight B., Gurney Norman, and Katherine Ledford, eds. 1999. *Confronting Appalachian Stereotypes: Back Talk from an American Region.* Lexington: University Press of Kentucky.

Blackshire-Belay, Carol Aisha, ed. 1992. *Language and Literature in the African American Imagination.* Westport, CT: Greenwood Press.

Bloom, Harold. 1994. *Black American Women Fiction Writers.* New York: Chelsea House.

Cabbell, Edward J. 1991. "The Soulful Side of the Mountains: A Sense of Place in Afro-Appalachian Writings." In *Honoring Our Past: Proceedings on the First Two Conferences on West Virginia's Black History,* edited by Joe W. Trotter and Ancella Radford Bickley, 357–78. Charleston: Alliance for the Collection, Preservation, and Dissemination of West Virginia's Black History.

———. 1995. "Black Diamonds: The Search for Blacks in Appalachian Literature and Writing." In *Appalachia Inside Out.* Vol. 1, *Conflict and Change,* edited by Ambrose N.

Manning, Robert J. Higgs, and Jim Wayne Miller, 241–45. Knoxville: University of Tennessee Press.

Carroll, Rebecca. 1994. *I Know What the Red Clay Looks Like: The Voice and Vision of Black American Women Writers*. New York: Crown.

Donahue, Jean, and Fred Johnson. 2001. *Coal Black Voices: A Documentary*. Media Working Group, Covington, KY. Videocassette.

DuBois, W. E. B. (1926) 1994. "Criteria of Negro Art." In A. Mitchell, *Within the Circle*, 60–68.

Dunaway, Wilma A. 2003a. *The African-American Family in Slavery and Emancipation*. Cambridge: Cambridge University Press.

———. 2003b. *Slavery in the American Mountain South*. Cambridge: Cambridge University Press.

———. 2008. *Women, Work, and Family in the Antebellum Mountain South*. Cambridge: Cambridge University Press.

Early, Gerald. 1999. "Ode to John Coltrane: A Jazz Musician's Influence on African American Culture." *Antioch Review* 57, no. 3 (Summer): 371–85.

Ergood, Bruce, and Bruce E. Kuhre, eds. 1991. *Appalachia: Social Context Past and Present*. Dubuque, IA: Kendall Hunt.

Ervin, Hazel Arnett, ed. 1999. *African American Literary Criticism, 1773 to 2000*. New York: Twayne.

Finney, Nikky. 1985. *On Wings Made of Gauze*. New York: Morrow.

———. 1995. *Rice*. Toronto: Sister Vision Press.

———. 1997. *Heartwood*. Lexington: University Press of Kentucky.

———. 1998. "Salt-Water Geechee Mounds." In *Bloodroot: Reflections on Place by Appalachian Women Writers*, edited by Joyce Dyer, 120–27. Lexington: University Press of Kentucky.

———. 2003. *The World Is Round*. Atlanta: Interlight Publishing.

Fisher, Stephen L., ed. 1993. *Fighting Back in Appalachia: Traditions of Resistance and Change*. Philadelphia: Temple University Press.

Gilyard, Keith, ed. 1997. *Spirit and Flame: An Anthology of Contemporary African American Poetry*. Syracuse, NY: Syracuse University Press.

Giovanni, Nikki. 1998. "400 Mulvaney Street." In *Bloodroot: Reflections on Place by Appalachian Women Writers*, edited by Joyce Dyer, 132–39. Lexington: University Press of Kentucky.

Grubbs, Morris Allen, ed. 2001. *Home and Beyond: An Anthology of Kentucky Short Stories*. Lexington: University Press of Kentucky.

Higgs, Robert, and Ambrose N. Manning, eds. (1975) 1996. *Voices from the Hills: Selected Readings of Southern Appalachia*. Dubuque, IA: Kendall Hunt.

hooks, bell. 1991. "Narratives of Struggle." In *Critical Fictions: The Politics of Imaginative Writing*, edited by Philomena Mariani, 53–61. Seattle: Bay Press.

Joyce, Joyce A. 1999. "*Bantu, Nkodi, Ndungu, and Nganga*: Language, Poetics, Music, and Religion in African American Poetry." In *The Furious Flowering of African American Poetry*, edited by Joanne V. Gabbin, 99–117. Charlottesville: University Press of Virginia.

Lewis, David Levering, ed. 1994. *The Portable Harlem Renaissance Reader*. New York: Viking.

McKay, Claude. (1928) 1987. *Home to Harlem.* New York: Harper. Reprint, Boston: Northeastern University Press.

Miller, Danny L. 1996. *Wingless Flights: Appalachian Women in Fiction.* Bowling Green, KY: Bowling Green State University Popular Press.

Miller, Jim Wayne. (1975) 1996. "A Mirror for Appalachia." In Higgs and Manning, *Voices from the Hills,* 447–59.

Mitchell, Angelyn, ed. 1994. *Within the Circle: An Anthology of African American Literary Criticism from the Harlem Renaissance to the Present.* Durham, NC: Duke University Press.

Mitchell, Felicia, ed. 2002. *Her Words: Diverse Voices in Contemporary Appalachian Women's Poetry.* Knoxville: University of Tennessee Press.

Neal, Larry. 1994. "The Black Arts Movement." In A. Mitchell, *Within the Circle,* 184–98.

Ovington, Mary White. 1994. "On Marcus Garvey." In Lewis, *The Portable Harlem Renaissance Reader,* 29–33.

Quashie, Kevin Everod, Joyce Laush, and Keith D. Miller, eds. 2001. *New Bones: Contemporary Black Writers in America.* Upper Saddle River, NJ: Prentice-Hall.

Smethurst, James Edward. 1999. *The New Red Negro: The Literary Left and African American Poetry, 1930–1946.* New York: Oxford University Press.

Smith, Barbara Ellen. 1999. "'Beyond the Mountains': The Paradox of Women's Place in Appalachian History." *NWSA Journal* 11, no. 3 (Fall): 1–17.

Turner, William H., and Edward J. Cabbell, eds. 1985. *Blacks in Appalachia.* Lexington: University Press of Kentucky.

Walker, Frank X. 2000. *Affrilachia.* Lexington: Old Cove Press.

———. 2004. *Buffalo Dance: The Journey of York.* Lexington: University Press of Kentucky.

———. 2005. *Black Box.* Lexington, KY: Old Cove Press.

———. 2009. *When Winter Come: The Ascension of York.* Lexington: University Press of Kentucky.

Wilkinson, Crystal. 2000. *Blackberries, Blackberries.* London: Toby Press.

———. 2002. *Water Street.* London: Toby Press.

THIRTEEN

Teaching the Poetry and Prose of Marilou Awiakta

GRACE TONEY EDWARDS

FROM HER EARLIEST YEARS MARILOU AWIAKTA has been an astute observer, listener, and storyteller. A Cherokee/Appalachian author in Memphis, Tennessee, she writes poetry and prose that range in subject matter from childhood memories of growing up in Oak Ridge during the days of the Manhattan Project,[1] to myths, legends, and stories of the Cherokee, to social, political, scientific, and environmental issues in contemporary society. She says that the three major strands of her life and thereby her writing are her Cherokee ancestry, her Celtic/Appalachian heritage, and her upbringing on the atomic frontier of Oak Ridge.

For her writing, she chose her middle name, Awiakta, given to her by her grandfather. It means "eye of the deer" and is also the Cherokee name for the vibrant flowering plant known as black-eyed Susan. She has written in some form virtually her whole life. As a youngster she declared to her mother that she wanted to be a writer. In response, her mother queried: "What will you do for the people?" Awiakta's answer has been the production of three published books and hundreds of published poems, essays, and articles. In demand as speaker, reader, and workshop leader, she frequently visits college and university campuses across the nation, Native American gatherings of various sorts, and literary, artistic, historical, religious, and civic groups.

Early Days into Adulthood

At age three, Awiakta composed her first poem, inspired by a butter-
fly in flight that suddenly fell dead at her feet. Her mother preserved her
daughter's words:

> Oh, Little Butterfly,
> how I wish you weren't dead,
> so that you could fly
> with other butterflies instead.[2]

Just three years later, she "published" her first short story, titled "Mr. and Mrs.
Honeybee Find a Home." Written in wartime, with housing at a premium, the
topic reveals the powerful influence of social issues even then on the thoughtful
child. The carefully lettered title page of the extant manuscript shows colorful
illustrations of bees and flowers by the author, whose name is highlighted in
bright red and blue double underlining. Already the budding writer perceived
the importance of identity and was clearly in pursuit of establishing her own.

Awiakta's parents, both with Cherokee ancestry, settled in Knoxville soon
after the baby's birth. Near the beginning of the United States' involvement
in World War II, a flurry of secret activity erupted in the misty mountains
just west of Knoxville. That flurry was to become the Manhattan Project, the
development of the atomic bomb by the United States government. Marilou's
father began work there, and in time, when housing became available, the
family moved to live "behind the fence" in Oak Ridge, Tennessee.[3] Marilou
was nine and old enough to absorb all the newness, excitement, pioneer spirit,
secretiveness, and sense of something hugely important in that place. As time
and events brought an end to the war, she thrived in that hub of scientific experimentation and advancement. Her interests leaned toward the artistic and
literary, but she recognized the great import of the scientific and appreciated
the community culture that acknowledged the essential coexistence of science
and art.

At the University of Tennessee, Marilou majored in English and French.
She met her husband, Paul Thompson, there, a premed student who eventually took her to live in Laon, France, to fulfill a long-nurtured dream. For
three years in France as a young wife and mother, translator, and liaison officer, she immersed herself in the culture and language she had studied. Oddly,

the strange new sounds and sights began to carry her in mind back home, to Oak Ridge, to the Great Smokies, to the mountain people she had grown up among. During a long seventeen-year hiatus from writing poetry, the people and experiences of her childhood and adolescence gestated until 1972, when, to answer a challenge, she wrote the poem "Prayer of Appalachia," which she entered in the Mid-South Poetry Contest. She won first place, the Jesse Hill Ford Award, and has written steadily ever since.

That poem became part of *Abiding Appalachia: Where Mountain and Atom Meet* ([1978] 2006),[4] a collection commissioned by St. Luke's Press in Memphis, where Marilou, Paul, and their three children were living by then and where she and her husband live today. Her "writing place" is an upstairs room called the Dwell—papered with pine boughs and lighted by a full-moon globe hanging over the IBM Selectric typewriter she prepares her manuscripts on. The lace-curtained windows open out into the branches of pin oaks to bring close the natural world that has long nurtured Awiakta's spirit. She relaxes in the Glen, a cozy sitting-room with a large-ceiling-to-floor window framing a secluded forest nook formed by evergreens and hollies meant to bring a semblance of her native East Tennessee into her Memphis home.

Scholar/professor Ernest Lee observed the "power of poetry in her home and in her person" when he took students to interview her. In a conference presentation, he addressed Awiakta, who was in the audience: "I think of *you* as a poem." He continued by quoting her: "The way I feel about poetry is that all of life is poetry. Part of my work as a poet is to listen for the poems in other people and, if they don't want to sing them themselves, to sing for them" (Lee 2000). And sing she does—for Native people, for Appalachians, for women, for the beleaguered, for Mother Earth, and more.

Awiakta is at her best when she sings in unison with other people or perhaps, more accurately, when she sings in rounds, or call-and-response. She thrives on interactivity and encourages audience participation in her presentations. In gathering material for her art and sharing the fruits of it, she exudes genuine warmth and interest in others, thereby establishing an environment fitting for gifts of word and seed that are this poet's trademarks. As example of the latter, she circulates personally among her audience, when size allows, to put a grain of corn in each person's hand and to offer a personal greeting.

> *Teaching Tip*: Give students an opportunity to see Awiakta on film and/or to hear her voice on audiotape. The Kentucky Educational Television production titled *Telling Tales* features a number of storytellers, among them

Awiakta. An abridged audio version of *Selu: Seeking the Corn Mother's Wisdom* is available with Awiakta herself as reader. For other resources, readers are directed to Radford University's McConnell Library, where Awiakta's literary papers are housed; and to Radford's Appalachian Regional Studies Center, where several locally produced videotapes, interviews, photographs, slides, and student-generated projects are located.

Teaching Tip: Early in the study of Awiakta's writing, have students make a personalized "Spirit Shield" in honor of Native American literature and culture. Drawing with colored pencils, crayons, markers, or paints, students depict graphically the images and values that are most important to them—the "stuff that feeds the student's spirit." In her own workshops, Awiakta suggests such generic earth items as tree, water, rock, mountain, bird, horse, and so on. However, she also encourages students to include humans and nonnatural items with special significance to the individual.

Making the Spirit Shield is an in-class activity. Upon completion, students post the shields in the classroom without commentary except for an identification of some sort—not the student's actual name, but rather an alias in keeping with the assignment (e.g., Falling Water, Little White Horse, etc.). (Curiosity always makes classmates guess whose shield is whose, but the secret should be maintained as long as possible.) At a later date in the study, after the students are comfortable with Awiakta's writing and one another, the teacher asks students to claim their shields and to explain to the class why they each have chosen the items that represent their spirit. This exercise can be adapted to fit virtually any age level and teaching situation.

Genres of Writing

Awiakta's eclectic interests and versatility in literary forms defy conventional genre categorization. Indeed, her blending of genres produced the prose poem in her first book, *Abiding Appalachia: Where Mountain and Atom Meet*, published in 1978 and reprinted in multiple editions since then.[5] That collection, which she considers to be the eye of her work, contains other poetic forms as well, including lyrical and narrative poems. Her second book, titled *Rising Fawn and the Fire Mystery* (1983), is a child's story of historical fiction, but widely read by audiences of all ages and used as a text in college classrooms and social therapy groups. Her renowned 1993 publication, *Selu: Seeking the*

Corn Mother's Wisdom,[6] combines poetry, myth, legend, fiction, personal essay, and philosophical treatise to create a truly multigenre book. As mentioned earlier, however, she says: "Everything I write is poetry. Life is metaphorical. The form comes from the thought." Even though a piece may appear as prose, in Awiakta's mind it is a poetic expression.

Teaching Tip: For illustration of specific genres, the following selections work well:

In *Abiding Appalachia* ([1978] 2006):

Prose Poems:	"My mountains are very old" (2)
	"The Removal" (7–8)
Lyrical Poems:	"An Indian Walks in Me" (3)
	"Smoky Mountain Woman" (13)
	"Prayer of Appalachia" (20)
	"Star Vision" (49)
Narrative Poems:	"The Prophet" (24–25)
	"Genesis" (26–27)
	"The Graphite Queen" (52–54)

In *Selu: Seeking the Corn Mother's Wisdom* (1993):

Fiction:	"Grandmother Ishtoua's Lesson"—The story of Rising Fawn (73–81)
Legend:	"The Last Day of Roland the Cherokee" (54–56)
Myth:	The Story of Little Deer (woven into the text; 29)
Poetry:	"The Coming of Little Deer" (109)
	"The Origin of Corn" (myth of Selu; 10–14)
	"The Birth of Selu" (myth of first man and first woman; 24–25)
	"Origin of Strawberries" (From "Cherokee Eden: Alternative to the Apple"; 118–19)
Personal Narrative/ Philosophical Treatise:	"Baring the Atom Mother's Heart" (personal story becomes philosophical; 118–19)
Oral Chants/ Interactive Poems:	"Boardwalk" (158)
	"Out of Ashes Peace Will Rise (7)
	"Anorexia Bulimia Speaks from the Grave" (193–94)

Major Issues and Themes

If all genres of Awiakta's writing are ultimately poetic, what of the content? How is that categorized? Awiakta is at base a historical/philosophical autobiographer. She writes from and about her own experiences but broadens those to represent her ethnic groups, her gender, her community. Within the designation of autobiography/history/philosophy, five major issues or themes emerge in Awiakta's writing:

1. Oak Ridge history: personal and global contexts
2. Gender relations
3. Environment, nature, and science in society
4. Balance and harmony—unity in diversity
5. Native American philosophy, history, custom

Several of these divisions overlap, with writings easily fitting more than one category. The last theme—Native American philosophy, history, custom—actually infuses all of her work as a basic part of the character of Awiakta, through her ethnic heritage, upbringing, and choice. The following sections discuss in detail portions of the two major books, focusing on the issues and themes listed above, as well as further exemplifying genre types.

I. ABIDING APPALACHIA: WHERE MOUNTAIN AND ATOM MEET ([1978] 2006)

In its ninth printing in 2006, *Abiding Appalachia* braids together the three strands of Awiakta's personal heritage—Cherokee, Appalachian, and scientific. Her poetry presents issues from the oldest and newest cultures of a large and diverse group of people. Starting with the natural habitat and moving to government secrets of the early 1940s, she writes in the opening prose poem:

> *My mountains are very old. When the Rockies birthed*
> *bare and sharp against the sky, the Smokies were already*
> *mellowed down, mantled with forests, steeped in mist,*
> *like ancients deep in thought. And to their foothills*
> *in my childhood days men brought the atom—to split it*
> *and release a force older than the earth, older, perhaps,*
> *than time itself. Where mountain and atom meet is*
> *to some a place in Tennessee—Oak Ridge, a city that*

> came suddenly and fenced itself and drew around it
> ridges of oak and pine to guard the reactor that in
> secret split the atom. (2)

She continues with the mystery of the Cherokee influence so prevalent in that place:

> But to me, where mountain and
> atom meet is a spirit beyond time and place, a spirit
> that abides in the mountain, in the atom, in the hearts
> of my people—the Cherokee and pioneers and other folk
> who through the years have come to call the mountains
> home. I have seen traces of this spirit but the spirit
> itself I have not seen. Like the sacred deer of the
> Cherokee it is from everlasting . . . invisible . . . abiding
> in the quick of mystery. And so I call it by the ancient
> name—Awi Usdi, Little Deer. (2)

Teaching Tip: Four of the themes mentioned above can be introduced in this poem. I list them here with slight modifications to fit the specific piece:

1. Environment of ancient mountains and the incursion of "new" science
2. History of Oak Ridge and the Manhattan Project (World War II)
3. Diversity of people who have come into the place
4. Cherokee myth of Awi Usdi, Little Deer

Each theme carries the possibility of research for the students and sharing findings with classmates. Since these are subject areas addressed throughout the whole volume of poetry, students need to learn the significance of the history in order to fully appreciate the rest of the collection.

Native American Philosophy, History, and Custom; Balance and Harmony—Unity in Diversity

The collection is loosely organized into four parts with topics moving from Cherokee to Appalachian to atomic experiences, and finally to a blending of the three. Awiakta's credo poem, "An Indian Walks in Me," comes near the beginning and proclaims her heritage and philosophy: a quest for balance and harmony, for unity and wholeness. She closes with these lines:

Long before I learned the
universal turn of atoms, I heard
the spirit's song that binds us
all as one. And no more
could I follow any rule
that split my soul.
My Cherokee left me no sign
except in hair and cheek
and this firm step of mind
that seeks the whole
in strength and peace. (*Abiding*, 3)

Autobiography, yes, but representative of a greater whole than the poet herself. Following her identification with the Cherokee, she introduces Little Deer:

From the heart of the mountain he comes, with his head held high in
the wind.
Like the spirit of light he comes—the small white chief of the Deer.
(*Abiding*, 5)

Revered for his sense of justice, protection, and direction in time of need, Little Deer, or Awi Usdi, is significant in the mythology of Native people. Indeed, Awiakta herself has chosen the emblem of Little Deer leaping inside the orbit of the atom as her personal insignia. She wears this tangible evidence of her blended cultures in a pendant of silver on a background of black. Little Deer, with his wisdom and guidance, is never far from the heart of the poet.

Oak Ridge History: Personal and Global
From Little Deer to the Trail of Tears, from the sad story of Tsali to the mountain settlers who follow the Cherokee, the collection moves toward the Oak Ridge story. In the third segment of the book, Awiakta describes the foretelling of "a city on Black Oak Ridge." The prophet is John Hendrix, a farmer who, around 1900, had a vision of Bear Creek Valley being filled with "great buildings and factories" that "will help win the greatest war that ever will be" (*Abiding*, 24). John's neighbors were skeptical, but forty years later his prophecy came to pass, much as he had described. In "Genesis" Awiakta says, "A frontier was a-borning" on Black Oak Ridge:

> Thousands of people streamed in.
> Bulldozers scraped and moved the earth.
> Factories rose in valleys like Bear Creek
> and houses in droves sprang up among the trees
> and strung out in the lees of ridges.
> A great city soon lay concealed among the hills.
> > Why it had come no one knew.
> > But its energy was a strong and constant hum. (*Abiding*, 26)

The "hum" drew Awiakta's family to live behind the fence, a symbol not of oppression but of protection and freedom—freedom for children to run and play in field and wood, protected "as if our own kin patrolled the fence" (30). She describes the much coveted house of their own, a "B" cemesto cabin with two bedrooms to accommodate two adults and two same-gender children ("Cemesto Cabin: Frontier '45" [*Abiding*, 29]). The lettered cemestos were single-family prefabricated houses, erected, some say, at the alarming rate of one hundred every thirty minutes. The immediate need to house seventy thousand inhabitants produced remarkable results. Other types of dwellings included multiple-family buildings, flattops, hutments, and barracks. Most of these continue to be occupied today in Oak Ridge, though vinyl may cover cemesto and garages may crowd into basements.

Awiakta's writing in both *Abiding Appalachia* and *Selu* attests to the significance of the houses and wooded lanes in establishing the sense of security and community in that strange, yet familiar, place. A favorite story is about moving to the new house. On a cold December day just after Christmas, the family climbed the ridge of South Tampa Lane to find smoke rising from the chimney of their designated house. The movers had started a fire in the fireplace to greet and warm them on their arrival, and they had set up their beds to provide a place of rest. The men themselves were gone—mountain men, Awiakta is quick to add—for they appreciated the family's need for privacy in this special moment of arrival in a new home.[7]

Another prevalent memory from Awiakta's childhood days is the boardwalk. In the hastily built city with unpaved streets, mud abounded. Boardwalks were laid to provide footpaths and, for an imaginative child, a great resource of sensory images. In "Boardwalk," her favorite audience-participation poem, Awiakta revels in sound, touch, and smell imagery, evident both in the child experiencing and the adult recalling. From the echo of steps, both her own and others, to the slipperiness of wet wood, to the smell and touch of drying wood, she contrasts the gifts of this living organic substance with the unyielding nature of concrete. Her poem concludes:

> Boardwalk . . . boardwalk . . .
> Step, step . . . talk, talk . . .
> Concrete
> won't talk to me
> won't give to me
> won't play with me
> won't fight with me
> won't do
> for me. (*Abiding*, 32)

The playful nature of this poem runs through others spoken from a child's perspective; yet the same reflection on serious issues in the six-year-old's "Mr. and Mrs. Honeybee Find a Home" surfaces repeatedly. "Test Cow" indicates the child's knowledge of the dangers of radiation and at the same time her compassion for the radioactive cow "locked behind a fence. . . . It hurts my heart / that I can't even stroke her head / but as mother said, / radiation's just not friendly" (*Abiding*, 33). "Disaster Drill" recalls not only the dangers of living on the atomic frontier in wartime, but other removals from other times: Anne Frank, the Cherokee, Tsali. ". . . not for real . . . no bomb is falling . . . / no seal broken at the lab . . . a drill./ But we leave school, climb the hill/ lie in the ditch – we are removed" (37). And "Mother's Advice While Bandaging My Stubbed Toe" counsels,

> If you go barefoot in the world
> you have to take bad stubs in stride—
> or hide in shoes. "Be plucky, like an Indian,"
> that's what my papa said to me. . . .
> Be wary, but run on. (*Abiding*, 36)

These poems are clearly autobiographical, but also clearly more: they convey history of an important place and time from an insider's point of view; they speak philosophy from considered reflection and perhaps even racial memory.

Teaching Tip: This group of poems provides excellent choral or individual oral reading opportunities for students in the classroom. Awiakta's poetry is aural;

it needs to be read aloud. Engaging students in round-robin reading or another method of interactivity fosters their sense of ownership of the poetry.

Environment, Nature, Science in Society

The last segment of *Abiding Appalachia* features the adult poet's perspective. She weaves together the strands of her life experience, including her own children as visitors in the cemesto cabin, now a white-sided cottage. She makes a pilgrimage to prophet John Hendrix's grave. She acknowledges change and loss, but recognizes progress and growth. The emphasis of this section is plainly on the power of the atom and the skill of those scientists who dared to experiment and discover. A visit to the reactor that actually split the atom introduces the Graphite Queen, also known as the Loyal Lady: "Reactor Regina," "a boarded structure, tall and temple-like," "an altar, majestic, immense," "she met her end—standing, with life itself fading slowly . . . slowly. . . . Standing as becomes a queen whose power was of the light itself" (*Abiding*, 52–54). Despite the fading of the Loyal Lady, she is not gone, we learn, but reigns still, reincarnated in a new form:

> In a nearby valley
> a new queen reigns.
> She is a deep pool
> clear and still
> and from the slender cylinder
> of her heart
> a blue glow rises,
> a glow they call
> Cerenkov's fire. (*Abiding*, 55)

Awiakta closes her collection with "Where Mountain and Atom Meet." Representative of the forces of nature and of scientific experimentation, the poem depicts the mountain and the atom as powerful entities exuding from the "great I Am / that gathers to its own/ spirits that have gone before" (*Abiding*, 56). Serving as an epilogue for the whole book, Awi Usdi, the Ancient White, appropriately is the last character on the stage:

> *I see him coming . . .*
> *leaping from the heart of the mountain*
> *leaping from the eye of the atom . . .*

the white deer follows an ancient path
leaving no print on the ground. . . .
Deep calls to deep
And the mountains call their children home. (*Abiding*, 57,
emphasis in original)

Several themes abound in this last section: Cherokee myth, legend, and philosophy as evidenced in the lines just quoted; a reverence for the advances of science as depicted in the poems about the splitting of the atom. Though I have not emphasized poems about women, Awiakta's awareness of and admiration for her own gender are plain. It is, however, to the next book that we turn for precise attention to this theme.

II. SELU: SEEKING THE CORN MOTHER'S WISDOM (1993)

Native American Philosophy, History, Custom

Choosing as her title character the powerful image of Selu, the Cherokee Corn Mother who has analogues in other Native cultures as well, Awiakta explores the giving nature of this female prototype. The Cherokee myth of Selu's birth shows her stepping down, fully grown, from a stalk of corn, bringing with her an ear of the sweet vegetable and singing a lovely song. She befriends Kanati, the lonely, bored solitary male, who heretofore has sought solace in excessive hunting. She prepares a meal, using his meat and the sweet corn she has brought, and thus is born a marriage of balance and harmony, mutual respect between male and female, a take-and-give-back philosophy between nature and humankind. This is the lesson Selu teaches throughout Awiakta's book. In the author's own words:

> Woman and man represent cardinal balances in nature. Among these balances are:
> • the balance of forces—continuance in the midst of change;
> • the balance of food—vegetables and meat;
> • the balance of relationships—taking and giving back with respect (*Selu*, 25).

The myth of Selu continues with her demise in human form but regeneration in a stalk of corn growing from her grave—hence the Cherokee word *Selu*, meaning both "Corn-Mother" and "corn." Her death comes as a consequence of her grandsons' breaking the law of respect; however, she offers them instructions on how to redeem themselves by preserving and planting the corn. Following her instructions, they produce abundant crops. And even today Selu continues to feed the people around the world with her plentitude (*Selu*, 10–14).

Gender Relations; Balance and Harmony—Unity in Diversity

The Selu story is a straightforward Native American myth of origin; the teachings of Selu, a female, offer a philosophy of life: strength, balance, harmony, respect. The condition of women in early Cherokee society begs emulation. In the poem titled "Song of the Grandmothers," Awiakta writes:

> I am Cherokee.
> My people believe in the Spirit that unites all things.
> I am woman. I am life force. My word has great value.
> The man reveres me as he reveres Mother Earth and his own spirit.
> (*Selu*, 93)

Throughout the book *Selu*, Awiakta stresses the participation and leadership of the Cherokee women in the Great Council, in the sacred dances, in the home, in the marriage, in the field, even in battle. The coming of the white man and his concept of woman's place, however, bring change. In a poignant poem depicting the circumscribed role of women, she asks:

> If the hand that rocks
> the cradle rules the world,
> why does the mother pace
> row on row of white crosses,
> seeking the one
> that stakes her son motionless
> in his lidded box? (*Selu*, 85)

In "Anorexia Bulimia Speaks from the Grave," Awiakta assumes a strongly activist position as she advocates "busting out" from bound feet, bound breasts, bound waists. But to contemporary young women she says, "They've got your soul in a bind...." She goes on to say that they want you to starve yourself to fit some unnatural societal image; they don't want you "to take on weight" because "you might start throwin' it around." Her resounding crusade cry is

Feed your body.
Feed your soul.
Feed your dream.
BUST OUT!!! (Selu, 193–94)

Awiakta's humor energizes her poetry, even with subject matter as serious as this. Another chuckle-inducer is called "On Being a Female Phoenix":

> Not only do I rise
> from my own ashes,
> I have to carry them out!" (*Selu*, 135)

Woven amid the sparkling humor of *Selu* comes sensitive poetry address-ing love and sacrifice between the sexes. "Motheroot," written in 1978 for Mari-lou's husband, Paul, speaks of giving and support within a marriage, but applies to other relationships as well. Brief and simple, its message is profound:

> Creation often
> needs two hearts
> one to root
> and one to flower
> one to sustain
> in time of drouth
> and hold fast
> against winds of pain
> the fragile bloom
> that in the glory
> of its hour
> affirms a heart
> unsung, unseen. (*Selu*, 184)

Special in its personal connection to Awiakta and Paul, "Motheroot" has been honored through an inscription in stone at the University of California Riverside. A plaza beside the Humanities and Social Sciences Building fea-tures a curving black slate walkway through landscaped orange and kumquat trees. On one side of the black slate is inscribed the whole of "Motheroot" in Indian red, with the poet's name, "Marilou Awiakta," and the book's title, "*Selu*," following. The poem keeps notable company; on the other side of the walkway is a quotation from Virgil's *Georgics*.

Another love poem with personal overtones is titled "Selu and Kanati: Marriage" and carries a note identifying the mountainous twin peaks as the Chimney Tops in the Great Smoky Mountains. Awiakta writes, "One peak is softly rounded, one is sharp. Their beauty is their balance." The poetic description is of a spectacular natural landmark; the title suggests human counterparts:

> Two peaks
> alone ... apart ...
> yet join at the heart
> where trees rise green
> from rain-soaked loam. . . .
> Two peaks
> they stand against the sky
> spanned by a jagged arm of rock
> locked in an embrace
> elements cannot destroy
> or time erase. (*Selu*, 117)

The poem gains in significance when one knows that at the Chimney Tops, Paul Thompson proposed to Marilou Bonham and presented her with an engagement ring that led to marriage. As Awiakta the poet writes of the balance in the two separate peaks joined at the heart, surely Marilou the woman is considering two individuals joined in union of mutual support and sustenance: "Creation often / needs two hearts / one to root / and one to flower" (*Selu*, 184).

> *Teaching Tip*: In writing workshops, Awiakta often asks students to write "seed thoughts" in response to her poetry. These may take any form the student chooses, (e.g., journal entry, exposition, short story, poem). Since many of the poems discussed in the preceding section address issues that students are personally interested in/concerned about, I suggest a writing exercise of their own "seed thoughts," which they could then share orally with classmates, either as a whole-class activity or in small groups. Another step could be an in-house "publication"—either in print or perhaps via electronic means such as a document camera or PowerPoint presentation.

Environment, Nature, Science in Society

Just as Awiakta celebrates the female gender, so does she celebrate nature, sometimes combining the two as in "Smoky Mountain-Woman," a poem attributing feminine characteristics of strength and persistence to the mountain. Her final line could refer to either entity, woman or mountain: "Time cannot thwart my stubborn thrust toward Heaven" (*Selu*, 183).

In an activist mode, Awiakta the environmentalist warns of dire results from an incautious and disrespectful use of natural resources in "When Earth Becomes an 'It'" (*Selu*, 6). "Dying Back" chillingly describes the "standing people" on the mountain turning "brown in the head" from "acid greed / that takes the form of rain / and fog and cloud." At the same time, the "walking people" in the valley are "blank-eyed" and "dying back / as all species do / that kill their own seed" (5). The poet's humor flashes in "Mother Nature Sends a Pink Slip," but her message is grim. In memo format, the address reads,

> To: Homo Sapiens
> Re: Termination

The memo poem gives the reasons for this drastic action as noncompliance with management goals and objectives. Three warnings over the past decade have not brought about change; hence, the final lines of the memo:

> Your failure to take appropriate action
> has locked these warnings into
> the Phase-Out Mode, which will result
> in termination.   No appeal. (*Selu*, 88)

Balance and Harmony—Unity in Diversity; Environment, Nature, and Science in Society

Bleak as this message is, Awiakta's hope springs eternal. Just as she recognized while but a child the power of the atom to destroy as well as to help and heal, she acknowledges the curative powers of restoring balance and harmony in our relationship to the earth and to one another. One entire section of her book, titled "When the People Call Earth 'Mother,'" is filled with anecdotes, legends, myths, historical accounts, interviews, and personal narratives exemplifying obedience to the law of respect, restoration of balance and harmony, unity in diversity. She calls on the good nature and common sense of her Native people; she points to the thoughtfulness and generosity of wise statesmen; she applauds the respect, caution, and daring of cutting-edge scientists.

In the conclusion of her multigenre book, she entitles her penultimate section "Selu Sings for Survival." Here she celebrates the remarkable work of Dr. Barbara McClintock, corn geneticist, who discovered the process of "jumping genes" among chromosomes, who preached the philosophy of considering the wholeness of the organism rather than only isolated parts, and who eventually won a Nobel Prize for her groundbreaking work. Awiakta says McClintock knew firsthand Ginitsi Selu, the corn and the Corn-Mother—the wisdom, the philosophy, and the grain itself. She helped the modern world to accept and understand the gift of "Ginitsi Selu, Corn, Mother of Us All" (*Selu*, 326).

> *Teaching Tip:* Current environmental issues and science in society issues can generate research to parallel or complement the information in *Selu*. This is an ideal opportunity for interdisciplinary collaboration between science and literature teachers.

Thus the story comes full circle—from a sacred origin myth of the Cherokee to a singularly important scientific discovery, brought to fruition in each case by a female protagonist. The "telling" comes from Awiakta, a Cherokee/Appalachian female poet who, in the words of scientist Rupert Cutler (1995), may provide for the ethnic/gender equality movement, and consequently the environment, a similar impact as that rendered by Rachel Carson's *Silent Spring* (1962).

Conclusion

As evidenced throughout this essay, Marilou Awiakta offers her writing as a gift to her readers, listeners, family, and friends. She is an author who does not separate herself from her subject matter, nor from her audience. She and her work are eminently teachable; her poetry and prose are accessible; she deals with issues historical and current, literary and scientific; she connects. Scientist John C. Nemeth summarizes as follows:

> This artist brings to her work a manifest medley of art and science that gathers the joy, sorrow, contentment, and achievements of her peoples, the technology of her region and nation, and the majesty of her land into a study of truth, a painting, a chant of Appalachia, past, present, and future.

An unabashed proponent of nuclear power's life-saving, life-quality enhanc-ing character, in *Selu: Seeking The Corn Mother's Wisdom*, she describes a hum from beneath the surface of Oak Ridge, a sound of nuclear might, a source of strength that she translates to powerful thinking and writing.[8]

Through her skillful blending of old and new, she gives us all leave to recite with her, and believe with her, these words, this concept:

> Long before I learned
> The universal turn of atoms, I heard
> The Spirit's song that binds us
> All as one. ("An Indian Walks in Me," in *Selu*, 190)

Notes

Portions of this essay first appeared in *Her Words: Diverse Voices in Contemporary Ap-palachian Women's Poetry*, edited by Felicia Mitchell and published by the University of Tennessee Press in 2002.

1. The Manhattan Project, a secret program of the U.S. War Department, ultimately resulted in the production of the atomic bomb used during World War II. For more in-formation, see the sources on Oak Ridge in the reference list.

2. Marilou Awiakta, interview by author, Memphis Tennessee, 16 September 1999.

3. The fenced area of approximately 90 square miles, or 60,000 acres, came to be called the Oak Ridge Reservation, a U.S. government designation not related to American Indian reservations.

4. Hereafter cited parenthetically in text as *Abiding*.

5. The most recent incarnation of *Abiding Appalachia* is a 2006 reprinting of the book by Pocahontas Press of Blacksburg, Virginia. All citations in this essay refer to page num-bers in the latest printing.

6. Hereafter cited parenthetically in text as *Selu*.

7. Awiakta interview, 16 September 1999.

8. John C. Nemeth, "Awiakta, Marilou (1936–) Poet, Author, Lecturer," Manuscript version for *Encyclopedia of Appalachia* (Abramson and Haskell 2006). An edited, condensed version appears in the published work.

References

Awiakta, Marilou. (1978) 2006. *Abiding Appalachia: Where Mountain and Atom Meet.* Blacksburg, VA: Pocahontas Press.

——. 1983. *Rising Fawn and the Fire Mystery.* Memphis: Saint Luke's Press. Golden, CO: Fulcrum (2007).

——. 1992. "My Country Childhood." *Countryside* (March): n.p.

———. 1993. *Selu: Seeking the Corn-Mother's Wisdom*. Golden, CO: Fulcrum.

———. 1995. "Grandmothers." In *The Oxford Companion to Women's Writing in the United States*, edited by Cathy N. Davidson and Linda Wagner-Martin. New York: Oxford University Press.

———. 1998. "Sound." In *Bloodroot: Reflections on Place by Appalachian Women Writers*, edited by Joyce Dyer, 40–51. Lexington: University Press of Kentucky.

Carls, Alice-Catherine. 1997–1998. "Polyphony, Harmony, and Color: Awiakta's 'Vital Poetry.'" *Poesie Premiere* 9 (Winter): 1–4. English translation of French essay introducing a thirty-page collection of Awiakta's poetry in French translation.

Carson, Rachel. 1962. *Silent Spring*. New York: Houghton Mifflin.

Cutler, Rupert. 1995. Review of *Selu: Seeking the Corn-Mother's Wisdom*, by Marilou Awiakta. *Now and Then* (Spring): 37.

Edwards, Grace Toney. 2000. "The Hum of Black Oak Ridge in the Poetry of Marilou Awiakta." Paper and slide presentation, Appalachian Studies Association Annual Conference, 24–26 March, University of Tennessee, Knoxville, TN.

———. 2002. "Marilou Awiakta: Poet for the People." In *Her Words: Diverse Voices in Contemporary Appalachian Women's Poetry*, edited by Felicia Mitchell, 17–34. Knoxville: University of Tennessee Press.

Johns, Vicki Slagle. 1997. "Of Atoms and Appalachia: Marilou Awiakta's Cultural and Scientific Heritage Permeates Her Writing." *Tennessee Alumnus* 77 (Winter): 7–9.

Keller, Paulene. 1999. "Marilou Awiakta: Native American, Appalachian Heritage and the Atom." *Women's News of the Mid-South* 7 (1999): 12–13.

Lanier, Rene Parks, Jr. (1986) 2006. "The Enchanted World of Marilou Awiakta." Afterword to Awiakta (1978) 2006, 58–64.

Lee, Ernest. 2000. "Sources of Light in Awiakta's *Selu*." Paper presented at Appalachian Studies Association Annual Conference, 24–26 March, University of Tennessee, Knoxville, TN.

Lumpkin, Shirley. 2000. "Backlighting Wisdom with Humor: The 'Twinkles' in Awiakta's *Selu*." Paper presented at Appalachian Studies Association Annual Conference, 23–26 March, University of Tennessee, Knoxville, TN.

Nemeth, John C. "Awiakta, Marilou (1936–) Poet, Author, Lecturer." Manuscript version for *Encyclopedia of Appalachia* (Abramson and Haskell, 2006). See Additional Resources for Teaching for publication information on this work.

Sadler, Marilyn. 1994. "A Woman of Substance." *Memphis* 19 (September): 26–26, 85–87.

Vaschenko, Alexandr. 1995. Review of *Selu: Seeking the Corn-Mother's Wisdom*, by Marilou Awiakta. *North Dakota Quarterly* 62 (Summer): 229–32.

Additional Resources for Teaching

Abramson, Rudy, and Jean Haskell, eds. 2006. *Encyclopedia of Appalachia*. Knoxville: University of Tennessee Press.

American Museum of Science and Energy, Oak Ridge, Tennessee. http://www.amse.org.

Awiakta Collection. Videotaped interviews and performances, photographs, slides, critical analyses, print materials. Appalachian Regional Studies Center Archives. Radford University, Radford, VA.

Awiakta Papers. Appalachian Collection, McConnell Library, Radford University, Radford, VA.

Awiakta, Marilou. 1995. *Selu: Seeking the Corn-Mother's Wisdom.* Audio Literature. Excerpts from the book read by author on two audiocassettes.

Duncan, Barbara R. 1998. *Living Stories of the Cherokee.* Chapel Hill: University of North Carolina Press.

Edwards, Grace Toney, JoAnn Aust Asbury, and Ricky L. Cox, eds. 2006. *A Handbook to Appalachia: An Introduction to the Region.* Knoxville: University of Tennessee Press.

Ehle, John. 1997. *Trail of Tears: The Rise and Fall of the Cherokee Nation.* New York: Anchor Books.

Gosling, F. G. 1994. *The Manhattan Project: Making the Atomic Bomb.* Energy History Series. United States Department of Energy.

Mankiller, Wilma. 2004. *Every Day Is a Good Day: Reflections by Contemporary Indigenous Women.* Golden: Fulcrum.

Mankiller, Wilma, and Michael Wallis. 1993. *Mankiller: A Chief and Her People.* New York: St. Martin's Griffin.

Miller, Danny, Sandra Ballard, Roberta Herrin, Stephen D. Mooney, Susan Underwood, and Jack Wright. "Appalachian Literature." In Edwards, Asbury, and Cox 2006, 199–216.

Mooney, James. 1992. *James Mooney's History, Myths, and Sacred Formulas of the Cherokees.* Fairview, NC: Bright Mountain Books.

———. 1996. *Myths of the Cherokee.* Mineola, NY: Dover.

Nemeth, John C. "Awiakta, Marilou." In Abramson and Haskell 2006, 1046.

Overholt, James, ed. 1987. *These Are our Voices: The Story of Oak Ridge, 1942–1970.* Oak Ridge: Children's Museum of Oak Ridge.

Shurbutt, S. Bailey. 2005. "Where Mountain Meets Atom, Within the Healing Circle: The Writing of Marilou Awiakta." *Journal of Appalachian Studies* 11 (Spring/Fall): 195–204.

FOURTEEN

Toward "Crystal-Tight Arrays":
Teaching the Evolving Art
of Robert Morgan's Poetry

ROBERT M. WEST

ROBERT MORGAN HAS WRITTEN POETRY of distinction for
more than forty years: his first book, *Zirconia Poems*, appeared in 1969; and in
2011 he brought out his fifteenth collection, *Terroir*. His poems have often first
appeared in such prestigious venues as *Poetry*, the *Southern Review*, the *Georgia
Review*, and the *Atlantic Monthly*, and have been reprinted in many anthologies. Readers familiar with Appalachian literature have long counted him an
important Appalachian poet. Special issues of *Appalachian Heritage, Iron Mountain Review, Pembroke Magazine*, and *Southern Quarterly* have spotlighted his
work. The two existing book-length studies of Appalachian poetry, Rita Sims
Quillen's *Looking for Native Ground: Contemporary Appalachian Poetry* (1989), and
John Lang's *Six Poets from the Mountain South* (2010), each devote a full chapter
to him. Raised in the Western North Carolina community of Green River,
in rural Henderson County, Morgan usually writes about the landscape and
culture of rural Appalachia; he has also written many poems about objects or
about scientific concepts. Critical writing about his work has naturally tended
to concentrate on those interests.

However, students and other readers may find another aspect of his
oeuvre just as interesting: how his ideas about poetry's sound and structure
have developed over his long career. To focus on that issue is to highlight his

theoretical and technical sophistication as a poet, and the gradually sharpening distinction he makes between the sound of prose and the sound of verse. Given the persistent stereotype of Appalachian people as unlettered and ignorant, attention to Morgan's artistry (and to his self-conscious cultivation of that artistry) can be highly enlightening, both to students from beyond the region and to those who have grown up within it. They learn not only that an Appalachian writer has produced a body of poetry very much worth reading (a lesson they could learn by studying any number of Appalachian poets), but also that he has pursued and achieved a kind of formal mastery that invites readers to compare him to many of the great American and world poets whose work precedes and informs his own. We can say that one way he commands respect for Appalachian experience is by adopting forms that themselves command respect.

One of Morgan's most widely reprinted poems is a brief ars poetica, one that makes a good introduction to a discussion of his prosody's evolution. "Honey" was originally published in the September 1991 issue of the *Atlantic Monthly*, and the Pulitzer Prize–winning poet (and future US poet laureate) Charles Simic then selected it for *The Best American Poetry 1992*. The Nobel Prize–winning Polish poet Czesław Miłosz selected it for his popular anthology *A Book of Luminous Things* (1996), and at the date of this writing it has been featured three times by Garrison Keillor on his daily *Writer's Almanac* program. Morgan included it in his 1996 chapbook, *Wild Peavines*; in his 2000 book, *Topsoil Road*; and also in his 2004 retrospective, *The Strange Attractor: New and Selected Poems*. It has even drawn a film adaptation, a 2002 animated short by Gail Noonan. The poem offers a set of instructions for culling honey from beehives, but those instructions double as advice to aspiring poets. Anyone familiar with Rilke might suspect as much from the outset. In *Letters to a Young Poet*, Rilke says of God that "as bees gather honey, so we collect what is sweetest out of all things and build Him" (1984, 62); later, in a famous letter to his Polish translator, Witold von Hulewicz, Rilke remarks that "we are the bees of the invisible," transforming the visible world by incorporating it into the poet's sensibility. Indeed, "Honey" does turn out to be a poem about transformation, but not so much transformation of the material into spirit, as transformation of one kind of language into another.

"Only calmness will reassure / the bees to let you rob their hoard," Morgan's poem begins, adding, "If you go near bees / every day they will know you": this may be literally true, but it is also good metaphorical advice from a deliberate craftsman, one who believes the muses are most apt to visit those who court them persistently. And an admonition several lines later, "Resist greed," applies as much to an impatient young poet as to a beekeeper. But the conceit becomes unmistakable in the poem's concluding lines, in which the honey has at last been discovered:

> With the top off
> you touch the fat gold frames, each cell
> a hex perfect as a snowflake,
> a sealed relic of sun and time
> and roots of many acres fixed
> in crystal-tight arrays, in rows
> and lattices of sweeter latin
> from scattered prose of meadow, woods. (Morgan 2000, 53)

With that ending, Morgan really tips the poem toward the figurative and strongly encourages us to reread "Honey" as an extended metaphor for poetic composition. From "scattered prose," we are told, are made "crystal-tight arrays," "rows and lattices of sweeter latin." It bears noting that Latin is the language of Virgil, whose long poem about agriculture, *The Georgics*, includes in book 4 a substantial section on bees and beekeeping. But why does Morgan's poem use a lowercase *l* in "latin" instead of the capital letter? Likely to avoid invoking the actual, specific language, which virtually no contemporary poet would be writing in, while still bringing in its association with order: after all, for centuries Latin was the language of government, the church, and science—the medium of Augustus, Augustine, and Linnaeus. Prose, then, is implicitly defined as ordinary language "scattered" all around us, and poetry is its "perfect" ordering, its refinement and arrangement. Significantly, it is just as the poem approaches the words "crystal-tight arrays" that its own arrangement turns most crystalline: though the poem had previously coalesced into metrical regularity only for a line or so at a time, it suddenly locks into iambic tetrameter (*daDUM-daDUM-daDUM-daDUM*) for the final four lines. The penultimate line deviates from that pattern slightly, but only slightly: the third syllable of "lattices" asks for and naturally receives some promotion, and the line ends with an extra, unaccented syllable, but our sense of the tetrameter is left quite intact. Thus "Honey," which we could call Morgan's letter to any young poet, enacts through its prosody the very discovery it describes, introducing the bee-made "crystal-tight arrays," their "rows / and lattices" just as its language becomes most metrically ordered.[1]

Before going further, let me say that I have taught the reading and analysis of poetry (including Robert Morgan's) at three universities varying in size, public/private status, and admissions selectivity. Two are within Appalachia as defined by the Appalachia Regional Commission, and the exception is only a two-hour drive beyond the ARC boundary. Many of my students at all three institutions have been very bright, literate, and motivated young men and women. Yet few to none have known anything about prosody before beginning their study with me. I gather that most of their high school teachers and many of my own colleagues at the college or university level do not address poetic form in their teaching. To ask these students to scan a line of verse is like asking them to listen to a passage of music and then identify the time signature, when no one has ever explained to them the concept of musical measure. In fact, it is very much like that, since the concepts of musical and poetic measure are essentially the same, and both are apparently widely untaught. In 2000, I tried to teach a freshman class about meter by drawing the analogy to its musical counterpart, only to be told by my students that they had never had music instruction in their local schools.

Of course, there are many wonderful teachers who themselves never received a good background in meter and other aspects of poetic form, and who therefore feel uncomfortable dealing with aspects of it in class. Perhaps they would like to teach students something about the sound structure of a poem and find a way to relate that meaningfully to what the poem is saying, but they lack the knowledge and confidence to do so. Fortunately, there are many good guides available to help those teachers and any other interested readers. A popular one is *Perrine's Sound and Sense: An Introduction to Poetry* (Arp and Johnson 2010), and Paul Fussell's *Poetic Meter and Poetic Form* (1979) is also highly regarded. My students and I have found entertaining and very useful a little book by the English poet James Fenton: *An Introduction to English Poetry* (2002). Also worth keeping on hand is a one-volume standard reference with entries for terms related to poetry. One such reference is *A Handbook to Literature* (12th edition 2012), produced by Robert Morgan's longtime friend, the poet William Harmon; it offers readable and reasonably thorough entries for terms related to poetry and other kinds of literature, and is likely to suffice for most teachers and other readers. For those with a special interest, the *New*

Princeton Encyclopedia of Poetry and Poetics (Preminger and Brogan 1993) offers definitive treatments of poetry-related concepts. Of course there are many other resources available; these are just a few that might help prepare teachers and students for lessons relating to form in Robert Morgan's work, or indeed any other poet's.

"Honey" asks us to imagine "crystal-tight arrays," and anyone teaching that poem could point out that Morgan has long favored crystallization as a metaphor for poetry writing. In a 1978 entry in "Mica," a published selection from his notebooks, he declares, "I would take the filth and stinky cans and sawdust bags, soot and broken bulbs, and crush the mess into a compact ingot, into a fleshy diamond" (1993, 122). In his 1980 short essay "Some Sentences on the Line," he writes that poetic "lines are the gathered bits of the original shattered diamond," and he goes on to say, "I like the idea that by breaking sentences into lines we can have something of crystalline perfection in the living voice. Motion and stillness at once" (1993, 4). In his 1991 essay "The Gift of Pause," he explains that poetry "is the perfect crystal lattice of language grown on the solution of prose" (1993, 19), and in an entry from "Mica" dated that same year, he writes that "the ruled space of a great poem is a kind of periodic chart, implying in compact symbols a whole universe, animated, elusive, changing, even while arranged in lattices permanent as crystal" (1993, 123).

Although Morgan has long defined his aims as a poet in terms related to crystal structure, his ideas of what "crystallization" means in practice have changed dramatically over the years. If we look for crystallization in the poems of his first two books, *Zirconia Poems* (1969) and *Red Owl* (1972), we can point to the extraordinary premium they place on compression and brevity. Sometimes these imagistic, free-verse poems eschew complete sentences in favor of staccato fragments. For instance, "High Country," which opens *Zirconia Poems*, begins, "In the hills, dead springs, blue flame of sky. The horizon goes all the way around" (1969, 3). The same book's final poem, "Junkyard after Storm," begins, "Among the broom and rusting hoods, / dead radios. / Dripping goldenrod" (1969, 40). In some poems, metaphors are fired off and quickly abandoned rather than developed; an example is "Rain, Drunk," where "the air is a bass string, / a coal of sound in the mind" (1969, 7). Any number of poems from those first two books would exemplify the same techniques just as well.

His third book, *Land Diving* (1976), is quite different, being made up of poems that tend to be longer, more discursive, and more committed to complete sentences as units of meaning. These are the firstfruits of Morgan's employment at Cornell University, which he has often said was a much more talkative environment than what he had known in North Carolina. As he became more of a talker, he says in an interview with Suzanne Booker, his poems "began to get more conversational, longer in wavelength and plot," until he found he "talked too easily": his work had lost the compression which he had identified with poetry. His solution for that crisis was to begin writing in rhymed forms, which "recovered the necessary resistance for lines" (1993, 136). Stanza shapes and rhyme schemes imposed a new kind of rigor on his writing, and thereby restored the distinction between conversational and poetic language. It is easy to see how the regularity of the stanza could suggest his ideal of the "crystal lattice." That said, it is worth noting that the regularity he achieves in these poems is more often visual than aural: the combination of frequent enjambment, slant rhyme, and lack of meter mutes the rhymes for listeners. We see rhymes we don't hear. Consider the opening of "Concert," a poem cast in quatrains following an *aabb* rhyme scheme:

> When Aunt Wessie played she
> reached into the keys with heavy
> arms as though rooting tomato
> slips, sinking hands in to
>
> the wrists . . . (1976, 10)

The "crystalline" structure is visible but inaudible here, and remains virtually inaudible through the rest of the poem to any but the most sensitive ears. It's worth noting the irony that the poem's music is as subtle as Aunt Wessie's was loud.[2]

Most students have been trained since middle childhood to think of reading as a private activity done silently, and so some may not at first grasp the distinction between rhyme *seen* and rhyme *heard*. Try reading aloud to them "Concert" or another such "visually rhyming" poem from *Land Diving* (1976; three such are "After Church," "Rice," and "Copse"), without letting them look at the text. Then do the same with a free-verse poem from the same book (such as "Steep," "Horseshoe, NC," or "Pumpkin"). Ask if they can tell which of the two poems is cast in rhyming stanzas. They have a fifty-fifty chance of being right or wrong, so some are bound to guess correctly, but after the exercise most will surely agree that it's difficult or impossible to tell anything about the poems' structures based on the way they sound.

This approach to versification remains Morgan's practice for the next few books, with his poems often adopting and cleverly fulfilling rhyme schemes, though often in ways more apprehensible by the eye than by the ear. A celebrated poem in this mode is his "Chant Royal," named after its form, which is French in origin and which the *New Princeton Encyclopedia of Poetry and Poetics* (Preminger and Brogan 1993) dates back to the twelfth century. The form requires five eleven-line stanzas rhyming *ababccddedE*, with the capital "E" indicating a refrain repeated at the end of each stanza, and the poem concludes with a five-line envoi rhyming *ddedE*. Except for the word ending the refrain, no word may be repeated as a rhyming word; given the fact that English is more difficult to rhyme in than French is, it's hardly surprising that Morgan uses slant as well as perfect rhyme to fulfill the form's requirements. *A Handbook to Literature* (Harmon 2012) credits Morgan's poem as the first serious example of the form in English. Commemorating the life of Morgan's maternal grandfather, "Chant Royal" begins,

> Born in a notch of the high mountains where
> a spring ran from under the porch, on
> the second of April just one hundred years
> ago this month, my grandpa was a weak one
> to start with, premature, weighed a scant
> two pounds twelve ounces. So fragile the aunt
> who tended that first night feared to move
> him except for feeding and the placing of
> diapers. He slept near the fire in a shoebox
> with one end cut out. Against the odds he would prove
> adequate for survival, withstanding all knocks. (1987, 65)

The poem's compact and compelling biography of the author's grandfather gives teachers and students much to discuss. It can be good to begin by inviting comments on the title. What does Morgan gain by titling the poem after its form? One reasonable response would be that by calling attention to the poem's form, Morgan is notifying his readers that he is playing a certain game, hoping they will familiarize themselves with its challenging rules (unless they happen to already know them), and then credit him with having succeeded.

Another would be that Morgan's use of the form and invocation of its name honor and elevate his grandfather by suggesting that this family patriarch was kingly in his toughness and his achievements. Another would be that, by signaling his awareness of a medieval French poetic form, Morgan shows that an Appalachian background and sophisticated learning can go hand in hand.

Further discussion could address the degree to which the poem's rhymes are audible: as with "Concert," the frequent enjambment, lack of meter, and frequent use of slant rhyme act together to obscure the fact that this is a poem that follows a rhyme scheme. For many listeners, the only noticeable aspects of the poem's structure would be the recurrence of its refrain, and that refrain's sometimes audible rhyme with the words in the *e* position ("shoebox," "raw," "unlocks," "mock," "rock," and "unorthodox"). Ask students what they think of the subtlety of the poem's adherence to the rhyme scheme. Some may take issue with the notion of an inaudible rhyme, and these may question whether Morgan has actually fulfilled the form's requirements; others may tell you that they find rhyme a distraction from a poem's meaning, and these may credit Morgan with having satisfied the form's requirements in such a way that leaves the poem's narrative content easily accessible. Though you may have your own opinion one way or the other, keep in mind that poets and critics of the highest stature have disagreed about such issues; you can help your students articulate their thinking without trying to settle what is, after all, an unsettled argument.

A shorter poem about which you could have a similar discussion is Morgan's "Earache," first collected in the limited-edition chapbook *Bronze Age* (1981). Like "Chant Royal," it is reprinted both in *Green River: New and Selected Poems* (1991) and in *The Strange Attractor: New and Selected Poems* (2004). In "Earache," Morgan recounts a childhood affliction that nothing would ease, 'til a group of people gathered to pray over him (1991, 9; 2004, 120). A reader paying little heed to the form would likely find the narrative captivating, but attention to that form (and Morgan's manner of fulfilling its requirements) would lead to a richer appreciation of his artistic achievement. "Earache" is an unusual kind of sonnet called a terza rima sonnet, one adopting the interlocking terza rima of Dante's *Divine Comedy* before concluding with a rhyming couplet: the rhyme scheme is *aba bcb cdc ded ee*. The most widely read poem in English that adopts the form is Percy Bysshe Shelley's "Ode to the West Wind," which is made up of five terza rima sonnets. By using a verse form associated both with Dante and with one of the chief English Romantic poets,

Morgan elevates this poem's testimony to the effectiveness of faith healing, giving it dignity and credibility. It is difficult to label as "simple" and "ignorant" anyone who demonstrates a deep familiarity with high culture as he tells of his experience.

A very different form Morgan masters during this period is the pantoum (sometimes spelled "pantun"). Originally a Malayan form, the pantoum was imported into European literature by French orientalists, especially Victor Hugo. Pantoums consist of any number of quatrains, with the first and third lines of each quatrain being repetitions of the second and fourth lines of the preceding quatrain; in the final quatrain, the second and fourth lines must be the first and third lines of the first quatrain, but this time in reverse order. Morgan's books have included four pantoums: "Mica Country" and "Audubon's Flute" in *Sigodlin* (1990); and "Hearth" and "Oxbow Lakes" in *Topsoil Road* (2000). Again, by writing in a form of international origin, Morgan gives emphatically unprovincial treatment to what some readers might consider provincial subject matter.

At the same time that Morgan was exploring forms involving rhyme and other repetition, he also began to write unrhymed, enjambed syllabic poems, a technique he discusses in some detail in his essay "Good Measure" (1993, 6); there, too, the poem's arrangement into lines is more a matter of the seen than of the heard. Examples of such poems are "Lightning Bug," "Rearview Mirror," "Vietnam War Memorial," and "Ghosts in the Carpet," to name just a few reprinted in Morgan's latest retrospective, *The Strange Attractor* (2004). In explaining these poems' form to students, keep in mind that now and then Morgan deviates from the syllable count he establishes as each poem's rule: for instance, a poem with lines usually eight syllables long may contain a few lines with seven or nine syllables. Ask your students, if Morgan's poems in rhyming and repeating forms represent one approach to crystallizing language, what about these unrhymed, enjambed syllabics—a form with no sound effects at all? You may need to point out that, even if this form means nothing to a reader, it must have affected the way the poem was written, and probably affected what the poem ended up saying.

With his emergence in the '90s as a prolific and successful writer of prose fiction, Morgan's verse technique underwent a fundamental shift. Just as his need to distinguish his poetry from his talk led to the first major change in his poetic practice, so his need to distinguish his poetry from his prose led to the second. The problem seems to have been this: What was the difference between verse and prose if they sounded the same? To solve that problem he adopted a new (yet very old) means of pursuing his ideal of crystal structure.

In 1989, Morgan published his first book of prose, a fine short story collection titled *The Blue Valleys*. Since then he has published nine additional prose books: two more collections of short stories, five novels, a book of essays and other prose about poetry, a biography of Daniel Boone, and a study of the United States' westward expansion. Yet he has hardly abandoned writing poems: over the same period, he has published two substantial chapbooks, three full-length collections of new poems, and two "new and selected" volumes. During this period he found a new approach to crystallizing language, a way that distinguishes it most sharply from prose: he began to write in meter.

The transition was gradual, and took place over the space of about a decade. His 1990 book, *Sigodlin*, includes a number of poems that approach metrical regularity here and there; one, "Hayfield," stands out as a poem that is almost uniformly iambic, and interestingly it invokes both crystallization and honey:

> it is the sap
> in grass that must be cut and left
> to crystallize in fibers, preserving
> like honey in a mummy's chest
> the blade and vein intact (1990, 12)

However, it is in his next full-length collection, *Topsoil Road* (2000), that Morgan repeatedly demonstrates an interest in meter. There are poems here that recall the earlier work by combining enjambed, largely unmetrical lines with rhyme schemes: the sonnet "Care," for example; or "Polishing the Silver," a poem in quatrains rhymed *abba*, like *In Memoriam* stanzas. Along with such poems, though, there are several strictly metrical poems: "Blowing Rock," "Squatting," "Family Bible," "Wind from a Waterfall," "Snake Fence," "Harvest Sink," and "The Grain of Sound" all deviate from iambic rhythm only rarely, if ever. Just as rhymed stanzas—even highly enjambed ones—had offered Morgan a clear distinction between poetry and talk, now meter offered him a clear distinction between poetry and prose. It is fitting that this transitional collection includes

"Honey," which, as noted above, finds its way to metrical regularity just as it evokes "your" discovery of the bees' own "crystal-tight arrays."

You might try reading aloud a couple of the metrical poems from *Topsoil Road* after explaining what iambic rhythm is. Tell your students that, generally speaking, every second syllable in each line will receive a stress; tell them too that this means they should hear, with few exceptions, a rhythm that sounds like *daDUM* repeated again and again. After reading, ask them what the effect of that steady rhythm is. Some students may say they find it propulsive or compelling, and thus tending to increase their interest; on the other hand, a few may say they find it monotonous. Regardless, most students will probably agree that the effect is a solemnizing or dignifying one, and you might ask about the consequences of the rhythm's application in poems about regional subject matter, such as "Squatting" and "The Grain of Sound." Students may need you to recall for them that this is the rhythm of most of the "great" poems in English—a quality shared by *Paradise Lost*, "To His Coy Mistress," *An Essay on Man*, "Ode on a Grecian Urn," and Emily Dickinson's poems, as different as those all are. By writing in meter, and predominantly iambic meter, Morgan finds a new way to crystallize his lines, and he also finds a new way to exalt what he writes about—both in terms of the sound of the rhythm itself, and also in terms of the body of poetry he invites us to set next to his own.

Morgan's commitment to meter has only become clearer since *Topsoil Road* (2000). Metrical poems make up over half of the "new" section of *The Strange Attractor: New and Selected Poems* (2004), and both his chapbook *October Crossing* (2009) and his latest full-length collection, *Terroir* (2011), consist of metrical poems entirely. Any of those three collections would make fine adoptions for a course studying Appalachian literature; each would give teachers and students plenty to examine, discuss, and write about, with regard both to *what* the poems say and to *how* they say it. We need to focus attention on both, so that students can grasp the evolution and achievement of this important Appalachian poet.

Notes

An earlier, shorter, and in important respects very different version of this essay appeared as "A Study in Sharpening Contrast: Robert Morgan and the Distinction between Prose and Poetry," in the Robert Morgan special issue of *Pembroke Magazine* 35 (2003): 77–81. My thanks to editor Shelby Stephenson for publishing that earlier essay.

1. For a different perspective on the lattice metaphor in Morgan's work, see Graves 2007.

2. In some work from this period, Morgan adopts a regular-looking stanza that forgoes not only meter but also any attempt at any kind of rhyme. A good example of a poem that employs this completely visual stanza is "Face," one of several poems Michael McFee discusses helpfully in his overview of Morgan's poetry, "'The Witness of Many Writings': Robert Morgan's Poetic Career" ([1990] 2006).

References

Arp, Thomas R., and Greg Johnson. 2010. *Perrine's Sound and Sense: An Introduction to Poetry.* Belmont, CA: Wadsworth.

Fenton, James. 2002. *An Introduction to English Poetry.* New York: Farrar, Straus and Giroux.

Fussell, Paul. 1979. *Poetic Meter and Poetic Form.* New York: McGraw-Hill.

Graves, Jesse. 2007. "Lattice Work: Formal Tendencies in the Poetry of Robert Morgan and Ron Rash." *Southern Quarterly* 45 (1): 78–86.

Harmon, William. 2012. 12th ed. *A Handbook to Literature.* New York: Macmillan.

Lang, John. 2010. *Six Poets from the Mountain South.* Baton Rouge: Louisiana State University Press.

McFee, Michael. (1990) 2006. "'The Witness of Many Writings': Robert Morgan's Poetic Career." *Iron Mountain Review* 6 (1): 17–23. Reprinted in McFee, *The Napkin Manuscripts: Selected Essays and an Interview,* 164–80. Knoxville: University of Tennessee Press.

Miłosz, Czesław, ed. 1996. *A Book of Luminous Things: An International Anthology of Poetry.* Orlando, FL: Houghton Mifflin.

Morgan, Robert. 1969. *Zirconia Poems.* Northwood Narrows, NH: Lillabulero Press.

———. 1972. *Red Owl.* New York: W. W. Norton.

———. 1976. *Land Diving.* Baton Rouge: Louisiana State University Press.

———. 1981. *Bronze Age.* Emory, VA: Iron Mountain Press.

———. 1987. *At the Edge of the Orchard Country.* Middletown, CT: Wesleyan University Press.

———. 1989. *The Blue Valleys: A Collection of Stories.* Atlanta: Peachtree Publishers.

———. 1990. *Sigodlin: Poems.* Middletown, CT: Wesleyan University Press.

———. 1991. *Green River: New and Selected Poems.* Hanover, NH: University Press of New England for Wesleyan University Press.

———. 1993. *Good Measure: Essays, Interviews, and Notes on Poetry.* Baton Rouge: Louisiana State University Press.

———. 1996. *Wild Peavines.* Frankfort, KY: Gnomon Press.

———. 2000. *Topsoil Road.* Baton Rouge: Louisiana State University Press.

———. 2004. *The Strange Attractor: New and Selected Poems.* Baton Rouge, Louisiana State University Press.

———. 2009. *October Crossing.* Frankfort, KY: Broadstone Books.

———. 2011. *Terroir.* New York: Penguin.

Preminger, Alex, and T. V. F. Brogan, eds. 1993. *The New Princeton Encyclopedia of Poetry and Poetics.* Princeton, NJ: Princeton University Press.

Quillen, Rita Sims. 1989. *Looking for Native Ground: Contemporary Appalachian Poetry.* Boone, NC: Appalachian Consortium Press.

Rilke, Rainer Maria. 1960. *Selected Letters.* Edited by Harry T. Moore. Garden City, NY: Doubleday.

———. 1984. *Letters to a Young Poet.* Translated by Stephen Mitchell. New York: Random House.

Simic, Charles, ed. 1992. *The Best American Poetry 1992.* New York: Macmillan.

CONTRIBUTORS

ERICA ABRAMS LOCKLEAR is an assistant professor in the Literature and Language Department at the University of North Carolina at Asheville. She is the author of *Negotiating a Perilous Empowerment: Appalachian Women's Literacies* and has also published articles in the *Southern Literary Journal*, *Crossroads: A Southern Culture Annual*, *Community Literacy Journal*, and *North Carolina Folklore Journal*. She teaches American, Southern, and Appalachian literature, first-year writing, humanities, and courses in the Women, Gender, and Sexuality Studies program at UNC Asheville.

THERESA BURRISS is chair of Appalachian Studies and director of the Appalachian Regional & Rural Studies Center at Radford University. She has published several articles on the Affrilachian writers in such journals as *Appalachian Heritage* and the *Iron Mountain Review*, along with a chapter in *An American Vein: Critical Readings in Appalachian Literature*. She served as cultural consultant and storyteller for two of choreographer Deborah McLaughlin's multimedia dance performances. The first, *Eating Appalachia: Selling Out to the Hungry Ghost*, was an artistic response to mountaintop-removal coal mining. The second, *Sounds of Stories Dancing*, addresses Appalachian out-migration and displacement from home.

RICKY COX teaches Appalachian folklore, American literature, and an introductory course in Appalachian Studies at Radford University in Radford, Virginia. As an associate of RU's Appalachian Regional and Rural Studies Center, he coordinates the Farm at Selu, a living history site representing 1930s farm life in Southwestern Virginia. He earned an Associate in Applied Science degree in Machine Technology from New River Community College and a BA in history and an MA in English from Radford University. He is a contributor to the *Encyclopedia of Appalachia* and a coeditor of *A Handbook to Appalachia: An Introduction to the Region* (University of Tennessee Press, 1996), with Grace Toney Edwards and JoAnn Asbury. *The Water-Powered Grist Mills of Floyd County, Virginia: Illustrated Histories, 1770–2010* coauthored with the late Frank Webb, was published by McFarland Press in early 2012.

GRACE TONEY EDWARDS is professor emeritus and research faculty associate at Radford University in Radford, Virginia. She retired from RU as director of the Appalachian Regional Studies Center and professor of Appalachian Studies and English in June 2010. Dr. Edwards is senior editor of *A Handbook to Appalachia: An Introduction to the Region* (2006) and is author of more than one hundred book chapters, journal articles, and review essays.

ELIZABETH ENGELHARDT is associate professor of American Studies and Women's and Gender Studies at the University of Texas at Austin. She is the author of *The Tangled Roots of Feminism, Environmentalism, and Appalachian Literature* (2003) and the editor of *Beyond Hill and Hollow: Original Readings in Appalachian Women's Studies* (2005) and the republication of Grace MacGowan Cooke's *The Power and the Glory: An Appalachian Novel* (2003). Her most recent works are a collaborative book, *Republic of Barbecue: Stories Beyond the Brisket* (2009), and her own *A Mess of Greens: Southern Women and Food* (forthcoming).

PATRICIA GANTT is a professor of English at Utah State University, where she serves as associate dean for the College of Humanities and Social Sciences and as associate head of her department. Her scholarly interests are in writers of color, memoir, oral history, and teaching literature. She is series editor of the *Student's Encyclopedia of Great American Writers*, a five-volume resource for secondary students and their teachers, and she has frequently published on Wilma Dykeman, August Wilson, and the Federal Writers' Project. Her memoirs can be heard on Utah Public Radio.

TINA L. HANLON teaches English at Ferrum College and the Hollins University Summer Graduate Program in Children's Literature. She has published essays on folktale adaptations, picture books, and fiction for children. She coedited the anthology *Crosscurrents of Children's Literature* (2006) and directs the website AppLit: Resources for Readers and Teachers of Appalachian Literature for Children and Young Adults.

JOHN C. INSCOE is the Albert B. Saye Professor of History at the University of Georgia. He has written widely on nineteenth-century Appalachia. His most recent books are *Race, War, and Remembrance in the Appalachian South* (2008) and *Writing the South Through the Self: Explorations in Autobiography* (2011). He is currently at work on a book-length study of Appalachia on film.

R. PARKS LANIER JR. retired from Radford University, Virginia, in 2009 after teaching English there for thirty-seven years. His poetry and essays on Appalachian themes have appeared widely in the region. In 1991, he edited *The Poetics of Appalachian Space* (University of Tennessee Press) with contributions from fourteen Appalachian scholars. He served five years as president of the Appalachian Writers' Association and received its award for "Outstanding Contributions to Regional Literature." For twenty years, he produced archival videos for Radford University's Highland Summer Conference. For fifteen years, he was sponsor of the Selu Writers' Retreat at Radford.

JEFF MANN's poetry, fiction, and essays have appeared in many publications, including *Prairie Schooner, Shenandoah, Laurel Review, The Gay and Lesbian Review Worldwide, Crab Orchard Review,* and *Appalachian Heritage.* He has published three award-winning poetry chapbooks, *Bliss* (1998), *Mountain Fireflies* (2000), and *Flint Shards from Sussex* (2000); two full-length books of poetry, *Bones Washed with Wine* (2003) and *On the Tongue* (2006); a collection of personal essays, *Edge: Travels of an Appalachian Leather Bear* (2008); a novella, *Devoured,* included in *Masters of Midnight: Erotic Tales of the Vampire* (2003); a book of poetry and memoir, *Loving Mountains, Loving Men* (2005); and a volume of short fiction, *A History of Barbed Wire* (2006), which won a Lambda Literary Award. He teaches creative writing at Virginia Tech in Blacksburg, Virginia.

FELICIA MITCHELL has taught English and creative writing at Emory & Henry College since 1987. She currently serves as department chair. Her academic writing has focused on Women's Studies, poetry, and teaching with technology. She edited *Her Words: Diverse Voices in Contemporary Appalachian Women's Poetry* (University of Tennessee Press, 2002). A poet, she is the author of several chapbooks, including *The Cleft of the Rock* from Finishing Line Press of Kentucky (2009). For ten years she wrote a weekly column for *Washington County News* based in Abingdon, Virginia.

EMILY SATTERWHITE is the author of *Dear Appalachia: Readers, Identity, and Popular Fiction since 1878* (University Press of Kentucky, 2011). Her articles have appeared in *American Literature, Appalachian Journal,* and *Journal of American Folklore.* She is an assistant professor at Virginia Tech, where she teaches Appalachian studies, American Studies, and popular culture.

LINDA TATE holds a PhD in English from the University of Wisconsin-Madison. For many years, Linda was in the Department of English at Shepherd

University in Shepherdstown, West Virginia. In 2006, she moved to Colorado, where she joined the faculty in the University of Denver's Writing Program. Linda is now based in Boulder, Colorado, where she works as a freelance writer and editor. Linda is the author of *A Southern Weave of Women: Fiction of the Contemporary South* (University of Georgia Press, 1994) and *Power in the Blood: A Family Narrative* (Ohio University Press, 2009). She is also the editor of *Conversations with Lee Smith* (University Press of Mississippi, 2001). In 2003, Linda was named the West Virginia Professor of the Year.

ROBERT WEST is an associate professor of English at Mississippi State University, where he also serves as associate editor of *Mississippi Quarterly: The Journal of Southern Cultures*. His essays and reviews relating to Appalachian literature have appeared in *Appalachian Heritage, Appalachian Journal, Asheville Poetry Review, The Carolina Quarterly, Iron Mountain Review, Journal of Kentucky Studies, Pembroke Magazine, Publications of the Mississippi Philological Association, Southern Quarterly*, and other venues.

INDEX

Index

Index